EDUCATION, MANAGEMENT, AND PARTICIPATION

New Directions in Educational Administration

SHERRY KEITH
San Francisco State University

ROBERT HENRIQUES GIRLING
Sonoma State University

Allyn and Bacon

Boston   London   Toronto   Sydney   Tokyo   Singapore

For our students who deserve a better world;
for our teachers who have given us the faith to seek a
better world;
for all administrators who are trying to create a better
world;
and for our families who have given us the strength to
believe.

Production Administrator: Annette Joseph
Production Coordinator: Holly Crawford
Editorial-Production Service: Lynda Griffiths, TKM Productions
Cover Administrator: Linda K. Dickinson
Cover Designer: Suzanne Harbison
Manufacturing Buyer: Louise Richardson

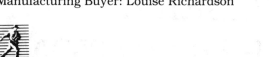

Library of Congress Cataloging-in-Publication Data

Keith, Sherry.
    Education, management, and participation : new directions in
educational administration / Sherry Keith, Robert Henriques Girling.
        p.   cm.
    Includes bibliographical references and index.
    ISBN 0-205-12623-5
    1. School management and organization—United States—Case
studies.   2. Teacher participation in administration—United States—
Case studies.   3. Community and school—United States—Case
studies.   I. Girling, Robert Henriques.   II. Title.
LB2805.K38   1991
371.2'00973—dc20   90-42297
                                                                    CIP

Printed in the United States of America
10 9 8 7 6 5 4 3 2 1   95 94 93 92 91 90

Photo Credits: Chapters 1, 4, 5, 7–10, © Frank Siteman 1990; Chapter
6, A. T. & T. Co. Phone Center.

Contents

PART II: THE PRACTICE OF PARTICIPATORY SCHOOL MANAGEMENT

Foreword

The call for educational reform has been ringing in our ears for over a decade. Schools are not serving the nation's increasingly diverse population. Dropout rates among secondary students have increased nationwide; failure to learn basic skills seems to be the rule rather than the exception among the less privileged segments of each new generation. Although physical capacities of our school systems have expanded, educational capacities have stagnated and in many instances declined. The centralization of educational administration in large district-level offices, which are perceived as out of touch with and unresponsive to the needs of students, teachers, and school-site administrators, has come under sharp criticism by teachers' unions, parents, and scholars as one of the chief reasons why our schools are failing. Recently reformers have begun to hail a new solution for revitalizing the schools: school-based management and school-site empowerment.

School-site empowerment is the new set of catchwords in our educational jargon. Almost every professional conference of educators is bedecked with discussions on school-site empowerment. For those of us who see the school site as the jewel of the educational system rather than just a place to satisfy the compliance requirements set out by federal and state agencies and central offices of school districts, even the words seem important. However, as with many educational concepts, the idea has become trivialized by its own rhetoric. To a large degree the term *educational empowerment* has begun to look like the Queen's words in *Through the Looking Glass*. Alice exclaimed to the Queen that she was confused because the Queen used the same word to mean very different things. The Queen responded that a word means whatever she wants it to mean.

School-site empowerment is now one of the Queen's words in that it has virtually no universally accepted meaning. It means what the speaker wants it to mean. Worse yet, it is often confused with teacher empowerment and shared decision making at the school site, without any attempt to build the capacity of the school to make shared decisions. School leadership is unprepared for such a process, and the central office does not have the capacity to provide the information, technical assistance, systematic staff development, and evaluation to support that process. Yet, school districts across the country are "empowering" their schools and staffs to take responsibility for school outcomes without providing the resources, training, decision-making discretion, systems of accountability, and other requirements for making such a process function and succeed.

The potential of the movement to empower teachers and principals at the school-site level is great, but is yet to be fully proven. As a theory of organizational effectiveness and as practiced in other segments of the public and private sectors, here in the United States as well as in other countries, there is much that could be usefully applied to our schools. To realize this potential will require resources and a sustained effort in the design, training, and implementation of school-site management systems. It will also require a careful working out of ideas among practitioners as to what empowerment means in the context of the day-to-day administration of schools.

This book represents one of the first major attempts to buttress the concept of empowerment by discussing its requirements for decision-making authority and the establishment of school capacity to make decisions. Through the establishment of a set of principles, techniques, and case studies, Sherry Keith and Robert Girling provide a framework for action at both the school-site and district levels. Although they focus on the crucial role of district and school-site managers, the book is clear about the need to provide deep and meaningful involvement of teachers in organizational, instructional, and curriculum decisions. The thrust of *Education, Management, and Participation* is on establishing the capacity of schools to take responsibility for the education of their students by adopting processes that work for the staff, students, and parents. Decision-making authority is combined with responsibility for results and the need to establish the capacity of the school system to support such changes. Since central office personnel are expected to collaborate with school sites in addressing problems, it also represents an opportunity to enhance the professionalism of central office staff by placing emphasis on their contributing to a solution rather than being policy compliance officers.

Keith and Girling have illuminated an approach to education that is more exciting and professionally challenging than the present "rules-bound" approach. They have also shown us the principles and processes that we need to embrace to make it happen. Most of all, they have provided rich case illustrations to support the processes that they suggest. Educational managers, teachers, other staff, parents, and students will find their approach to be productive, gentle, humane, and in the interest of all of us.

Henry M. Levin
Professor of Education
and Economics
Director, Center for Educational
Research at Stanford
Stanford University

Preface

We have written *Education, Management, and Participation* in order to present a rationale for methods of participative, school-based management. The book is intended for three main groups: students of educational administration preparing to be school-site and district managers, in-service trainees at the school and district level, and individual educational professionals. The book draws on current research findings with regard to school improvement and integrates them with contemporary management theory. We incorporate case studies of a variety of schools and school districts in order to provide an illustration of how theory can be applied in practice. At root we present a theory of management as well as practical tools that will serve to guide administrators and teachers toward changing educational structures and administrative processes. These changes are not sought as ends in themselves but as ingredients needed to transform the performance of schools—vital institutions in our social life.

This book focuses on participation as the most productive avenue toward restructuring and developing better schools; participative management refers to the regular and significant involvement of employees in decision making. We draw on a wealth of research and experiences of colleagues and practitioners who are currently using a variety of participative strategies, including site-based management, team building, and school restructuring, to empower the entire school community (teachers, parents, and site-level administrators). Our research has indicated that a participatory approach can provide productive solutions to such concerns as the need to improve the quality of instruction under conditions of financial restraint, the need to attract and retain talented people within the teaching profession, and the need to prevent the wholesale exodus of the growing number of at-risk students.

The central question that guided our research is: How can schools be managed in such a way as to encourage students and develop and fully use the diverse talents of those professionals who dedicate their lives to education? What we have found can be summarized in three principles. First, teachers want recognition and an opportunity for professional growth. Second, teachers are more productive and make a better contribution to the educational team if they are made to feel that they are central to the success of the entire organization. And third, successful schools incorporate leadership that is responsive to teachers' opinions.

Overview of the Book

Our text focuses on three elements of participatory management in educational settings. We summarize the evidence and individual case studies that illustrate the efficacy and operation of participative management and we discuss the necessary conditions and methods used by administrators for implementing this approach. The book is organized into 11 chapters; the chapters bring together parallel lines of research in education and management in order to delineate ways in which participation may enhance educational effectiveness by improving the quality of working life within schools. Six classic aspects of management are included in this book: goal setting, leadership, problem solving and decision making, motivation, performance appraisal, and staff development. In addition, chapters on planning and school finance, managing school-community relations, collective bargaining, and building a participative organization provide the reader with additional applications of the theoretical structure established in the first chapters. We have summarized a wide range of studies on participation in organizations in education as well as in other sectors of the economy. In an effort to make participatory concepts relevant to educators, we describe participatory practices in detail and exemplify their application in schools.

Chapter One: Schools as Organizations; Educators as Managers. Chapter One focuses on schools as organizations, past and present, and the changes that have created organizational demands for a new approach to management. We also review the evolution of management theory over the past century, particularly as it applies to education, and set the stage for our subject: participatory management in education.

Chapter Two: Participatory Management in Education. This chapter begins with the question, What is participative management? By examining the different concepts that describe participation, we develop a framework for understanding the ways in which teacher participation can contribute to overall school improvement. A second question follows: How does employee participation actually influence the organization in terms of the work environment and productivity? Here, we review the research findings on employee participation in a variety of organizational settings, including schools. Our third question is: How important is teacher participation to effective school management? Participation is presented as the key to teacher empowerment and professionalization, two major concerns of educators across the nation today. Finally, we examine the steps that must be taken and the possible pitfalls any school should avoid when considering a move toward a more participatory organization. A concluding case shows how one Washington school district used a participative school-based approach to develop a districtwide master plan.

Chapter Three: Leadership. This chapter discusses trait theory, path-goal theory, and contingency theories of leadership. Following a review of the findings to date on leadership, we ask, What are the attributes of leaders in effective schools? How do they spend their time? How do they see their roles as managers? Finally, we examine the question of leadership in participatory organizations.

Some critics of participation are fearful that increased employee involvement means a decrease in managerial activities and signals the demise of leadership. On the contrary, our findings indicate that the participatory organization is not leaderless, nor are leaders in participatory organizations powerless. We find that the roles and responsibilities of the leader/manager change and grow to include more emphasis on human relations, staff motivation, staff development, and client satisfaction. In schools, the effective leader can be particularly involved with improving the content and process of teaching, along with developing an organizational vision and acting as an agent of change. Finally, we examine the practice of the educational leader/developer and identify the essential role that constituent participation plays in effective situational leadership. The chapter concludes with a case study of Redwood City School District.

Chapter Four: Motivation. This chapter is devoted to the complex issue of human motivation in the context of school improvement and teacher performance. We know that certain characteristics of the teaching force (e.g., age and experience) create motivational challenges for school-site managers. Moreover, the organizational features of schools as well as certain characteristics of the teaching profession (e.g., isolation and flat career paths) also make for inherent motivational problems. We present three salient process theories of motivation—expectancy theory, goal theory, and behaviorism—along with two content theories—needs hierarchy and motivation-hygiene theory. In conclusion, we examine the implications and application of these theories with regard to the potential of greater teacher participation in school-site management.

Chapter Five: Solving Problems and Making Decisions. Chapter Five describes three key techniques for building participatory organizations: organizational goal setting, employee-centered problem solving, and decentralized decision making. We describe the techniques in detail and apply them specifically to schools. Setting goals is central to moving any organization forward and gaining commitment from its members for change and improvement. The diverse and sometimes conflicting goals of schools can be brought under control when teachers and administrators are mutually involved in specifying goals for their school. This chapter describes a school-based, goal-setting process evolving from teacher-administration collaboration.

Subsequently, we examine two related processes central to the management of effective organizations: problem solving and decision making. In hierarchical, bureaucratic organizations, problem solving and decision making are often functionally distinct as well as hierarchically differentiated (i.e., school principals may propose solutions to overcrowding at their school site, but decisions regarding any given proposed solution are likely to be referred to the district level). Participatory management focuses on articulating problem solving with decision making at the school-site level. This linkage is a key aspect of involving teachers and creating a professional work environment. We present techniques that build the link between the problem-solving process and decision making, such as quality circles and work teams. The chapter concludes with a case study that illustrates problems that may arise in using quality circles.

Chapter Six: Planning and Managing School Finance. Because school finance creates an overriding framework for the management process, Chapter Six analyzes how school finance works, the planning and budgeting process, and the theory of financial decision making. Since we view the school as a financial unit, fund raising at the site level and decentralizing school finance are considered as important aspects of school-based management. The concluding case illustrates how parents were involved in fund raising at a California school.

Chapter Seven: Professional Growth and Staff Development. A participatory organization is built, not born. Staff development plays a crucial role in constructing the participatory organization as well as upgrading professionalism among individual teachers. This chapter examines the relationship between staff development and professional growth in the context of career ladders and merit pay. After establishing a broad framework for staff development in the first sections of the chapter, we turn to the planning and management of staff development programs. We answer the questions, Who should attend? and What should the content be? The concluding sections of the chapter focus on two methods of staff development: coaching and mentoring.

Chapter Eight: Evaluation: Teachers, Programs, and Schools. This chapter examines related but distinct aspects of evaluation that confront the school manager: school and program evaluation on the one hand and the appraisal of individual teacher performance on the other hand. The first part of the chapter examines issues related to school and program evaluation: What should we evaluate? Who should be involved in an evaluation? What are the technical aspects of an evaluation? The latter part of the chapter focuses on evaluating the performance of teachers and includes a discussion of suggested criteria for measuring teacher effectiveness. The chapter concludes with an examination of four appraisal techniques and a description of the appraisal process.

Chapter Nine: Managing School-Community Relationships. Client responsiveness is identified as one of several distinguishing features of excellent organizations. Professional literature suggests that schools do not always act to place the needs of their students at the forefront of organizational priorities. As education seeks to respond to public expectations, we need to find ways in which schools can respond to and more effectively engage their clientele—students, parents, and the community. This chapter examines the concepts of client responsiveness and community involvement. Professional/client advocacy and partnership models of school-community relationships are examined, along with the benefits of community involvement. In addition, developing and orchestrating involvement from a site administrator's perspective is treated in the context of school-based management. The possibilities for building client-responsive schools are considered in terms of learning options, curricular focus, and sense of continuity. We also discuss the barriers schools confront when attempting the change.

Chapter Ten: Labor-Management Relations: Collective Bargaining and Beyond. Collective bargaining has become an increasingly central aspect of educational administration over the past three decades. Chapter Ten analyzes the functional imperative behind the rise of collective bargaining, gives a brief history of teachers' organizations, and provides an understanding of why teachers have been impelled toward unionization. We also examine the impact of collective bargaining on school management. The chapter concludes with an examination of alternative labor-management strategies that are beginning to emerge in education, including mutual gain bargaining and policy trust agreements.

Chapter Eleven: Restructuring for Participatory Management: Change and Stability. This chapter brings together the themes covered in the preceding chapters and offers guidance on when to begin initiating management changes in schools. We address such questions as, Who is responsible? What changes should come first? What needs to be done to get started and how long might it take? To respond to these questions, we incorporate theory presented throughout the text as well as the experience of the groups that have embarked on the process. These concepts are illustrated in two case studies.

Case Studies

As a result of our fieldwork with practicing administrators at the school-site and district levels, we have accumulated a wide range of educational management cases that illustrate a number of the principles and practices with which the text is concerned. We have included these cases, sometimes as an introduction to a chapter, other times as illustrations within the chapter itself or as concluding examples of concepts, issues, and themes the chapter has presented. As educators, we are partial to using case materials as a learning device. For those interested in the case approach as an instructional tool, we have included an Authors' Note at the onset of the cases to orient the readers' attention to key issues. In addition, a discussion of teaching with the case method is included in the appendix to the text.

Acknowledgments

This book incorporates the findings from extensive field research. It is based on countless hours of interviews with principals, teachers, superintendents, and district administrators. In addition, we have conducted a survey of management practices in 21 schools, along with interviews and observations, in an effort to identify the impact that school-site management practices have on student performance outcomes. Many people have generously contributed insights while patiently helping us to fathom the management issues that trouble the school administrator, plague the school teacher, and befuddle the parents and students. We gratefully acknowledge the many educators who have contributed directly to this work: Barbara Armstrong, Charles Benson, Guy Benveniste, Bert Bower, Ralph Boyce, David Bradford, Patricia Brown, Bob Buethal, Barbara Chriss, Terry Corpuz, Deb Edginton, Bob Gabriner, Wilda Gardella, Rick Girling, Milton Gordon, Jim Gray, Judy Guilkey-Amado, Jim Guthrie, Paul Guzman, Betty Halperin, Ken Hill, Sally Hurtado, Judith Kell, Rob Kessler, Kathy King, Julie Koppich, Henry Levin, Angela MacGregor, Susan Martin, Karen Nelson, Earl Newton, Georgia Squires, Pat Wiman, Judy Wright, Richard Zimmer, and the staff of Berkwood Hedge School.

In addition, we would like to acknowledge the role of our students in our course, Management Workshop for Educators and Training Professionals; Nina Gabelko of UC Berkeley's SUPER Project, who invited us to share our formative ideas with their School Administrators Institute; and Professors Hans Weiler and Martin Carnoy of Stanford University, who invited us to extend our views with international administrators in the context of their summer institutes with educational professionals from around the world. Our research team, Ann Katz, Bill Hefferman, Lisa Petrides, and Lynn Baker, assisted us in collecting empirical data. John Haehl and Howard Barkan graciously provided guidance in analyzing the data we collected under a grant from the Chancellor's Office of the California State University System. We wish to acknowledge those individuals who reviewed the book for Allyn and Bacon: Constance Gordon, Trinity College; Larry Hughes, University of Houston; Stefan Krchniak, Southern Illinois University; Thomas McGreal, University of Illinois; Lou Romano, Michigan State University; and Lynn Turner, East Texas State University.

We would also like to acknowledge the encouragement that we have received through the years from our parents, Ken and Helen, and Clara and Keith, as well as the joyous exuberance and love of learning from our children, Chalyn and Sean, which has served to inspire and sustain our energy throughout this project.

Last and certainly not least was the thoroughly professional assistance provided by Arin Pereira. Her endless patience and good humor in typing the numerous drafts of this book were truly remarkable.

CHAPTER ONE

Schools as Organizations; Educators as Managers

Introduction

Schools, like businesses, families, or political parties, are organizations. In some ways schools and businesses are alike, yet in other ways they are strikingly different. Since the management of schools and school systems is the topic of this book, we will begin by developing a common understanding about the characteristics of schools as organizations. What type of organization is a school? What functions does the school play in the context of contemporary U.S. society? Answers to these questions will produce a type of still-life drawing of the school as an organization.

To develop effective means of managing schools, however, a more panoramic perspective is needed. Schools exist within a larger context: Most public schools are part of a school district and the school district belongs to a statewide "system" of education. Moreover, the statewide system of education belongs to an entity that is frequently referred to as the "nation's system of education." An awareness and understanding of how individual schools fit into a larger organizational system, which is often referred to as the "educational system," is essential for effective management practice.

Organizations and organizational systems, just like people, exist in time and space, and they change in terms of their characteristics over time. An effective approach to management of any organization takes into account the movement of history, the realization that organizations are dynamic, and the knowledge that the management of an organization must be able to accommodate change, and in many instances actually be a stimulus for change. Schools and school systems have changed as organizations, although historians debate the degree to which their basic organizational characteristics have been transformed. The focus on change is like a motion picture; it gives educators an understanding of some of the dynamics of schools and school systems.

In this chapter we consider schools as organizations and organizational systems before turning to the major theme of the text: a participatory approach to school management. Moreover, as an introduction to the theme of participatory management, we also consider the evolution of different theories of management, particularly in the context of educational administration. This overview is intended to help future educational managers situate themselves as managers and their schools as organizations in the context of tradition and change. The text incorporates the findings of the rapidly expanding volume of interdisciplinary social science research in several areas: school effectiveness, managerial style and competence, and employee participation in a variety of workplace organizations. However, we firmly believe that managers need a sense of where management theory has come from as well as how schools and school systems, as organizations, have changed over time in order to be able to plan and direct where they might able to go in the future.

Schools as Organizational Systems

What Is an Organization?

There are several approaches to defining or describing an organization. One is to describe the organization in terms of its structure: Who is part of the organization and how are those members related to one another? If we take schools as our case in point, several salient structural characteristics emerge. One is the division of labor among various people who work at a school. There are the teaching staff, the support staff, and the administrative staff. Moreover, schools actually belong to a larger organizational system—the school district. And the district has its own array of specialized personnel: administrators (e.g., the superintendent, the business manager or director of personnel); professional specialists (e.g., the curriculum coordinator, the testing and evaluation specialist, the bilingual curriculum specialist); and support staff (e.g., district maintenance workers, clerical staff, and transportation workers). Another aspect associated with the division of labor that characterizes the structure of schools generally implies a set of hierarchical relationships among the various people who work within the system. The superintendent is at the top of the structure and is assumed to have the maximum amount of authority, responsibility, and autonomy. In a perfectly hierarchical system, authority, responsibility, and autonomy diminish as one moves from the top toward the bottom of the system. In reality, there is not a perfectly hierarchical organization or organizational system. Schools and school systems tend to be hierarchical but they also have important organizational quirks that lead to more autonomy at lower levels of the system, even though authority and responsibility are hierarchically structured.

Formal Organizations

A school is also a good example of a *formal* organization. Formal organizations, in contrast to informal organizations, persist over time and have explicit rules or procedures that govern key aspects of the organization, such as who can be a member of the organization, how members are recruited or selected, the roles of each member and what expectations members are required to fulfill. Within a formal organization, such as a school, informal organizations or groups frequently emerge. This may be a grouping as small and informal as a few teachers who have lunch with each other and meet outside of working hours regularly, or as structured and broadly based a school fund-raising committee that may eventually become a formally organized educational foundation.

Public Sector Organizations

Although schools are a workplace for their employees, as organizations they belong to the "public" sector. This means that they are governed by a public entity, usually a publicly elected school board. The procedures that govern many of the basic organizational processes are not necessarily controlled at the level of the workplace (i.e., the individual school site). On the one hand, many of the policies and procedural features that characterize public schools are determined by the school board, at the level of state or even federal policy or law. On the other hand, day-to-day operations, problem solving, and decision making take place at the school-site level.

Functions of Schools

Another approach to understanding an organization is to view the organization in terms of its processes and functions. Generically speaking, all organizations have a common function: to create the possibility for members of the organization to cooperate (Blau and Scott, 1962). Moreover, all organizations can also be described as having to establish procedures that promote the basic cooperative function with which they are concerned: (1) selecting a leader/leaders; (2) determining roles to be played by each member (division of labor); (3) setting organizational goals, and (4) selecting procedures for achieving these goals.

At first glance, schools would appear to have specific functions that distinguish them from other social organizations, such as businesses, churches, families, or political parties. Traditionally, the function of formal schooling has been described as educating the next generation in the specifics of basic academic skills (e.g., literacy, numeracy) and passing on knowledge of the society's history and culture (what has more recently been referred to as *cultural literacy*). Dreeben (1968) has described the functions of schooling in terms of socializing the child in the dominant attitudes and practices associated with modern, industrial society. He identifies these as independence (from the family); achievement (according to standards of merit defined by a socially recognized authority—in this case, the educational system itself); universalism (approaching individuals in terms of socially significant characteristics such as sex, age, ethnicity, etc.), and specificity (development of specialized interests vis-à-vis other people that are considered appropriate to the highly specialized division of labor in industrial society).

Over the past three decades, both the traditional academic function and the socialization function of education have been subject to severe scrutiny and criticism by educators, social scientists, and the general public. Critics have argued that schools have an overriding but, nevertheless, hidden agenda, which is to reproduce the broader social structure of society (Carnoy and Levin, 1976; Bowles and Gintis, 1976). That structure is based on racial, sexual, and social-class inequalities.

The debate over the goals and functions of education has profoundly influenced the school as a workplace organization. To begin with, schools have become increasingly scrutinized by the public in terms of what they teach (i.e., the curriculum). Second, schools have become a battleground in terms of who should have decision-making power over organizational structure, organizational procedures, and organizational resources. Third, schools that were once (until the mid-twentieth century) very local in terms of their orientation, policy making, and resource generation have come to be increasingly regulated and financed by state and federal authorities. At the same time, they have come to be amalgamated in expanding networks—school districts—that are bureaucratic in nature.

Evolution of the Educational System

We have already mentioned how individual schools have become increasingly amalgamated into larger organizational networks: the school districts, as well as the state and national systems of education. Educational managers, whether at the school site or district level, must be well informed with respect to ways in which these networks overlap and interact with each other to function effectively. Perhaps the adage "You must know the system in order to change it" is most appropriately applied in this instance.

The educational system has several arenas of action: the school, the district, and the state and federal governments. In addition, there are other forces, both within the system and outside it, that can have a determining influence on what takes place inside the school on a day-to-day basis. Among these are teachers' unions and local boards of education at the district level; the legal system at the local, state, and federal levels; and legislative bodies at the state and federal levels.

Stability and Change in Schools

Organizations, like people, are born, develop, and change. As organizations transform through growth and development, the ways in which they are run and managed may also change. A dynamic picture of schools will provide an appreciation of how their organization and management have evolved, why these changes have occurred, and what forces press toward the transformation of the current organization and management of schools.

Size, Scale, and Control

During the first half of the nineteenth century, schools in the United States were less plentiful, but more varied from both an organizational and a managerial perspective than they are known to be today. Public education was primarily rural throughout most of the 1800s. Moreover, it was generally not bureaucratic in structure. Teaching was an incipient profession, and the "educational establishment" was largely the domain of lay promoters and concerned citizens. The prototypic school of the nineteenth century was the one-room school house. This model could be readily found from the Atlantic seaboard to the Pacific coast. The 1850 census illustrated this clearly, reporting approximately 80,000 public schools and only 90,000 teachers—a ratio of slightly more than one teacher per school.

Teachers were characteristically young, poorly paid, and, by modern standards, considerably underqualified for their posts. Few were educated beyond the primary level. Tyack and Hansot

(1982) write that it would be inappropriate to consider these early educators as part of a profession or as employees of an organized educational system. Teachers were a highly mobile workforce and apparently did not usually stay long in any given post. A concerted effort was made in Massachusetts to make teaching a more stable occupation. In that state, historical records indicate that in 1860 one out of every five adult women had at same point passed through the school-house doors and lingered temporarily as a teacher (Tyack and Hansot, 1982). "Normal" or teacher training courses persisted as the dominate form of professional preparation until the end of the century. One survey of twenty leading universities in 1890 revealed only two courses in educational administration, and membership of the nation's leading professional association, the National Education Association, did not exceed 350 until 1884.

Neither the state or federal government exerted much formal or informal control over education until well into the twentieth century. Again, Tyack and Hansot point out that the United States Office of Education, which was founded in 1867, had a staff of six and a budget of $13,000. It's principal function was to collect and publish statistics. Even at the end of the nineteenth century, most state departments of education had no more than two officials, one being the superintendent. This is estimated to be about one non-teaching official per 100,000 students enrolled in public schools.

By the beginning of the 1990s, the educational landscape had been greatly transformed. Nationwide, the combined elementary and secondary school population has grown to nearly 46 million pupils. The number of public schools has stabilized at around 84,000. Although the actual number of schools has declined since 1890, school size has grown to an average of 424 pupils at the elementary level and 696 pupils at the secondary level. Administratively, there are more than 15,500 districts across the nation, ranging in size from fewer than 300 pupils to more than 50,000 pupils (U.S. Department of Education, 1989).

Teaching and the administration in public schools have become highly professionalized compared to one century ago. The elementary/secondary teaching force is now three million strong, with 99.7 percent of teachers having completed a university education and 51 percent with some type of graduate-level training in education. An estimated 90 percent belong to one of the two national teachers' organizations: the National Education Association (NEA) and the American Federation of Teachers (AFT). Nationally, there are over 133,000 principals of elementary and secondary schools. Although the overwhelming majority of administrators at the school and district levels are drawn from the ranks of the teaching profession, most states require specialized, graduate-level training in educational administration as a prerequisite for appointment to an administrative post.

State and federal educational agencies have expanded in terms of their size, scope of function, and financial influence. In 1989, the U.S. educational system cost $353 billion, with expenditures on public and private precollegiate schools costing $212 billion. Expenditures for each elementary and secondary school student were $5,246. On a nationwide basis, state departments of education currently finance about 49.8 percent of K–12 expenditures, the federal government contributes 6.4 percent, and local governments provide the remaining 43.9 percent. As organizations, both state and federal authorities have grown dramatically in size and function since the 1890s. There are 4,800 employees in the Department of Education at the federal level. State departments of education, in conjunction with state legislatures, now set a wide range of educational policies with regard to curriculum and instruction, educational finance, professional credential standards and practices, student testing, and organizational evaluation. The federal authorities have, by contrast, been principally concerned with specialized programs such as the Elementary and Secondary School Act of 1964, with the objective of providing additional funds to assist educationally disadvantaged students across the nation.

Management

The approaches to organizing as well as managing this vast, loosely coupled national educational complex have also changed and become far more uniform and solidified since the late nineteenth century. Katz (1971) has convincingly argued that although the educational system in the United States has grown dramatically in the past century, by about 1880, the U.S. education had acquired its fundamental structural characteristics and has not altered significantly since that period. During the period from 1800 to 1885, there were several competing approaches to organizing and managing schools, including what Katz labels as paternalistic voluntarism, democratic localism, corporate voluntarism, and incipient bureaucracy. Katz argues that by the end of the nineteenth century, bureaucracy was no longer incipient; it had come to be viewed as the one best way of organizing the burgeoning educational system at local, state, and federal levels. This is not to say that the other approaches have disappeared entirely: Democratic localism is the underlying approach of the "community control over the schools" movement that emerged in the 1960s and early 1970s, whereas strands of corporate voluntarism were invoked in the 1980s to fill the vacuum of a decline in the federal government's financial involvement in education.

Before we examine various managerial theories and their implications for educational administration, it is important to understand the broader social dynamics that created the initial impetus for growth and change. These include the shift of the U.S. economy from predominantly agricultural to a diversified basket of economic activities with great emphasis on manufacturing and heavy industry. Accompanying this shift was the urbanization of the population. In 1890, one half of the nation's population was rural; a century later, three-fourths was urban, with an estimated 65 percent of Americans living in cities/urban complexes of more than one million people (Bureau of the Census, 1949, 1987). Thus the urbanization of education has been one of the forces driving education toward greater scale, both at the school and district levels. The waves of immigration, in response to the acute need for labor in the rapidly expanding industrial sector of the economy, also had a profound impact on the organizational and managerial features that grew up and solidified around schools. Immigrants—many from peasant backgrounds in Europe—were concentrated in urban, industrializing areas of the country. Tremendous social and political pressures rose to absorb the children of the immigrants into U.S. society and prepare them for their future in an increasingly industrialized occupational landscape. The idea of the school as preparation for factory life, and later for the corporate world, became popular among educational leaders and social reformers in the late nineteenth and early twentieth centuries (Callahan, 1962; Spring, 1972).

With the educational sector growing so rapidly throughout the nineteenth century and with the extension of public elementary schooling to the majority of the population, it was inevitable that new organizational forms beyond the individual, self-administered community school would arise. The bureaucratic model of organization is based on an increasingly specialized division of labor. This occurs in the schools as well as between schools and local, state, and federal administrative bodies. Moreover, the chief characteristics of bureaucracy triumphed in education: hierarchy, written laws, policies, regulations, and procedures for the key aspects of running schools (e.g., selecting teachers, defining curriculum and instructional practices, assigning authority and responsibility for decision making, etc.). Nevertheless, vestiges of other organizational and managerial paradigms are still seen in today's educational system.

By understanding both how much and how little the educational system has changed over the past two hundred years, one can begin to appreciate the enormity of the challenge facing educators today, especially those who are concerned with its transformation and improvement. Educational professionals need to ask themselves, What are the forces that may be presently pressing the system toward change?

There is no doubt that the schools and the educational system at large have been under tremendous internal and external pressures and have changed even in this brief passage of time. Demographic forces still impinge upon the educational system, but in a different manner than in the past. Educators are no longer faced with an expanding system of elementary and secondary schools. In fact, the 1970s and 1980s were periods of largely unanticipated retrenchment for educational organizations. The numbers of students moving through the system declined dramatically. Meanwhile, projections for the 1990s call for a moderate rate of growth in the school-age population. Schools, like the economy, are likely to encounter a steady scenario, with less growth than at any time in nearly two centuries.

Although the growth rate of the educational system has slowed considerably, the demand and expectations for educational services have become much more complex than ever before. Many school districts in the large urban areas across the nation have extremely diverse clientele groups—linguistically, culturally, racially, and socioeconomically. Whereas in the nineteenth century the views of educational reformers calling for homogenization of the highly diverse immigrant population remained unchallenged, the obliteration of heterogenity is no longer an unquestioned goal for schools. Increasingly, the school system is being pressed to evolve ways to tailor its curriculum and instructional practices to a diverse clientele. These pressures are likely to continue into the future. Not only do they mean an intensified quest for new approaches to curriculum and instruction but they call for new approaches to organization and management.

Social Demand and the Schools

Together with other changes in the social terrain of U.S. society, such as the changes in family structure and the employment of women outside the household, schools are being pressed to expand the range of services they offer as well as tailor the traditional academic curriculum to different student client groups within the same school or district. The demand will grow for preschool, extended school daycare, and year-round school. Within the school system itself the change in the composition of the teaching force, which is older, more highly educated, and better trained, has created pressure for changes in which the way school site-problems are resolved, the manner by which change is instituted, and the method by which decisions are made. The relative stability of the teaching force, compared to one hundred years ago, and the trend toward the professionalization of teaching (a topic explored more fully in Chapters Two, Six, and Seven) bring inevitable pressure on administrators at the site, district, and state levels. The power gained by teachers through the growth of collective bargaining is unlikely to decline. This power can be a highly positive, creative force for school improvement or it can become a major stumbling block for the advancement of the quality of educational services, as well as the quality of working conditions for teachers themselves.

These forces call for a variety of changes in the way schools are organized and run. For instance, the idea that bigger is better will be increasingly challenged. Recent research questions the traditional assumption that large schools or large school districts are more efficient in terms of resource utilization or more effective in terms of maximizing student learning (Kenny, 1982). There will be more interest in returning to smaller organizational units that combat the depersonalization of large educational bureaucracies and may give teachers, students, and parents a greater say in the educational process. There will also be more pressure for schools to become more varied in both their organizational style and educational offerings. Magnet schools, educational vouchers, cooperative learning-based curricula, and bilingual education are all elements of the same force impinging upon schools to pay more attention to the needs of their clients and to the design of their programs, facilities, and organizations accordingly. Finally, it is very likely that the continued financial pressure on public schools will not abate. Because a declining proportion of the electorate will have children in school, it will continue to be difficult to convince voters to spend more money on educational services that they perceive to have no direct benefit to them—or that they perceive to be ineffective. This leads to a related force—the drive to improve the quality and effectiveness of schools in ways that are measurable. Like it or not, educators and particularly educational managers will face a rising demand for external accountability.

Inevitably, this view of the changing face of education ends with a complex array of challenges that confront the contemporary educational manager. The degrees of freedom for change are not unlimited. Professional educators need to develop both a clear analysis of what is needed and strategies for organizational management and change. Developing such an analysis depends on an understanding of management theory as applied to educational administration.

Management Theory and Education: An Overview

In an arena as complex as the management of organizations, knowledge of some basic principles is helpful. Theory is simply that—a principle or set of principles that account for or attempt to explain the relationship between two or more observable facts or events.

Scientific Management

Management theory has been evolving for the past one hundred years, beginning with Frederick Taylor's school of scientific management in the late nineteenth century. Scientific management was concerned with improving the efficiency of the work process. Taylor originally focused on time-and-motion studies in factory settings. His ideas spread rapidly. Early in the twentieth century they began to take hold among educational administrators. The "Gary Plan," also known as the "Platoon School of Gary, Indiana" (1908), was an effort to infuse the school curriculum with John Dewey's pedagogic practice of linking the academic program to the study of nature, art, music, and industrial education while simultaneously increasing the efficiency of the school. The plan was widely discussed by school administrators across the nation and adopted in more than 600 schools in some 126 cities. The connection between the Gary Plan and scientific management was made by Superintendent Wirt, the plan's author, in an article appearing in the *American School Board Journal* (February 1911). He stated, "Reduce the first cost of your school plants and the actual per pupil cost of school maintenance . . . while adding manual training, nature study, music, drawing, playground and gymnasium equipment and specially trained teachers for each of these departments" (Callahan, 1962, pp. 129–130). Wirt then went on to explain how his own improved school "machine" operated with a doubling of the number of pupils in the school plant at any given time.

Although the scientific management approach swept the nation until the early 1930s, it had recognizable limitations. With the focus on efficiency and productivity, it was more suited to a factory-type organization than to a school with complex functions to carry out and multiple services to provide. More important, however, was the limited focus of scientific management on the factors that actually affect both the efficiency and overall effectiveness of an organization. By focusing exclusively on improving the techniques of work, scientific management neglects other important dimensions of management. These were recognized by other management theories including the classical school of management, the systems theory of management, and later the human relations/behaviorist theories.

Classical Management Theory

Classical management theory approached management from an organizational perspective. Based on Max Weber's study of bureaucracy, theorists like Henri Fayol, Mary Parker Follett, and Chester Bernard emphasized the need to find guidelines for managing increasingly complex organizations with various divisions and subdivisions that are not necessarily all located at the same site. These organizational theorists were both observers of and, to some extent, advocates of bureaucracy. For instance, Weber viewed bureaucracy as the ideal organizational form, with its emphasis on rationality, technical competence, and clearly defined organizational structure with clear lines of authority and responsibility. This approach to management is most closely embodied in the superintendency model of school administration.

The Superintendency Model of School Administration

The superintendency model of school administration presents the principal as a strong leader whose responsibilities are extremely wide-ranging. The principal, acting alone, anticipates and identifies problems, analyzes their causes, and decides on an effective course of action to resolve them. The principal is knowledgeable about all aspects of curriculum and instruction, providing direction and feedback on the performance of the faculty. Armed with insight and full understanding of staff needs, the principal must plan for staff development in a constant quest to improve the quality of instruction offered in the school.

Central to the concept of superintendency is the practice of *oversight*. Oversight implies review from above. The responsibility for oversight is vested in superiors, whether they be foremen, supervisors, quality control agents, or principals. Contemporary studies of how principals spend their time suggest that oversight predominates. For example, in Montgomery County Public Schools approximately 60 percent of a principal's time was spent in oversight-related activities (Montgomery County Public Schools, 1975). Meanwhile, only 15 percent was directed toward instructional leadership—the main variable that empirical studies have consistently associated with effective schools (Brandt, 1987).

According to this approach the principal must personally motivate the teaching staff and be the guardian of staff morale. Responsibilities of the principal also include goal setting, planning, and evaluation functions on an organizationwide basis. In addition, the principal has key public relations functions with parent groups, the community, the district office, and the school board. Under conditions of budgetary restraint, the dynamic principal should try to acquire added resources for the school to supplement local, state, and federal funding.

One might logically ask, "What's wrong with all of this?" Such a job description for the school-site administrator is both overwhelming and unrealistic. Particularly, when empirical findings have indicated that a manager cannot typically supervise the work of more than six to eight persons effectively or be substantively responsible for more than three to four functional areas in an organization. This classical approach has important limitations when one considers the complex task of school management. It underutilizes the very asset that schools, as organizations, possess—a professionally qualified and often highly experienced human resource base (i.e., the teachers). This limitation is addressed by systems theory, human relations theories, and the participatory model of management, which is to a large extent founded on the systems and the human relations/behaviorist theories of management.

Systems Theory

The systems theory of management advocates that the manager view the organization as an unified system. The analogy comes from biological sciences: The organization is like an organism composed of a variety of subsystems, all of which are interrelated. Moreover, a change in one subsystem is likely to result in changes in other subsystems. Systems theories discuss organizations in terms of synergy (the cooperation resulting from the interaction among parts); communication flows and feedback among and within subsystems and the larger system; and the degree of openness or closure of the entity vis-à-vis the external environment. Weick (1976) chose to identify school districts as examples of "loosely coupled" systems. The label connotes the interaction among the schools—which are the subsystems of the larger school district "system." Each of these subsystems operates with relative autonomy. The synergy among schools in this respect is at a low rather than a high level and interdependence among schools is limited. Systems theory presents a wholistic perspective on the organization, encourages managers to view their work from this vantage point, and focuses on organizational relationships. However, it lacks perspective on the individual within the organization. This theme is taken up by the human relations school of management.

Human Relations/Behaviorist Theories

Since the famous Hawthorne studies conducted by Elton Mayo in Western Electric's Hawthorne plant between 1924 and 1933, more and more attention has been focused on the factors influencing human behavior in the workplace. The Hawthorne studies revealed that increases in worker productivity were not primarily attributable to technological innovation or to the type of time-and-motion improvements stressed by Taylor's scientific management approach. Rather, productivity improvements seemed to be traceable to the specific attention workers received when they were part of an "experimental" situation. This finding began to point management theorists toward the study of human behavior as a product of psychological and sociopsychological influences. Rensis Likert (1961) was among the social psychologists who studied the impact of work organization on workers' attitudes and job satisfaction in the 1940s and 1950s.

The human relations/behaviorist approach views productivity, efficiency, and effectiveness as social rather than simply technical concerns. It focuses not on what the manager does per se but on the manager's *style* of interaction with employees (see Chapter Four) and on the importance of social as well as work relationships among members of an organization. Although human relations-based management theory became a well-established approach as early as the 1960s, it has diffused more slowly than some of its predecessors. This is partially due to the complexity of understanding human behavior that frequently leads to conflicting recommendations for action. Also, it is often difficult to convince managers that focusing on managerial style and human relations can have a substantial positive impact on an organization's productivity and effectiveness. The human relations/behaviorist approach to management underlies, in part, the participatory model of school management with which we are concerned in this text. Unlike the other theories already mentioned, it is only beginning to be diffused into the field of educational administration.

The Participatory Model of School Management

In contrast to scientific management and the superintendency model of educational administration, participative management is characterized by school-level planning and decision making linked to professional accountability. The role of the administrator includes that of facilitator, organizer, listener/communicator, resource person, as well as organizational leader. The role of teachers, individually and collectively, encompasses the identification and prioritization of goals and needs with respect to classroom instruction and organization of "production" within the school, development of strategies to meet goals and needs, resolution of problems in the implementation of instructional and organizational goals, and participation in evaluating progress and results. Within the participatory model, the staff members are active in identifying their professional development needs, and they may even help to train and develop each other. Moreover, motivation, morale, and job satisfaction are shouldered exclusively by "the management." Teachers and administrators work together to improve the quality of the work environment, creating conditions for more effective teaching and learning, and identifying and changing those aspects of the work process that are viewed as inimical to quality performance.

Participative management is highly consistent with the current quest for substantial qualitative improvements in educational outcomes because it may provide the means for permitting the commitment of teachers, parents, and administrators to work together to resolve problems and articulate educational goals. Moreover, it is likely to be the most effective managerial vehicle for implementing sustained reform. Whereas support for this thesis as well as a detailed treatment of participative management in the context of education is the subject of this book, a brief introductory discussion is in order. The analysis draws on several lines of research. First, the research literature on school effectiveness provides us with knowledge regarding effective school leadership. Second, the domain of organizational theory offers new directions of research about professionals in organizations, employee participation, human relations, and organizational development.

School Effectiveness and Participation

Over the past decade a number of studies have attempted to identify the common features of highly effective schools (Purkey and Smith, 1983; Cohen, 1982; MacKenzie, 1983; Edmonds, 1979; Madaus et al., 1981; Cohn and Rossmiller, 1987). Much of this research emerged in response to the 1966 publication of the congressionally commissioned study, *Equality of Educational Opportunity* (Coleman, 1966). Known as the Coleman Report, the research upon which the report was based indicated that schools make little difference in the educational outcomes of students measured by standardized tests. Significant factors were identified as the student's family and social class background. In recent years a growing body of empirical research and case analyses of turn-around schools suggest that the school's organizational climate is more important than the results from the Coleman Report originally implied. The school effectiveness research indicates that "organizational characteristics of schools account for 32 percent of between school variance in student achievement" (Rosenholtz, 1985). This means that as much as one-third of the students' gain or loss on achievement tests can be accounted for by the quality of school management.

The findings of these studies exhibit a remarkable consistency. Emerging from this work is the importance of organizational structure, leadership, and the organizational culture. Embedded in these features of effective schools is the importance of collaborative planning and collegial relationships among teachers, which break down the isolation traditionally associated with teaching (Lortie, 1975) and promote a sense of unity and purpose in the school environment. Where there is a strong sense of community and a sense of being part of a supportive community, one observes a greater commitment to achieving educational goals (Lightfoot, 1983).

Leadership practices of the principals in high-performing schools include helping to establish clear goals, providing a vision of the good school, and encouraging teachers by assisting them in finding the necessary resources to carry out their jobs. Successful schools are also marked by teacher-directed classroom management and decision making as well as supportive collegial interaction (Purkey and Smith, 1983; Brandt, 1987).

To summarize, the well-managed school, as evidenced by student performance and teacher perceptions, exhibits a culture of mutually reinforcing expectations, trust, staff interaction, and participation in the development of instructional goals, curriculum, and classroom practice. Because of these findings, the California Commission on the Teaching Profession (1985) concluded that the participation of teachers in key aspects of school management is supported both by a growing body of research on effective schools and accumulating evidence from the field of business management.

Why is participation so crucial? MacKenzie (1983, p. 10) states, "Any curriculum works better if it is implemented with enthusiasm. Here the overall climate and atmosphere of the school can be seen as a crucible for the personal efficacy of those who work there." Teachers at one school, involved in a team-building project, reported that a major change resulted from mere participation. This was increased awareness of the various concerns of different faculty members, making the implementation of new teaching patterns and approaches to curriculum more effective. Nevertheless, this is still an exceptional situation. Few teachers believe that they have the decision-making authority that they need to be effective. The earlier cited California study determined that although 96 percent of teachers in that state believe they should participate in determining what is taught at school, less than half (41 percent) reported an opportunity to do so (Koppich, Gerritz, and Guthrie, 1985).

Professionalization and Participation

Teaching has been described as a profession beset with problems. Included among the list of problems identified by the California Commission on the Teaching Profession (1985) are: (1) low salaries and subordinate status within the school; (2) isolation in the classroom, with rare opportunities or incentives for collegiality; (3) increased conflict between teachers and administrators, inhibiting cooperation in school improvement; (4) deficiencies in professional training and support; and (5) the absence of appropriate professional standards to encourage quality teaching and public confidence.

To attract, motivate, and retain competent, dedicated, professional teachers under these circumstances is challenging, to say the least. The literature on organizations that are staffed in the majority by professionals (Benveniste, 1987; Shulman, 1986) reveals that there is shared leadership, self-regulation of both entry and promotion (Shulman, 1986), some choice and control over how work is organized, discretionary control over the use of time, and decision-making responsibilities linked to accountability.

Participation cuts across the characteristics of professionalized jobs. Professionals do not leave key decisions that affect the content and organization of work to others; they have latitude and discretion in the diagnosis of problems, design of solutions, and evaluation of effectiveness. Professionals establish their own system of quality control and performance evaluation. They share a common view of the general goals and scope of activity within their domain. The argument for participation as one of several select avenues to "professionalizing" teaching is strong and persuasive, especially when compared with well-established professions such as medicine, law, or university teaching.

Management, Organizations, and Participation

During the past century there have been strands of action and research with regard to employee participation in management of the workplace. The advent and spread of Frederick Taylor's "scientific" management, which emphasized specialization and routinization of the work process to improve production, stimulated another direction of research. Elton Mayo's now famous "Hawthorne experiments," mentioned earlier in this chapter, were designed to explore the factors affecting employee morale and productivity. The curious results revealed that personal attention paid to workers participating in the experiments as well as consultation with and veto power of workers in respect to work site changes were critical factors stimulating improved production performance. Mayo wrote, "The group unquestionably develops a sense of participation in the critical determinations and becomes something of a social unit" when the supervisor takes personal interest in each worker, communicates to the workers about improved performance, and urges the work group to "feel its duty [is] to set its own conditions of work" (Simmons and Mares, 1985, p. 29). This early foundation of the human relations school of management developed in reaction to the overengineering of the workplace encouraged by Taylorism.

There were isolated efforts to incorporate some of the early findings with regard to employee participation in plants and factories across the United States. Most of the efforts took the form of labor-management committees. Focused principally on how to increase production, the concerns of these committees were distinct from collective bargaining agreements of the times. Emerging from these early efforts was the Scanlon Plan developed by Joseph Scanlon (originally an accountant with LaPointe Steel Company and later a researcher at MIT in industrial design and relations), which set up a two-tiered participation scheme, with committees composed of labor and management representatives from each department in the enterprise meeting regularly to discuss production problems and make suggestions. A screening committee then reviewed and (usually) approved suggestions. Economic gains due to productivity increases were shared by using a ratio of dollar sales to total unit labor costs monitored weekly or monthly. Some 75 percent of any surplus was returned to each person's salary or wage. Since the plan rewarded the group rather than the individual, pressure to produce more or better came from employees and peers, rather than from management's insistence (Simmons and Mares, 1985).

The human relations approach to management began following World War II. A growing body of empirical research initiated by leading psychologists, such as Rensis Likert and Frederick Herzberg, linked employee satisfaction and productivity to the conditions of work, such as responsibility, opportunities for advancement and growth, social recognition, and pay. These advances in industrial psychology gave rise to more articulated theories of management.

In particular, Douglas McGregor of MIT developed the now popularized X and Y theories of management. Theories X and Y (discussed more fully in Chapter Four) represent two contrasting styles of management. Theory X, based on Taylorism and traditional hierarchical organizational structure, assumes that the average person does not like to work and will avoid doing so if possible. Therefore, people must be coerced with rewards and punishments and carefully supervised and directed by authority figures in the work setting. By contrast, Theory Y asserts that people are anxious to do a good job, seek learning opportunities and stimulation in the workplace, and want to assume increasing amounts of responsibility. To harness these impulses, the organization of work itself, along with the work environment, needs to stimulate the expression and use of imagination by all employees. The management style associated with Theory Y should be open, involve employees in identifying as well as solving problems, and give employees the opportunity to make decisions that directly affect their work.

Theories X and Y are the extremes at either end of a managerial continuum. Related to Theory Y management are two recent and important trends: the organizational development approach (OD), often associated with the quality of working life (QWL) programs, and Japanese management or Theory Z. Both OD and Theory Z strongly emphasize dimensions of employee participation as part of the management process.

The organizational development approach highlights the need to modify both the structure and process of human relationships within organizations to achieve better performance results. Recent work by Bradford and Cohen (1984) found that high performance in business organizations comes about through building a "shared responsibility team" that both makes and implements decisions. Managers in these organizations share information with their employees, provide regular feedback (on achievements and areas for improvement), involve them in decision making, and support the upgrading of employee skills and knowledge. Creation of teams to solve organizational problems can change the nature of relationships between managers and employees as well as the way employees interact with colleagues.

Theory Z, associated with the Japanese style of management,

incorporates many of these same elements. William Ouchi (1982) describes Theory Z management in terms of four highly inter- dependent aspects:

1. *Commitment* within the organization to an overall philoso- phy which includes organizational goals and objectives and basic operating procedures.
2. Emphasis on *long-term association and development* with regard to both employees and goods or services being pro- duced. This long-term perspective assumes a highly stable workforce, mentoring relationships between new and experi- enced employees, slow promotions, and the opportunity to move around within the organization by working in different aspects of its operations.
3. *Trust* among all staff within the organization exhibited by a high degree of staff willingness to share information and work on joint employee-management projects.
4. *Participatory decision making* which involves employees at all levels of the organization.

Summary

Schools are complex formal organizations. They are situated within other organizational contexts: school districts and state- wide school systems. School administrators are managers within these organizational settings. The school system performs the vital function of mediating between the family and the formal so- cial order.

Management theory, as applied to education, has evolved over the years. Early approaches stressed scientific management and superintendency, with an emphasis on overseeing the entire range of schoolwide or districtwide activities. An unintended con- sequence of this approach is that it tends to smother broad-based creativity. In contrast, recent trends in management research and practice for nearly half a century demonstrate that more creative decisions and more effective implementation occurs in organiza- tions where information is shared, where managers and em- ployees are frequently jointly involved in the design and implementation of projects, and where management trusts and supports employees (Miller and Monge, 1986).

References

Benveniste, G. *Professionalizing the Organization.* San Francisco: Jossey-Bass, 1987.

Blau, P. M., and Scott, W. R. *Formal Organizations: A Comparative Approach.* San Francisco: Chandler, 1962, p. 10.

Bowles, S., and Gintis, H. *Schooling in Capitalist America.* New York: Basic Books, 1976.

Bradford, D., and Cohen, A. *Managing for Excellence.* New York: Wiley & Sons, 1984.

Brandt, R. "On Principal Leadership and School Achievement: A Conversation with Richard Andrews." *Educational Leadership* (September 1987).

Bruno, J., and Nottingham, M. A. *Collegial Teams.* New York: Lexington Books, 1976.

Bureau of the Census. *Historical Statistics of the United States, 1789–1945.* Washington, D.C.: U.S. Department Printing Office, 1949.

Bureau of the Census. *Statistical Abstract of the United States, 1988.* Washington, D.C.: U.S. Department Printing Office, 1988.

California Commission on the Teaching Profession. *Who Will Teach Our Children?* Sacramento, CA, 1985.

Callahan, R. E. *Education and the Cult of Efficiency.* Chicago: University of Chicago Press, 1962, pp. 129–130.

Carnoy, M., and Levin, H. *The Limits of Educational Reform.* New York: David McKay, 1976.

Cohen, M. "Effective Schools: Accumulating Research Findings." *American Education* (January-February 1982): 13–16.

Cohen, E., and Rossmiller, R. "Research on Effective Schools: Implications for Less Developed Countries." *Comparative Education Review* 31(August 1987): 377–399.

Coleman, J. S. *Equality of Educational Opportunity.* Washington, D.C.: U.S. Government Printing Office, 1966.

Department of Education. *Digest of Educational Statistics.* Washington, D.C.: U.S. Government Printing Office, 1989.

Dougherty, V. *State Programs of School Improvement, 1983: A 50-State Survey.* Denver: Educational Commission of the States, October 1983.

Dreeben, R. *On What Is Learned in School.* Reading, MA: Addison-Wesley, 1968.

Edmonds, R. "Programs of School Improvement; An Overview." *Educational Leadership* (December 1982): 4–11.

Kenny, L. W. "Economies of Scale in Schooling." *Economics of Education Review* 2 (1982): 1–24.

Koppich, J., Gerritz, W., and Guthrie, J. W. "A View from the Classroom: California Teachers' Opinions of the Teaching Profession and School Reform Proposals." Paper prepared for the California Commission on the Teaching Profession, 1985.

Likert, R. *New Patterns of Management.* New York: McGraw-Hill, 1961.

Lightfoot, S. L. *The Good High School.* New York: Basic Books, 1983.

Lortie, D. *School Teacher.* Chicago: University of Chicago Press, 1975.

MacKenzie, D. "Research for School Improvement: An Appraisal of Some Recent Trends." *Educational Researcher* (April 1983): 5–16.

Madaus, G., Airasian, P. W., and Kellaghan, T. *School Effectiveness: A Reassessment of the Evidence.* New York: McGraw-Hill, 1980.

McGregor, D. *The Human Side of Enterprise.* New York: McGraw-Hill, 1960.

Miller, K., and Monge, P. R. "Participation Satisfaction and Productivity: A Meta-Analysis." *Academy of Management Journal,* 29 (1986): 727–753.

Montgomery County Public Schools. *Report of a Study of the Principalship in Action in the Montgomery Public Schools.* Rockville, MD, 1975.

Ouchi, W. *Theory Z.* Reading, MA: Addison-Wesley, 1982.

Purkey, S. C., and Smith, M. S. "Effective Schools—A Review." *Elementary School Journal* 83 (1983): 427–452.

Rosenholtz, S. J. "Effective Schools: Interpreting the Evidence." *American Journal of Education,* 93 (1985): 352–388.

Shulman, L. S. "Those Who Understand Knowledge Growth in Teaching." *Educational Researcher,* (February 1986): 4–14.

Simmons, J., and Mares, W. *Working Together: Employee Participation in Action.* New York: New York University Press, 1985.

Spring, J. *Education and the Rise of the Corporate State.* Boston: Beacon Press, 1972.

Tyack, D. B. *The One Best System: A History of American Urban Education.* Cambridge, MA: Harvard University Press, 1974.

Tyack, D. B., and Hansot, Elisabeth. *Managers of Virtue: Public School Leadership in America, 1820–1980.* New York: Basic Book, 1982.

U.S. Department of Education. *Digest of Educational Statistics.* Washington, D.C.: U.S. Government Printing Office, 1989.

"US Schools Called Costly and Inefficient." *San Francisco Chronicle,* August 24, 1989, p. A19.

Weick, K. "Educational Organization as Loosely Coupled System." *Administrative Science Quarterly* 22 (1976): 1–14.

Wise, A. et al. *Case Studies for Teacher Evaluation: A Study of Effective Practices.* Santa Monica, CA: RAND, 1984.

Wolcott, H. F. *The Man in the Principal's Office. An Ethnography.* New York: Holt, Rinehart and Winston, 1973.

CHAPTER TWO

Participatory Management in Education

Introduction

In March of each year, all of the schools in the Vallejo Unified School District in California meet for a one-day retreat to formulate their plans for the coming year. A teacher/administrator team with 5 to 10 members from each school meets to discuss their accomplishments of the preceding year and their goals for the coming year. In March 1988, four teachers, the principal, and two district resource staff formed the team for Beverly Hills Elementary School. Unlike its namesake in wealthy southern California, Beverly Hills Elementary is located in a working-class urban neighborhood. The school has 450 children, 13 teachers, 2 resource staff, and 1 principal. The mood of the meeting was one of restrained excitement. Several issues were under consideration, including how to link the math and language arts curriculum with the school's strategy for professional staff development. Following a lively discussion of possibilities, Barbara Armstrong, the principal, summed up: "Pass the word to the others—if there is a conference you would like to attend, there is conference money for math and language arts."

In discussing what is different about Beverly Hills School, now that a style of participative management has been introduced, teachers offered a range of perceptive impressions. "What we do is to treat everyone as a source of creative input. Teachers share their ideas; if you give an idea to one person, it spreads," said one teacher. Another added, "In other schools, I would never talk about what I did in the classroom; I would be open to attack. Here, I receive daily support from Barbara and everyone else." What the staff does is continuously self-renewing. By celebrating what they do well, by visiting each other's classrooms, and by sharing ideas, a climate of trust, cooperation, and a willingness to try new ideas has evolved. Even more important, with the added input and effort of teachers, the district reports rising California Academic Performance (CAP) scores.

This chapter begins by explaining participative management and examining different concepts and frameworks for analyzing employee participation in organizations. Subsequently, we turn to the issue of how participation actually influences an organization's employees and its productivity. To address this issue, we present an overview of the research done to date in both schools and other organizational settings. We then focus on the importance of participation in school settings as the key to teacher empowerment and professionalizing the work environment. Finally, we examine the steps to take and the possible pitfalls schools will need to consider as they move toward a participatory management program.

What Is Participatory Management?

Participatory management refers to regular and significant employee involvement in organizational decision making. Employees are involved in setting goals, resolving problems and making decisions that affect the entire organization as well as their individual jobs, establishing and enforcing performance standards, and making sure their organization is on target in terms of responding to the needs of the clients it serves.

Recent developments in management theory have placed increasing emphasis on the importance of employee involvement in the planning and decisions that affect their work. Employee participation has become central to some of the most successful private corporations such as Hewlett Packard and W. L. Gore Associates, makers of Goretex. With the emphasis on educational quality, there is a search for methods to overcome chronic organizational problems that plague the schools as well as invigorate school personnel with enthusiasm for school renewal.

Participatory management departs from the recognition that contemporary organizational life is highly complex. Observing that it is not possible for managers to have answers for the myriad problems and issues that arise in connection to the work of their organizations, participatory management asserts that managers must turn to the specialized knowledge and firsthand experience of their employees if the organization is to flourish. Participatory principles of management rest on the concept of shared authority by which managers delegate power as well as responsibility to their employees.

The degree of power and responsibility delegated is variable. Experience shows that employee participation in management ranges from the proverbial suggestion box to more advanced forms of industrial democracy, including European workers' councils that have complete control over every aspect of management and decision making. The German codetermination program has been in existence since the early 1950s, requiring an equal number of employee- and management-appointed directors for all large companies. In Europe, participatory management was designed to change the adversarial character of labor relations. Measured by the relative labor peace in Scandinavia and West Germany, where it is predominant, there has been considerable success.

Studies of participatory management can be grouped into those that utilize a cognitive model of participation and those that use an affective model of participation. *Cognitive* models propose that participation produces increases in productivity by bringing higher-quality information from different areas and levels of the organization to bear on strategic decisions. In contrast, *affective* models assert that productivity gains are the result of improved worker satisfaction and its relationship to motivation. Working in a participative climate results in improved employee attitudes, which reduce resistance to change while increasing worker motivation through the satisfaction of higher-order needs (see Chapter Four). "When management accords the workers participation in any important decision, it implies that workers are intelligent, competent, and valued partners. Thus, participation directly affects . . . the perception of being valued, the perception of common goals and cooperation" (French, Israel, and As, 1960, p. 5).

A Framework for Analysis: Management Styles and Educational Effectiveness

We propose a framework that combines the cognitive and affective approaches and relates them to educational effectiveness. The framework has three dimensions: management style, organizational environment, and educational effectiveness.

Management Style

Management styles can be variously characterized. (See Chapter Three for a detailed discussion.) For analytic clarity, we prefer to describe the variety of styles as ranging from nonparticipatory to participatory. Nonparticipatory styles can include such different forms of management as the laissez-faire and authoritarian approaches. Under laissez-faire management, the organization moves along under its own steam without specific direction from the leadership. Explicit goals are rarely set, problems are solved ad hoc by whomever is on hand, employees are expected to motivate themselves with little or no feedback on their performance, individuals must assume personal responsibility for their own career and professional development, and the most vocal clients get the lion's share of the organization's attention. The laissez-faire style of management may at times be accidentally participative. There is no explicit policy or organizational structure to support participatory processes.

An authoritarian style of management is generally posed as the mirror opposite of participatory management. The authoritarian manager retains all authority but may consult with or delegate some responsibility to employees. Goals are set, problems are solved, and decisions are made by the manager. Initiative is taken at the top and communication flows from the manager down the organizational ladder, but rarely from the employees upward. Both of these nonparticipatory management styles can be found in large organizations. School districts are no exception. One school may be managed by the laissez-faire dreamer principal and another by the autocrat—unless the district takes a position on management style and makes explicit policies, trains its administrators, and institutionalizes specific practices with regard to school-site administration.

Organizational Environment and Culture

When Susan Perez took over as principal of Las Alamedas Elementary School, the response of her colleagues in other parts of the district was typically, "Oh, so you're assigned there." Most of the staff had spent the past three years fighting an unpopular principal. Many were demoralized and somewhat cynical. Moreover, the new principal stated that the teaching staff generally felt the community did not care about the school. Consequently, many experienced teachers had ceased to engage fully their professional talents in the classrooms or to contribute to the school at large.

Contrast this ambiance to that of Berkwood-Hedge, an alternative teacher-owned elementary school. Teachers meet weekly to deal with all matters of school business, including curriculum and instruction issues, staff development, school finance and administration, and problems individual children or classes may be experiencing. The meetings are highly organized with a staff-generated agenda, and during two and a half hours often cover some 30 items. Individually and in committees, teachers volunteer to assume responsibility for nonteaching activities that they perceive will enhance the school as an educational institution. Teachers like one another and frequently socialize with each other and with parents of their students outside working hours.

These two examples illustrate elements of what has become known as *organizational culture.* Organizational culture can be defined as the philosophy and rules of the game of any given organization. This encompasses ideology, values, assumptions, beliefs, expectations, attitudes, and norms that bind the organization together and are generally shared by the employees. Together, these elements constitute explicit and implicit consensus within an organization as to how to solve problems and approach decisions (Kilmann, Saxon, and Serpa, 1986).

The professional work climate evolves from the dominant organizational climate. This climate is a complex mixture of staff morale, the amount of commitment to a common purpose as well as specific work ethics and standards, the degree to which competition or cooperation pervades the relations among staff members, and the frequency and tone of communication among members within the organization as well as between the organization and its environment. Studies of job satisfaction are often used as one indicator of organizational climate, whereas organization cultures are frequently studied by observational methods. Organizational culture in the educational settings is often reflected in a districtwide environment. Individual schools absorb the district culture, but may deviate from it in terms of their individual school climates.

Educational Effectiveness

Since the early 1970s, educational researchers have become interested in the topic of what constitutes an effective school. The effective schools' research has focused primarily on case studies of individual schools that seem to be working well. The objective of the research has been to identify factors endemic to the apparent effectiveness of the school. Relatively few studies of educational effectiveness have tried to relate factors thought to influence effectiveness to student learning outcomes. Educational effectiveness is a highly complex and much debated concept. Ultimately, it should be the measure of whether or not schools are doing a good job or a poor one. Educational outcomes are most easily measured by standardized test scores of pupil achievement in specific subject areas. This approach has been criticized for its unidimensionality as well as social, sexual, and racial biases. The results of the debate are far from conclusive (see Rowan, Bossert, and Dwyer, 1983; David, 1988; and Cohn and Rossmiller, 1987). To avoid entering the quagmire of the discussion, suffice it to say that our framework (see Figure 2.1) postulates that management style affects educational outcomes—both cognitive and affective—via its

FIGURE 2.1 • *Relationship between Management Style, the Organizational Environment, and Educational Effectiveness*

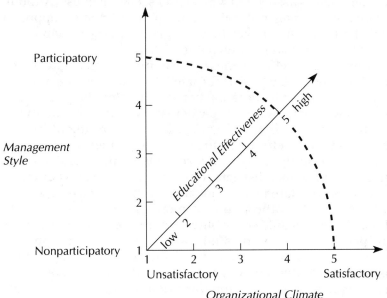

impact on the organization environment. Practitioners need to give careful consideration to designing school-level structures that are comprehensive.

Each of the three dimensions shown in Figure 2.1 is graduated along a continuum. Optimal educational effectiveness calls for an appropriate blend of management style and organizational climate. Management style affects the professional work climate, which is constantly interacting with general organizational characteristics. In most cases, management style is limited by organizational characteristics. For example, in some hierarchical organizations, it is generally difficult for line managers to diverge from highly formalized rules, procedures, and policies, whereas in less hierarchical organizations, management often has the latitude to improvise.

Figure 2.1 illustrates the interdependency of management style with organizational climate, which act together to influence the degree of educational effectiveness. If each of these is measured on a scale of 1 to 5 in which 5 is high, then the optimal score is a 5,5,5. This diagram illustrates that generally a high degree of educational effectiveness is associated with participative managerial styles and satisfactory organizational climate. Clearly, there are other factors associated with schools' effectiveness. Although a participative managerial style is not a panacea nor is it appropriate in all situations, it is nevertheless significant. (See Chapter Three for further discussion of this point.)

Educational effectiveness, measured by the outcomes the school or school district sets for itself, results from the interaction of management style, organizational characteristics, and the professional work climate. More participatory management styles appear to produce a better organizational environment, which in turn leads to more effective educational outcomes. In 1988–89, we conducted a study of 16 California elementary and secondary schools in six school districts to test the hypothesis that managerial style is correlated with educational effectiveness. Specifically, we tested the hypothesis that a more participatory style at the school-site level would contribute to more effective schoolwide student performance. In our study we measured educational effectiveness in terms of student performance on the California Assessment Program (CAP), a set of standardized school achievement tests that correct for variation in the students' socioeconomic status, racial background, and language spoken in the home environment.

Results from the research showed that schools in which the teaching staff reported that they were involved in developing the school's goals, making decisions, designing staff development plans, and learning from colleagues had significantly higher student performance on standardized test measures than others with less involvement (Girling and Keith, 1989). Qualitative data derived from open-ended interview questions provided further insight as to why some schools may perform better than others. The comments of teachers tell us how they are subjectively affected by certain working conditions. For example, one teacher at a school with relatively high CAP scores stated, "What makes our school unique is that the faculty works together and supports each other as well as working together for the children."

In another school that underwent a dramatic shift in its style of management, an influential teacher commented, "I am the school's rep to the management team whose job it is to create the budget for 1989–90, so I am feeling we are getting a great deal of say in it. It's *very* important because we had such a horrible time regarding budget matters last year, very adversarial. Now we are on an entirely different track and it's great."

Meanwhile, the role of feedback was highlighted by yet another teacher: "The management style at our school affects teachers by being so supportive. With *constructive* criticism, teachers are able to consistently improve." In contrast, a school with low CAP scores was characterized as "unresponsive to teacher concerns" and seemingly "afraid to communicate with teachers." Although this study is one among a very few that have attempted to relate student learning outcomes to management practices in the school setting, participatory management has been studied in a wide variety of organizational contexts. We will now turn to a brief examination of the findings to date.

What We Know about Participatory Management

As indicated earlier, the participative model of management focuses on the specific ways in which employees can be involved in the management process with the objective of improving the organization's productivity and overall effectiveness. Although participatory management does mean greater employee involvement in managing the organization, it does not negate the importance of managers or mandate that employees be involved in every aspect of managing the organization at all times.

There is a growing body of knowledge and empirical research that indicates a significant correlation between participatory management and employee satisfaction and organizational productivity (Miller and Monge, 1986; Anthony, 1978; Locke and Schweiger, 1979). A recent meta-analysis reviewed a wide range of both field and laboratory studies of participative management (Miller and Monge, 1986).[1] Following their detailed analysis of the data, the authors conclude that "participation has an effect on both satisfaction and productivity" (p. 748). The correlation of participation with productivity for the field studies was .27 ($p < .01$), whereas the effect of a participatory climate on work satisfaction was $r = .46$ ($p < .01$). These findings lend strong support and reinforcement to the findings of other researchers.[2]

Katzell and Guzzo (1983) reviewed 207 productivity experiments reported between 1971 and 1981 that involved employee participation. Among these, some 87 percent recorded evidence of improvement, whereas in 98 cases there was a significant improvement in productivity (nearly one-half of a standard deviation). Other studies have also found that participation in setting goals is an invaluable device for increasing a manager's knowledge, promoting "buy-in" to decisions, and improving the quality of action-oriented decision making (Latham and Locke, 1979). Lawler and Hackman's (1969) study of custodians showed that involving them in decision making on issues relevant to their work built their trust in the intentions of management. This in turn was reflected in lower absence rates than where autocratic style was used. Finally, the National Center for Employee Ownership (1987) found that labor turnover rate among participative, employee-owned organizations was less than 25 percent the rate of companies without participation plans.

These conclusions are encouraging, but they do not necessarily imply that all forms of participation will have a positive impact in every situation. On the contrary, the evidence suggests that participation requires a set of facilitating conditions. At this point it will be useful to consider the application and potential benefits of participative management in educational environments as well as some of the barriers and necessary conditions for effective participation.

Participation, Teacher Effectiveness, and School Quality

Research on educational effectiveness enhances one's understanding of how participatory management can affect school quality. One intriguing study of effective teaching surveyed teacher attitudes toward the management styles of their principals as well as student perceptions of effective learning related to the action of teachers (Greenblatt, Cooper, and Muth, 1984). The research revealed that schools in which the principal practiced a consultative management style through seeking the opinions of selected members of the staff (i.e., those who possess expertise or pertinent information and use the information in making and implementing decisions) also had the most effective learning environments.

Turning to the issue of school quality, a culture of mutually reinforcing expectations and activities is the critical variable. Figure 2.2 provides a summary of the core and facilitating elements that comprise the dimensions necessary for excellence in education, according to MacKenzie's (1983) survey of research on school improvement.

What is noteworthy about the list of items in Figure 2.2 is the number of elements that either presume or require a cooperative and participative environment. Among these are the following:

FIGURE 2.2 • *Dimensions of Effective Schooling*

1. Leadership Dimensions
   Core Elements
   1.1 Positive climate and overall atmosphere
   1.2 Goal-focused activities toward clear, attainable, and relevant objectives
   1.3 Teacher-directed classroom management and decision making
   1.4 In-service staff training for effective teaching
   Facilitating Elements
   1.5 Shared consensus on values and goals
   1.6 Long-range planning and coordination
   1.7 Stability and continuity of key staff
   1.8 District-level support for school improvement

2. Efficacy Dimensions
   Core Elements
   2.1 High and positive achievement expectations with a constant press for excellence
   2.2 Visible rewards for academic excellence and growth
   2.3 Cooperative activity and group interaction in the classroom
   2.4 Total staff involvement in school improvement
   2.5 Autonomy and flexibility to implement adaptive processes
   2.6 Appropriate levels of difficulty for learning tasks
   2.7 Teacher empathy, rapport, and personal interaction with students
   Facilitating Elements
   2.8 Emphasis on homework and study
   2.9 Positive accountability; acceptance and responsibility for learning outcomes
   2.10 Strategies to avoid nonpromotion of students
   2.11 Deemphasis of strict ability grouping, interaction with more accomplished peers

3. Efficiency Dimensions
   Core Elements
   3.1 Effective use of instructional time: amount and intensity of engagement in school learning
   3.2 Orderly and disciplined school and classroom environments
   3.3 Continuous diagnosis, evaluation and feedback
   3.4 Well-structured classroom activities
   3.5 Instruction guided by content coverage
   3.6 Schoolwide emphasis on basic and higher-order skills
   Facilitating Elements
   3.7 Opportunities for individualized work
   3.8 Number and variety of opportunities to learn

Source: D. MacKenzie, "Research for School Improvement: An Appraisal of Some Recent Trends," *Educational Researcher* (April 1983):8. Copyright 1983 by the American Educational Research Association. Adapted by permission of the publisher.

(1.1) a positive climate and overall atmosphere; (1.2) goal-focused activities toward clear, attainable, and relevant objectives; (1.3) teacher-directed classroom management and decision making; (1.5) shared consensus on values and goals; and (2.5) autonomy and flexibility to implement adaptive processes. It is apparent that a basis of participative strategic management can provide some of the essential ingredients for improving the quality of schooling. MacKenzie (1983) summarizes the findings from his survey of over 100 studies of school improvement with the following observation:

> *Any curriculum works better if it is implemented with enthusiasm. Here the overall climate of the school can be seen as a crucible for the personal efficacy of those who work there. . . . Staff interaction and participatory planning around the specific goals of instruction may help engender a more widely shared consensus on values and goals through which the achievement climate becomes self-sustaining. (pp. 10–11)*

Participation in School Settings

Education is a multifaceted activity; the tasks of educational managers at the school site and district level are becoming more complex and professionally demanding. Meanwhile, the concept of schooling is continually being transformed by a wide variety of environmental factors, from budgetary stringency to global learning. The manager in the educational system must be able to cope with and develop plans for budgetary allocation, provide feedback and assistance in curricular design, and set and enforce standards of educational quality.

These tasks call for educational managers to orchestrate a range of activities, from liaison between individuals and the management of interpersonal conflicts to providing teachers and superiors with required information. The site manager must be able to maintain a sense of order, anticipate and plan the allocation of supplies and equipment, coordinate and manage financial resources, and allocate students and teachers to instructional units. He or she must be involved in the design of curriculum and instruction. Additionally, the site manager must be concerned with hiring, evaluating, motivating, and developing the staff.

Barth (1980), a teacher and principal with over 20 years of experience, has written about the role of the elementary school principal. Citing a study of the Atlanta school system, he notes that fully 75 percent of a principal's time is spent on management tasks, liaison, and public relations; just 17 percent is devoted to instructional leadership; and the remaining 8 percent is distributed among miscellaneous activities. Barth comments on the staggering responsibility, which, together with a sense of isolation and intense time pressure, makes the principalship an extraordinarily complex and demanding job.

In the traditional, bureaucratically centralized style of management, employees are told to submit to authority, exercise self-control, and sacrifice for an uncertain future. Employees may perceive themselves to be vulnerable and powerless since communication is indirect and infrequent, and they are never certain what to expect next. Denied of opportunities for self-expression, employees sense boredom, repetition, and bureaucracy (Block, 1987).

Meanwhile, Levin (1988) has pointed to a number of negative consequences of traditional nonparticipative approaches to educational decision making.

> *The first is that district policies are typically made in a uniform fashion that ignores the enormous variety of student needs and characteristics that are actually found in the different schools of the district. . . . A second obstacle to effectiveness is that by placing both decisions and evaluation in a locus that is external to those who must implement the decisions, teachers and school-based educators cannot take responsibility for educational outcomes. Under these circumstances, it is easy to view educational outcomes [as] resulting from factors beyond the control of classroom teachers, since such teachers have little power to affect the planning, design, and evaluation of educational activities. . . . One could even argue that the present arrangement inures teachers to the particular needs of their schools and students, since they can do little about altering conditions to satisfy those needs. (pp. 10–11)*

One way out of the lacunae is to develop a strategic participative approach to management. In the United States, beginning in the mid-1980s, a growing number of individual schools, school districts, and school systems have begun to experiment with participative strategies and models that capitalize on the professional talents of the educational community—teachers, parents, and administrators.

Why Participation Works in Educational Settings

Two trends are serving to redefine the nature of work in schools: empowerment and professionalization (Benveniste, 1987; Little, 1987). Together they help to explain how a participatory management style enhances the educational effectiveness of schools.

Empowerment

Empowerment is rapidly becoming a catchword in educational parlance. Being empowered means to have choice and control. *Webster's* defines empower as "to give official authority of legal power to." This is perhaps the highest degree of empowerment. This maximum level of empowerment occurs in several of the cases we have studied. Teachers at Berkwood-Hedge School in Berkeley, California, act collectively and are empowered to have official and legal authority over every aspect of the school's management. At Riviera Junior High School in South Dade County, Florida, the school council has delegated authority. Legal responsibility, however, remains with the principal, who can be dismissed by a superintendent or school board that oversees action taken at the school level.

Empowerment has two dimensions: structural and psychosocial. *Structural* changes can affect the positional power and increase employee satisfaction. Flat, as opposed to hierarchical, organizations appear to increase satisfaction, especially when there is greater opportunity to exercise authority by all members of the organization. The possibility of participating in the definition of organizational goals and strategies contributes to a greater sense of mastery and esteem (Carpinter, 1971).

Kanter (1977) suggests why this strategy tends to be associated with improvements in productivity: When employees at lower levels of the organizational hierarchy have a chance to share in power from above, they feel greater fulfillment of their psychological needs, experience greater team identity, and are more cooperative. In turn, they become more participatory and more supportive of the autonomy and discretion of their subordinates. This increases the satisfaction and commitment of those below. Empowering teachers to address organizationally and educationally relevant matters unlocks hidden capabilities. Making knowledge about the organization, such as information about budgets or minutes of certain meetings, routinely available to teachers can promote the understanding and commitment of those at lower levels to the larger organizational goals.

The *psychosocial* aspect of empowerment refers to the degree to which the school community as a whole has a perceptual sense of control over its environment. This is somewhat different from *Webster's* usage. In some circumstances, the actual or perceived degree of control may exceed the legal. For example, as president of the faculty union, one of the authors experienced a situation in which the university administration chose to consult with the union prior to making certain decisions. There was no legal requirement for such consultation to take place; however, it was the *administrative style* of the university president and vice-president to follow this procedure. In this instance, the personalities involved influenced the level of empowerment. Nevertheless, that level of empowerment was fragile, subject to change whenever the individual officeholders changed or if the university administration should have a change of heart.

Thus the level of empowerment is comprised of a structural and a perceptual component. Full empowerment of teachers will require both. The key to full empowerment is that employees feel that the important aspects of their work environment are in their own hands. Under these conditions, they will sense a wider latitude for risk and innovation and will act boldly instead of repressing their ideas and suggestions. They will perceive their relationship toward a vision that is larger than themselves and will commit themselves to achieving that purpose.

Professionalization

It is not uncommon to hear educators complain that they are not treated as professionals. What does this mean? Professionals are characterized by a high level of specialized education and training, which is associated with a high level of technical competence and ethical standards. Teachers are professionals in that they have all six of the basic characteristics of professionals:

(1) application of skills based on technical knowledge, (2) advanced educational and training requirements, (3) some formal controls on entry to the profession, (4) existence of professional associations, (5) codes of professional conduct, and (6) a sense of responsibility for serving the public (Benveniste, 1987, p. 32ff).

To be treated as a professional implies that one has the opportunity to employ a full range of technical skills. Educators are generally well trained in communication, curriculum design, and interpersonal and group processes; many also have a range of specialized skills. Professionalization requires opportunities for teachers to manage themselves as professionals by (1) exercising a wide range of professional skills related to, but reaching beyond, the limits of day-to-day classroom teaching (e.g., curriculum design, planning and evaluation, materials selection); (2) working with peers on professionally related projects at the classroom or school-site level; and (3) playing a role in the professional evaluation of peers and their school as an organization. Beyond this, teachers will seek opportunities to expand their professional horizons by having input in nontraditional areas such as school-site planning, budget analysis, and resource allocation.

Where there is a high degree of professionalism in a school, three important events take place. First, more *initiative and innovation* occur. The Dade County School District in Florida developed a strategy of participative management. In Riviera Junior High School in South Dade County, the teachers' council responded to teachers' concerns that 60-minute periods were too long to hold the attention span of junior high students and changed the teaching day from six hour-long periods to seven 50-minute periods, which released teachers for 30 minutes of professional duties. At Miami's Campbell Drive Middle School, teachers voted to work an extra period each day without pay if administrators would agree to reduce class size. With union and administrative blessing, the change was put into effect. Second, a greater *sharing of information and ideas* may take place where there is a high degree of informal exchange, cross-training, and peer coaching among colleagues (Little, 1987). Members of the team learn professional skills from each other by exchanging information and working together. Third, *greater accountability* is evident in a professionalized organizational climate. Professionalism fosters a common code of standards among teachers, reflected in informally enforced quality norms. As one of our informants stated, "the *quality of instruction* becomes the ethic which inspires each and every teacher."

Toward a Participatory Management Program

Participation, like any substantive improvement, necessitates development and adoption of a program of activities. Several steps are critical, including the following:

1. *Develop a set of written values that summarize the organization's commitment of participative management.* Value statements can sometimes be mere public relations ploys or border on platitudinous banality. Yet, if a statement is developed through discussion with a wide range of employees, the statement can serve as a beacon of what it is hoped will be achieved. People can be moved by appeal to a higher sense of purpose; value statements can be part of that effort.

2. *Get the personal commitment of those at the highest level.* Strong leadership is needed to overcome the myriad barriers and roadblocks. Moreover, if the principal or superintendent is not committed, teachers will always question whether their involvement will be taken seriously. Several years ago, a group of teachers at one inner-city urban high school tried to establish a quality circle to deal with problems of student discipline. For a year, the group persisted with support from the principal and superintendent, finally producing a plan for improving school discipline. When the principalship changed, a new administrator fell upon the plan, adopting it without involvement of or credit to the originating group of teachers. Today, cynicism resounds among those original participants.

3. *Train teachers to develop the necessary skills so that they may participate in key management processes and decisions.* Participatory management, like teaching, is an artform when well practiced. However, it is based on specific skills and techniques. To develop these skills, teachers and managers need training and time to perfect them. Participatory management may feel clumsy and awkward to many at first, and may appear to be time consuming. Managers and employees must be willing to devote time and training resources to the creation of a working system of participatory management.

4. *Confirm that information flows up and down the organization.* Consultation is a two-way street. If an administrator gives the impression that consultation means only feeding information upward, then staff members may become resentful. If consultation involves sharing of ideas between principal and teachers,

the individuals will be more willing to consult. Moreover, not all teachers may want to be involved in decision making, but most will appreciate knowing that a colleague has been involved in the process.

5. *Begin with broad involvement in the planning process.* Changes in the Riveria Junior High School in South Dade County, Florida, came about because of broad-based participation in site-level planning and goal setting. Two critical success indicators are (a) the degree to which planning and goal-setting activities are open to members of the organization *at their discretion* and (b) the degree to which there is administrative commitment and follow through with regard to teacher participation. To illustrate, at one site, administrators selected all of the members of the school improvement team, which resulted in many teachers feeling a sense of exclusion from a fundamental and important process. At another site, administrators made an arbitrary decision on the teaching responsibility for department heads, an issue that the school improvement project had been studying for months. This led one participant to remark, "The administrators encouraged us to do months and months of work; they said they were 100 percent behind us, and then they go and do whatever they want. It's obvious that they were just giving lip service to our project; they never intended to abandon their old 'bosses know best' way of doing things" (Welsh, 1987, p. 47). The failure to translate goals into departmental and individual tasks is one of the most common reasons for the failure of strategic plans. Unless goals can be tied to the work activities of individuals and *unless those individuals accept the goals as their own,* it remains as an abstract idea. Participation transforms planning into a vital daily process. Giving staff members a greater voice in deciding how to confront work-related problems ensures a better understanding of organizational constraints and options.

Where this process is used, research shows that organizations are more likely to exhibit the characteristics of a healthy organization (Campbell, 1981). Such organizations manage their work within a framework of goals and plans and take decisions at or near the source of information. Consequently, they exhibit relatively undistorted communication and, because of the participatory process in setting goals and values, experience a minimum of conflictual win-lose behavior.

Barriers to Effective Participation

Clearly there are many advantages to using participatory management. Yet, if this is so, why isn't this a more prevalent form of school administration? Those who have had experience with trying to introduce participative approaches are well aware of the significant barriers that can block implementation. There are three fundamental types of barriers: organizational, managerial, and employee.

Organizational Barriers

Organizational barriers fall into two categories: philosophical and structural. *Philosophical barriers* relate to the values of the top management group. The philosophical values and the underlying belief set manifests what the leadership regards as important. Effective schools research has noted that a climate of openness, which encourages employees and teachers to contribute to a better organization, can nurture a host of substantial improvements (Rosenholtz, 1985). In this respect, the attitude of the leadership is a critical factor. When management encourages a climate in which teachers feel that the organization supports them in their endeavors, they do not feel threatened or subject to reprisal for honest mistakes.

One of the most important *structural barriers* is the existence of a reward system that penalizes participation. In some organizations, those who wish to participate and articulate those sentiments may be seen as "malcontents" or troublemakers who must be kept under control or excluded from a prestigious committee because they questioned the actions of a superior (Anthony, 1978).

A further potential barrier to effective participation is the availability of time. Without release from the press of ongoing work, it is difficult for employees to engage substantively in thinking through problems, researching possible strategies, and sharing their findings. Involving others in making decisions takes time—often more time than unilateral decisions demand. Therefore, the cost of better decisions is the additional time needed to make them. One very promising school improvement project in Alexandria, Virginia, fell apart because the majority of the initial participants dropped out as a result of additional time-consuming committee work without compensating release time (Welsh, 1987). If inadequate time is allocated for group decision making or if meetings are held after normal work hours, there is a barrier to effective participation.

Managerial Barriers

It is not uncommon for managers to want to change their management approach toward a more participative style. Often they do not know where to begin or what to do (Anthony, 1978). Lack of training and insecurity are two of the most common obstacles. Training involves both managers and employees in learning specific techniques of cooperative group processes such as problem solving or goal setting. Without appropriate training, a pseudo-participatory situation can arise. *Pseudo-participation* refers to the trappings of participation without the authority. For example, a superintendent in a rural district considered himself a participative manager. He called in principals to "consult" with them on decisions he was about to make. Yet, he never veered from his initial point of view. This false participation frustrated his subordinates.

Some managers are insecure or fearful of participative methods. They may believe that sharing their authority over certain decisions will diminish their power. Instead of taking pride in the accomplishments of their team, they resent or feel threatened by the superior performance of subordinates. As a result, they permit subordinates to participate in only the most mundane and tangential matters. Others are fearful that people will not perform and the job will not get done (Anthony, 1978). There is no simple formula for eliminating insecurity. Training and sustained exposure to successful implementation of participatory techniques by esteemed colleagues can ameliorate certain anxieties. Organizational incentives for participation can also help to motivate managers to change their style.

Employee Barriers

When we discuss participatory management with some teachers, they report that they just want to teach their classes without any added form of administrative responsibility. Participation is viewed as an increased workload. Research demonstrates that some members of an organization will be more predisposed to participate; others may actually feel "decisional saturation." A study of organizational decision making among teachers in western New York state found that about 20 percent of their sample felt decisionally saturated (Alutto and Belasco, 1972). The teachers in this category tended to be older females teaching at elementary levels in urban districts. They felt greater than normal conflict over the amount of time allotted for them to undertake professional activities. Thus participation may be viewed as another added task to an already intense work schedule.

A second barrier among employees in participative situations may be a perceived lack of professional competence. If teachers or other employees are professionally weak, participation may flounder. Moreover, employees should not be enjoined to participate in activities when special skills/knowledge they do not possess are required for satisfactory results. Although participation can extend a teacher's professional expertise and enrich one's work life, it cannot substitute for basic professional training.

Benefits of the Participatory Schools

If successfully pursued, a participative strategic process can avoid a number of administrative problems by providing five vital ingredients to an educational institution or system.

1. *Clarity of purpose.* Clearly defined goals promote a sense of internal agreement and commitment. Members of the staff will understand goals and be committed to their implementation because they have participated in their formulation. Participation in the design of strategy leads to more challenging goals and higher levels of motivation toward the attainment of those goals. This became clear as we conducted field research. In talking with teachers, principals, and district administrators at a variety of school sites, educators expressed a uniform enthusiasm for involvement in organizational goal setting. Likewise, participants in our "1988 Roundtable on Participative Management" at the University of California, Berkeley, stated that a major source of friction between teachers and administrators in nonparticipative settings was the lack of commitment to common goals.

2. *Greater commitment to and coordination of decisions.* Goals that are articulated and accepted can serve to coordinate the decisions and actions of teachers and administrators in a number

of related areas. Mutual goals provide a vital focus and point of reference for a wide range of future decisions. When individuals understand the objectives of an organization, they tend to be more committed to implementing those decisions (Lawler and Hackman, 1969).

3. *Effective conflict resolution.* Agreed upon goals provide a mechanism for resolving the inevitable conflicts that occur between organizational units or individuals. Goals provide a framework of overall agreement within which conflicts can be handled constructively.

4. *Ability to adapt to changing circumstances.* Collectively determined goals increase the organization's ability to respond with relative ease to a changing environment. A continuous goal-setting process that involves the school and district staff in an on-going self-evaluation of their responsiveness to client needs and the effectiveness of their program is a useful vehicle for administrators and staff to analyze jointly the changing conditions and to find solutions to common problems.

5. *Renewal.* The participative goal-setting process provides a continuous opportunity to renew the organization's energy level by providing a recurrent fresh assessment of its potential for excellence. In the words of Judy Guilkey-Amado, Director of Elementary School Improvement of the Vallejo (California) Unified School District, the participative goal-setting process "ensures that we perceive our schools as dynamic and not static institutions."

How to Develop a Participatory Management System

An organizational strategy encompasses a comprehensive plan of action that identifies goals and policies and links those goals to a plan of action. The strategy should serve as a guide for the allocation of resources, human as well as financial and physical. Any organization's strategy is closely related to the way in which decisions are made and problems are solved (see Chapter Five). In order for an organization to attain the benefits of participation and to develop a participative climate, an organizational strategy is fundamental.

As indicated in the opening vignette, the Vallejo City (California) Unified School District has attempted to pursue a participative approach toward strategic management. Planning for each year's activities begins in March of the preceding academic year. School-based teams of teachers and administrators get together for a two-day retreat to develop their annual school-site plan. With support from the office of the superintendent, each school begins by evaluating the accomplishments in the current year and identifying goals that can be achieved in the coming year. The plans of each school are combined and form the basis for the district's instructional improvement plan.

Our research has shown that participation is important in formulating goals that project the teachers' value systems. For example, at Beverly Hills Elementary School the reading skills goal was to have all students learning to read with understanding, think critically about what they read, and enjoy and respond actively to important literary works. One objective for attaining this goal was to hire and train three classroom aides to provide instructional support to individual students in emphasized reading skills. Goal setting begins with a diagnosis of the situation, the environment, and the needs of the organization. In this case, a parent-teacher survey (designed and carried out jointly) observed that classroom aides had proven exceptionally important in grades K, 1, and 2.

All organizations have multiple goals and objectives that exist in a complex hierarchy. At the uppermost strata is the institution's values objectives—a broad statement of values that it strives to achieve. Although organizational goals identify future targets according to contemporary theory and research, it is the climatic considerations—managerial style, teamwork, open communication, and a supportive atmosphere—that are the crucial determinants of successful administration.

Summary

Participatory management is a program for regular and significant employee involvement in organizational decision making. Effective management calls for a philosophical commitment to the participatory framework. Educational research has sought to uncover what factors are needed to produce an effective school. The research has identified a number of dimensions, however. At the core, uniting these dimensions is a common notion of participation, teacher involvement, and teamwork. The reasons why participation is central in educational settings lie in empowerment and professionalization. This chapter includes a list of steps that educational managers can take to develop a participatory management program, as well as barriers to participation that deserve consideration. A successful program of participation can avoid a number of administrative problems by facilitating greater clarity of purpose, coordination of decisions, better conflict resolution, and ability to adapt to changing circumstances.

Case Study ————————————————————————

Lake Washington School District Master Plan—A System for Growth and Change

(Authors' Note: This case illustrates how a districtwide school-based management plan contributed to the turnaround of the Lake Washington School District in Kirkland, Washington. What problems did the district face? What is the function of a master plan? What were the first steps taken by the district in the formulation of the master plan? What operating principles guided the planning process? What method was used to assist principals in developing their planning skills and what did the findings indicate? What is the meaning of the term marketing plan? *How is evaluation incorporated in the master plan? How did the planning process address the district's problems? Do you think this planning process is replicable in other districts?)*

Eleven years ago, Lake Washington School District was in a state of turmoil. The quality of education was perceived to be poor, parents and community members were highly dissatisfied, employees were jealous and distrustful, and the relationship between the teachers' union and the administration was adversarial.

Today things are different. Lake Washington School District has strong community support. The Parent-Teacher-Student Association has 9,000 members—the largest in the state, bond issues and levies pass with 80 to 85 percent margins, location within the district is a "selling point" for homes, and businesses often initiate partnerships with the schools. The district was one of four recognized by RAND Corporation in a nationwide study on teacher evaluation, and four of the district's schools have received excellence awards from the U.S. Office of Education. In addition, the teachers' union has just signed an extension to a three-year contract, guaranteeing two more years of harmony.

These dramatic changes resulted from the implementation of a districtwide master plan affecting every employee, every position, and every function of the school district.

Planning for Change

The Lake Washington master plan balances building-based decision making and administrative input, encourages collegiality, and is responsive to change. For each building, the district master plan is mirrored by a locally developed master plan, and each teacher is also developing a plan for his or her classroom.

The customary first step in master planning is to determine the needs of the community and develop a master statement. Before developing the master plan, the district conducted a school climate survey and a student needs assessment. Based on the results, the district adopted a mission statement emphasizing "what's best for the kids."

The administration wanted a master plan that would be responsive to changing needs and situations. Therefore, they emphasized relationships and interactions rather than rigid hierarchical structures or rules, believing that people are more flexible than policies and procedures. They developed operating principals that are people-oriented, providing guidelines for communication in areas such as cooperation, support, loyalty, disagreement, and initiative. For example, one of the guidelines on loyalty reads, "When we disagree, we will focus on issues, not people, and we will be open and honest. Each individual will use a process to resolve conflicts that is fair, just, and sensitive to the integrity of other people."

The Master Plan

The main functions of the master plan are to provide direction and to encourage people to see the gestalt of the workings of the district—to climb the "mental ladder" to get a better view of the interactions of the various parts of the whole. The plan provides a framework that defines daily operations and creates a sense of belonging through group decision making, common goals, and an emphasis on the synergistic relationship between the central administration and the building principals.

Lake Washington's master plan has 10 components that can be divided into three broad categories: planning, action, and accountability (see Figure 2.3). The *planning* function includes a community needs assessment, annual goals, budget allocation, and district policy. The *action* function includes administrator expectations and development, staff expectations and development, job description, staff selection, and program. The *accountability* function provides evaluation guidelines.

The final document serves as both a map and a set of guidelines for planned change. Yearly goals are established with input from faculty, administration, school board, community, and students. These goals reflect the changing needs of the district as a whole. Upon adoption by the school board, the goals become the job descriptions for the administrative staff for the coming year.

In addition to these 1-year goals, 5-year projections and 6- to 20-year visions guide the long-range planning specifically for facilities, instructional programs, implementation of technology, and total integration of a new core curriculum and essential skills training.

Master plans for the individual schools are similar to the district plans with 10 parallel components (see Figure 2.4). At the building level, planning teams include teachers, staff members, the principal, and sometimes students and the community. Specific school goals are developed based on district goals, forming job expectations for the principal and staff for the coming year.

FIGURE 2.3 • *Mission: Building the Management Team*

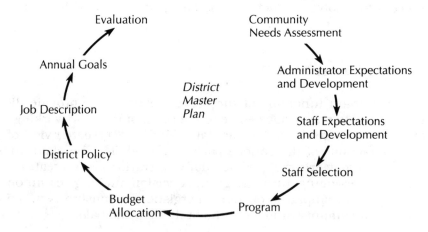

FIGURE 2.4 • *Mission: Developing the Building Team*

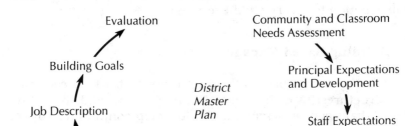

Principal Task/Time Analysis

To help principals develop planning skills, the district used a task/time analysis. Principals kept a log of their activities over a two-week period. Then central office administrators and principals developed a task/time model reflecting the ideal breakdown of activities during a day: instructional program development and assessment (24 percent), staff development (24 percent), student services (20 percent), positive school/community climate (20 percent), personal growth (8 percent), and operations (4 percent). Comparing how principals actually spent their time with this model indicated what changes were necessary to realize the ideal. This comparison resulted in additional secretarial support in all schools, a role redefinition so regular secretaries could assume more management responsibilities in the elementary schools, and the addition of an associate principal in each high school to provide instructional leadership.

The ideal relative time spent on each task reflects an emphasis on leadership. For example, ideally only 4 percent of a principal's time will involve operations, whereas 20 percent of his or her time will be devoted to creating a positive school/community climate—requiring such skills as motivation, promotion, communicating, and networking.

The task/time model, combined with the building master plan, has helped principals pursue district goals while allowing them to assess their own daily activities. The model helps them concentrate on their most important function: supervision of quality instruction for every child every day.

Building-Based Management

The key to this plan is the autonomy with which each principal structures his or her master plan. One of the district directives is that each principal should "develop community support for school and district programs by implementing a marketing plan." The principal responds to this and the task/time model by asking for faculty input and writing the proposed plan and implementation time line. Upon approval by the central administration, the plan is carried out according to schedule.

"Marketing plans" include the usual things, such as weekly coffees for 15 to 20 parents at a time, monthly open houses for parents and community members designed around specific themes or programs, and encouragement of teacher/parent school newsletters and brochures. But now each school has a marketing plan that supports the school goals and is uniquely fitted to the needs of the community. Some plans demonstrate considerable creativity and involve community members in both planning and implementation.

The third function of the district master plan is evaluation. Principals are evaluated by central office administrators based on the outcomes of the building master plans and the accomplishment of the action plans. The question is not only, Did you do it? but Did it work? and What evidence is there that it was successful? Principals in turn evaluate teachers based on an instructional skills model used within the district.

Every employee in the Lake Washington School District is evaluated at least once a year, with the individual's job description used as a criterion. The evaluation program is coupled with flexible staff development options oriented toward helping district personnel reach their full potential both personally and professionally. Pre- and postevaluation conferences are required, and all "unsatisfactory" ratings are remedied with a supportive development plan.

Why the Plan Works

The formula for developing and implementing a district master plan is simple and straightforward: Develop a mission statement, establish goals, outline activities to meet the goals, and evaluate the results. To effect remarkable changes in a school district, there must be a commitment to hiring the best people; providing training, development, and support for all staff; then trusting them to do their jobs. This means not only trusting the people themselves but trusting the staff selection and evaluation processes.

Lake Washington's master plan works because it achieves balance between central office and building-based management. The staff, following the same plan and process at all levels, has developed programs, found creative ways to solve problems, and established community ties—advances that could never have been achieved by directives from the central office. With the guidance of a master plan, an ineffective district has been transformed into a model for excellence.

This case was prepared by L. E. Scarr, Superintendent, Lake Washington School District, Kirkland, WA.

Endnotes

1. Meta-analysis is an analytical technique that can be used for numerically cumulating the findings of numerous research studies (Hunter, Schmidt, and Jackson, 1982).
2. The significance of $p < .01$ is that these results could be attributed to chance or happenstance with less than 1 percent probability. This then lends strong support to a claim for association between the variables.

References

Alutto, J., and Belasco, J. "A Typology for Participation in Organizational Decision Making." *Administrative Science Quarterly* (1972): 117–125.

Anthony, W. P. *Participative Management.* Reading, MA: Addison-Wesley, 1978.

Barth, R. *Run School Run.* Cambridge, MA: Harvard University Press, 1980.

Benveniste, G. *Professionalizing the Organization.* San Francisco: Jossey-Bass, 1987.

Block, P. H. "Empowering Employees." *Training and Development Journal* (April 1987):34–39.

Campbell, J. "On the Nature of Organizational Effectiveness." In P. S. Goodman and J. P. Pennings (Eds.), *New Perspectives on Organizational Effectiveness.* San Francisco: Jossey-Bass, 1981.

Carpinter, H. H. "Formal Organizational Structural Factors and Perceived

Job Satisfaction of Classroom Teachers." *Administrative Science Quarterly* 16 (1971):460–465.

Cohn, E. *Economics of Education.* Cambridge, MA: Ballinger, 1979.

Cohn, E. and Rossmiller, R. A. "Research on Effective Schools: Implications for Developing Countries." *Comparative Education Review* (August 1987):377–399.

David, J. "Use of Indicators by School Districts: Aid or Threat to Improvement." *Phi Delta Kappan* (March 1988):499–503.

Dewey, J. "Democracy and Educational Administration." *School and Society* 45 (1937):460.

French, J. R. P.; Israel, J.; and As, D. "An Experiment in a Norwegian Factory: Interpersonal Dimensions in Decision-Making." *Human Relations* 13 (1960):3-13

Girling, R., and Keith, S. "School Management Style and Student Performance: An Empirical Analysis." Final Report to California State University Committee for Research Scholarship and Creativity, September 1989.

Greenblatt, R. B.; Cooper, B.; and Muth, R. "Managing for Effective Teaching." *Educational Leadership* (February 1984):57–59.

Hunter, J. W.; Schmidt, F. L.; and Jackson, G. B. *Meta-Analysis: Cumulating Research Findings Across Studies.* Beverly Hills, CA: Sage, 1982.

Kanter, R. M. *Men and Women of the Corporation.* New York: Basic Books, 1977.

Katzell, R. A., and Guzzo, R. A. "Psychological Approaches to Productivity Improvement." *American Psychologist* 38 (1983):468-472.

Kilmann, R.; Saxon, M. J.; and Serpa, R. "Issues in Understanding and Changing Culture." *California Management Review* (Winter 1986):89.

Latham, G., and Locke, E. "Goal Setting—A Motivational Technique that Works." *Organizational Dynamics* (Autumn 1979).

Lawler, E. A., and Hackman, R. "Impact of Employees Participation in the Development of Pay Incentive Plans." *Journal of Applied Psychology* (December 1969):467–471.

Levin, H. "Finance and Governance Implications of School-Based Decisions." Mimeo, CERAS Stanford University, 1988, pp. 10–11.

Little, J. W. "Teachers as Colleagues." In V. Richardson-Koehler (Ed.), *Educators' Handbook: A Research Perspective.* New York: Longman, 1987.

Locke, E. A., and Schweiger, D. M. "Participation in Decisionmaking: One More Look." *Research in Organizational Behavior* 1 (1979): 265–339.

MacKenzie, D. "Research for School Improvement: An Appraisal of Some Recent Trends." *Educational Researcher* 12 (1983):5–16.

Madaus, G. F., and Airasian, P. W. *School Effectiveness: A Reassessment of the Evidence.* New York: McGraw-Hill, 1980.

Miller, K., and Monge, P. R. "Participation, Satisfaction, and Productivity: A Meta Analysis." *Academy of Management Journal* 29 (1986):727–753.

Mood, A. *Do Teachers Mike A Difference?* Washington, D.C.: Office of Education, U.S. Government Printing Office, 1970.

National Center for Employee Ownership. *Beyond Taxes: Managing an Employee Ownership Company.* Oakland, CA, 1987.

Purkey, S. C., and Smith, M. S. "Effective Schools—A Review." *Elementary School Journal* 83 (1983):427–452.

Rosenholtz, S. "Effective Schools: Interpreting the Evidence." *American Journal of Education* (May 1985):352–388.

Rowan, B.; Bossert, S. T.; and Dwyer, D. C. "Research on Effective Schools: A Cautionary Note." *Educational Researcher* (April 1983):24–31.

Weick, K. E. "Educational Organizations as Loosely Coupled Systems." *Administrative Science Quarterly* 21 (1976):1–10.

Welsh, P. "Are Administrators Ready to Share Decision Making with Teachers?" *American Educator* (Spring 1987):23–25, 47–48.

CHAPTER THREE

Leadership

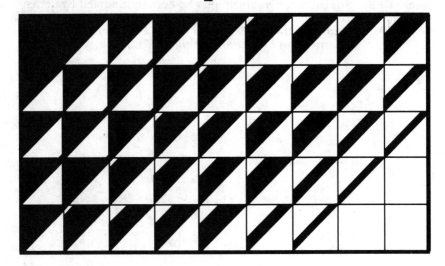

Introduction

In 1979, the Redwood City Board of Education in California appointed Dr. Ken Hill as its new superintendent. (See the case study at the end of this chapter.) Drawing on his training in organizational development, Superintendent Hill set out to map a strategy for uniting the school district around a set of common goals. He projected a vision of cooperative action to achieve curricular excellence. A 15-person committee, including members of the district management team, school board, teachers' association, and classified employees' union, developed a draft mission statement that was accepted only after it was discussed with each of the district's 14 schools. Using several task-specific committees consisting of administrators and teachers, the district developed a long-range plan, defined unified curriculum, and elaborated a plan for improving the teacher evaluation process. Hill subscribes to the participative style of leadership. "Everyone says change comes from the bottom up, but I feel there has to be a climate of leadership for expression of problems," remarks Hill, "We don't mind problems, we trust each other and try to solve problems together." Hill's style of leadership and its implicit value system of open communication, collegiality, participation, and risk taking contributes to a "can do" attitude that is sparking a new-found enthusiasm among teachers.

Since Plutarch turned his attention to the lives of his fellow Greeks, historians and researchers have sought to find out what makes leaders.[1] Over the years theorists have provided conceptions of what comprises a leader and what constitutes effective leadership. *Leadership* refers to a relationship between a leader and followers involving power, vision, and influence central to managers' success in daily work roles. Vaill (1987) states, "Our leaders are spiritual leaders among other things. They are the ones who suggest meanings in our activities, give us new images, visions, metaphors." Leadership is especially important in searching for ways of handling challenging situations.

This chapter focuses on leadership. Beginning by examining theories of leadership, we ask the questions, What makes a leader? and What confers the position of leadership on any given individual? We then discuss the different ways to lead, which broaches the issue of leadership style. Finally, we enter into an in-depth discussion of participatory leadership in general as well as applied in schools specifically.

Theories of Leadership

What is leadership? What role do leaders play? What does one have to know in order to be an effective leader? There are several classical theories of leadership, including trait theories, environmental theories, and behavioral theories. Each provides a different perspective on the factors that come together to create leaders.

Trait Theories

Classical thinkers like Aristotle asserted that leaders are born. "From the hour of your birth," he wrote, "some are marked for subjection, others for rule." Historian Thomas Carlyle, in his 1841 essay "Heroes and Hero Worship," viewed the leader as a person uniquely endowed with special qualities that capture the imagination of the masses. The assumption that the leader is endowed with special and superior qualities gave rise to a search to identify those traits common to the select few who were our born leaders.

Trait theories place emphasis on the personal characteristics of leaders. Research within the trait theory tradition tries to identify a set of personal characteristics that separate effective leaders from ineffective leaders. Recent studies on managerial traits conducted in the United States suggest the following qualities are associated with effective leadership: (1) supervisory ability, including planning, organizing, leading, and controlling the work of others; (2) a need for personal responsibility and occupational achievement; (3) creative and verbal abilities, including judgment, reasoning, and thinking; and (4) decisiveness in making decisions and solving problems.

Most trait theories suggest that a single leadership style is superior to other styles in all kinds of organizations (i.e., in corporations, hospitals, schools, and factories). However, researchers have been unable to establish a single leadership profile associated with effective managerial outcomes. Moreover, although the studies of leadership traits have provided interesting taxonomies, they fail to provide insight into how one might develop the necessary skills.

Environmental Theories

According to a more recent set of theories, leaders arise in times of need and are called forth as a result of time, place, and circumstance. Situations demand leaders and consequently the leader is the instrumental factor through which a solution is achieved (Mumford, 1909; Murphey, 1941). The conclusion of this school of analysis is that leaders are not born, but arise in large part as a product of circumstance. The problem with these *environmental theories* is that they leave unanswered a host of questions relating to the type of circumstance and whether any action taken by the circumstantial leader will prove effective. In order to answer these questions, one needs to plumb further.

Behavioral Theories

Still more recent theoretical approaches tend to be more complex. *Behavioral theories* focus on a combination of personal and situational variables or on the interaction between the expectations and perceptions of leaders and followers within differing organizational conditions. Based largely on comparative studies of effective and ineffective leaders, behavioral approaches, including most contingency theories and path-goal theory, suggest that effective leadership requires one to adjust his or her style to fit differing situations.

Behavioral research suggests that leader effectiveness is a product of the leader's motivations, the character of subordinate responses, and the circumstances of the leader-constituent interaction. Leader-constituent relationships are seen as intricate; some subordinates respond best when given more autonomy, whereas others want a high degree of direction. Differing managerial situations require different responses. The behavioral approach counters the hypothesis "that some men are born leaders, and that neither training, experience, or conditions can materially affect leadership skills" (Fiedler, 1972). Along with other behaviorists, Fiedler argues that leaders can be trained. He suggests that the most effective way to train leaders is by managerial rotation in order to provide them with a base of experiences on which to draw. Significantly, this theoretical approach supports the notion that almost every manager in an organization can perform effectively in a leadership role. Moreover, the ablest and most effective leaders do not always practice and hold to a single style. Rather, they will be supportive in personal relationships when that style is needed yet quick and authoritative when the situation calls for it.

Contingency Theory

Fiedler's taxonomy has led contemporary researchers to propose a contingency theory of leadership. *Contingency theory* defines good leadership as the ability to match the right leadership style to the situation. Utilizing the two styles of leadership (i.e., relationship oriented and task oriented), the contingency approach suggests that depending on the situational configuration, one of these styles will be appropriate. According to this view, there is no universal "good leadership"; rather, one type of leader will be a good leader in a given situation and may be viewed as a poor leader in another situation. Effective leadership is the appropriate response to a combination of the nature of the task, the environment, and the characteristics of the subordinates involved (Fiedler, 1968).

Path-Goal Theory

Another behavioral approach has been called the *path-goal theory* (House, 1971). According to path-goal theory, the effective leader is one who (1) clearly defines the goals to be attained, (2) recognizes or stimulates the group's identification with the goal, and (3) removes obstacles that could stand in the way of employees achieving these goals. All efforts are directed toward increased opportunities for personal satisfaction as the individual works toward and achieves the goal. The function of the leader is to assist team members by clarifying goals and clearing toward achievement of the goal. Different situations call for different styles of motivation in order to promote action and satisfaction of colleagues.

Leadership and Power

In summary, behavioral theories suggest that leadership is a complex phenomenon. Rather than depending primarily on individual characteristics, leadership is a set of appropriate responses to changing circumstances. Environmental theories, by contrast, emphasize that situations create leaders, rather than leaders emerging as those who respond effectively to a variety of situations. Trait theories tend to stress a set of personal characteristics possessed by the individual. These characteristics are thought to be trans-situational (e.g., the person with leadership characteristics will be a leader in many and varied circumstances).

Each of these theories offers insights into what constitutes leadership. Another important consideration is the relationship between leadership and power. Who or what empowers a leader? One of the most widely used analyses of the sources of a leader's power has been proposed by French and Raven (1959). They identify six bases of power:

1. Positional power, derived from the individual's position within an organization (e.g., principal, teacher, superintendent)
2. Expect power, based on an individual's command of relevant knowledge and skills (e.g., knowledge of history or mathematics, classroom management skills, understanding of curriculum, etc.)
3. Referent power, founded on personal attractiveness to colleagues or subordinates
4. Persuasive and reasoning power, which permits an individual to exercise influence over others
5. Reward power, based on an individual's ability to provide desired rewards, whether material or nonmaterial (e.g., promotions, resources, recognition, etc.)
6. Coercive or punitive power

Several or even all of these different power sources may be available to the positional leader (e.g., the school principal). Leaders may choose to use a narrow or a wide range of power sources. The different ways in which leaders choose to exercise power is closely related to our next topic of importance: leadership styles.

Leadership Styles

One of the many ways to visualize leadership styles is along a continuum (see Figure 3.1). At the two extremes are heroic and laissez-faire styles, with participative leadership as the golden mean. Each leadership style is characterized by a set of behaviors and results in certain consequences. These characteristics and consequences are summarized in Table 3.1.

FIGURE 3.1 • *Leadership Styles*

Heroic Leadership Style

Heroic leaders are found at one end of the continuum. They tend to function autonomously, make decisions by themselves, and are likely to be highly directive, providing specific instructions as to what and how tasks should be performed. Heroic leaders set goals, solve problems, and usually prefer that subordinates follow specified rules and regulations. They rely heavily on rewards, punishments, and positional sources of power to motivate subordinates.

Bradford and Cohen (1984) find that when leaders feel they must know everything and do everything, they are placed in a tragic role. The expectations of continuous "heroic" performance is a terrible burden and one that often leads societies and organizations to "consume their leaders." Heroic leaders become consumed through overwork, stress, and failure attributable to placing themselves in impossible roles. This approach tends to lower employee performance far below actual capacity. On the one hand, the heroic leader feels overly responsible; on the other hand, the subordinates feel underutilized, overcontrolled, and ultimately uncommitted. Bridges (1977) has found that school administrators tend to develop a concept of themselves that is both heroic and unrealistic. As a result, they underestimate the complexity of their organizational task and overestimate what they can do. Consider the following vignette:

> Marjorie is employed as a reading specialist. She reports to her principal, Bill, an individual who tries to keep complete control of all activities in his office. Every aspect of planning, from the budget to the smallest curricular detail, is watched closely by Bill. In one instance, Marjorie prepared a curricular plan for her school. Bill did not like the plan and told her to redo it, giving her all the data and conclusions that he expected to be in the plan. The problem with Bill's ideas is that they are somewhat out of date, reflecting views on educational development that were popular when he studied the field some 30 years ago. In his desire to control

TABLE 3.1 • Leadership Styles and Consequences

Laissez-Faire	Participatory	Heroic (Autocratic)
Characteristics		
No goal setting	Group goal setting	Leader sets goals
Decisions by avoidance	Group mechanism for making decisions	Leader decides
Ad hoc problem solving	Group mechanisms for solving problems	Leader solves problems
Self-motivation	Group efforts to identify motivators	Leader uses carrot and stick
No feedback on peer performace	Informal feedback on performance	Leader gives praise and appreciation
Individuals identify and seek professional opportunities	Organizationwide training and professional development assessment	Leader determines professional development needs
Most vocal client gets the response	Seeks staff input on various client needs	Leader decides on client priorities
Complete freedom of individual action	Leader gives suggestions	Leader gives orders
Leader provides materials and answers questions when asked	Leader stimulates self-guidance	Leader often uses nonconstructive criticism
Consequences		
Lack of organization	Friendliness	Hostility and discontent
Poorer quality and lower quantity of work	Spontaneity	Demands for attention result in leader stress and burnout
Frustration	Cohesiveness	Submissiveness
Aggression	Moderate productivity	High short-term productivity
Low group unity	High group unity	Low unity and high worker turnover

all information, Bill limits the interaction of teachers by personally attending all district meetings and seldom delegating. Any problems that crop up find Bill immediately on hand with a ready solution.

Powers and Powers (1983) note that if he or she is especially competent, the autocratic or heroic leader's behavior will be accepted as a necessary burden, but if not, "his tenure in office will be marked at least by hard feelings and discord and at the most by hatred and fear that can paralyze the operation he is supposed to make more efficient by his management" (p. 26).

When heroic leadership is the dominant mode, a number of undesirable and dysfunctional consequences are produced. Heroic leaders must maintain control over others since to lose that power entails a loss of ability to give orders that will be obeyed. Coercion, threats, and power plays are common and they often engender feelings of resentment and acts of confrontation. As one respondent in our study of administrative style and student performance stated, "The top-down style of management alienates us. There is a real 'us [administration]-they [teachers]' mentality. We are not working together to benefit students. We are locked in an adversarial relationship." Another respondent wrote, "Ignoring and not listening to teachers' ideas and concerns . . . does not allow for creative and innovative teaching, thus students do not get the benefit of a 'happy' rejuvenated teacher—one who is constantly learning and improving." Another teacher said that the authoritarian leadership in her school "[gives us] a depressing feeling of hopelessness and neglect."

Nevertheless, there are situations in which heroic leadership is necessary to achieve the desired outcome. A classic example is the event of a fire. To call a meeting or to consult carefully all the individuals involved would invite disaster! Consequently, no leader would or should be participative all of the time. (And conversely, no administrator is likely to be autocratic all of the time.) Autocratic and participative styles of management lie on a continuum of leadership or administrative types. They reflect important differences in outlook and predominant modes of response.

Laissez-Faire Style

In contrast to the heroic style of leadership, laissez-faire leaders are abdicating and often disengaged. The laissez-faire leadership style relies on a "let everyone do their own thing" philosophy. No vision of the organization's mission is projected nor are

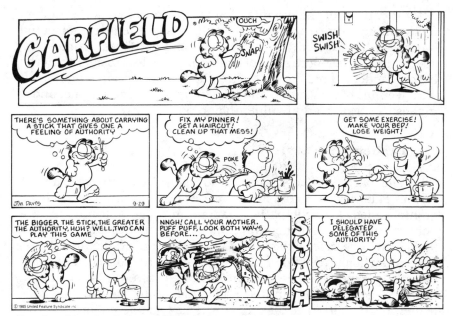

Reprinted by permission of UFS, Inc.

clearly defined goals and objectives communicated to members of the organization. Planning has little or no place within the laissez-faire approach. "Crisis" management, whereby the primary energies of the leader are devoted to dealing with one crisis after the next, is also closely associated with the laissez-faire style.

Leaders who exhibit a laissez-faire style are often individuals who have risen to a leadership role on the basis of assent through a bureaucracy rather than by virtue of demonstrated leadership abilities. The current lack of well-developed career ladders for teachers (see Chapter Seven) is frequently blamed for pushing competent teachers out of the classroom into administrative positions. These are too often the only positions of leadership as well as the only avenue of professional progress. Individuals may find themselves in a situation of positional power, with little desire to be an administrator and few leadership skills. This frequently results in a laissez-faire style of leadership.

Under a laissez-faire leader, there are no clear procedures for decision making, and supervision and feedback on performance is minimal. Moreover, laissez-faire leadership results in a power vacuum that almost inevitably leads to struggles among competing subordinates to exercise power and establish leadership based on referent power (French and Raven, 1959). This situation tends to draw members of the organization into a continual series of conflicts among competing factions and to sap energies that could otherwise be directed toward professional activities. In most respects, the laissez-faire style of leadership has less to offer than the heroic mode. It tends to leave members of an organization adrift with feelings of frustration and low group unity and morale, and it makes the organization vulnerable to power plays.

Participative Style

The participative style of leadership lies between the extremes of laissez-faire and heroic modes on the continuum of leadership styles. A participative leadership style is grounded in a behavioral model of leadership. The participative leader is flexible and able to exercise leadership skills as the context dictates. Moreover, a participative style relies on noncoercive sources of power, especially expertise, persuasion, reason, and rewards. Positional power is generally of limited consequence to the participatory leader, particularly because he or she has as one major objective the delegation of power and the sharing of responsibility when appropriate.

There are four key dimensions of a participative leadership style: creating and communicating a vision, building trust and organizational commitment, utilizing the organization's expertise, and developing the organization team (see Figure 3.2 and Table 3.2). Our research on effective schools indicates a positive correla-

FIGURE 3.2 • *Dimensions of Participative Leadership*

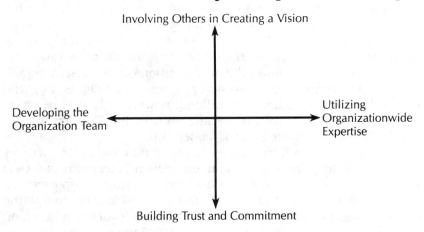

Involving Others in Creating a Vision

Developing the Organization Team

Utilizing Organizationwide Expertise

Building Trust and Commitment

TABLE 3.2 • Dimensions of Participative Leadership

Dimensions	Function of Participation	Case Study Illustrations
Creates vision	Provides a basis for consensus on goals. Establishes shared task orientation.	Redwood City School District (Chapter 3) Clair Lilienthal Elementary (Chapter 9) Lake Washington School District (Chapter 2) Hawthorne Elementary (Chapter 3)
Builds trust and organizational commitment	Establishes common understanding. Assures lateral as well as vertical communication.	Redwood City School District (Chapter 3) Lake Washington School District (Chapter 2)
Projects expertise	Establishes credibility. Maximizes use of employee talent. Distributes responsibility.	Hawthorne Elementary (Chapter 3) Orion Elementary (Chapter 8) Redwood City School District (Chapter 3)
Develops people	Encourages professional growth. Promotes organizational goals. Distributes responsibility.	Beverly Hills Elementary (Chapter 7) Vallejo School District (Chapter 6) Redwood City School District (Chapter 3)

tion between involvement of teachers and the teachers' union in creating a vision and setting school goals, utilizing teacher expertise in problem solving, building trust through involvement in curriculum design, and developing the organizational team through providing valuable feedback. Each of these concepts is discussed in the following section on participative leadership in school settings.

Participative and Team Leadership in School Settings

To a large extent, the nature and degree of participation by employees in schools are determined by the leadership style of the formal or "positional" leader (i.e., the department chair, the principal, or the district superintendent). The formal leader creates the atmosphere and gives the appropriate signal to his or her staff that participation is genuinely desired. Effective participative leadership centers on four characteristic activities: creating a vision, building trust, utilizing expertise, and developing the team.

Creating a Vision

One vital dimension attributed to a participative leadership style is vision. Participative leaders work with their staff to create a vision of their organization by assessing the current position and establishing some solid goals for the future. In interviews, teachers often mention that outstanding leaders in their lives have an infectious enthusiasm that is communicated to everyone around them. They emphasize that it is possible to move toward an improved situation, and that the organization can do more and achieve what others may consider an impossible dream. Hickman and Silva (1984) highlight the idea of vision and explain that building a vision necessarily involves contact with employees at all levels of an organization in order to understand their concerns. Manasse (1984), an organizational consultant to school systems, writes:

> *Effective principals have a vision of their school and of their role in making that vision a reality. . . . To be successful in managing the goal setting process and achieving commitment and consensus among staff, effective*

leaders use well developed analytic and intellectual skills in guiding staff in the process of identifying problems, and political and managerial skills to resolve conflicts and make the planning process work. (p. 44)

Judith Kell worked effectively with teachers to project a new vision of an inner-city school in San Francisco (see Box 3.1). The result was a renewed sense of effectiveness throughout the school.

BOX 3.1 • *Hawthorne Elementary School*

Hawthorne Elementary School is located in the heart of San Francisco's Mission District. The neighborhood is predominantly Hispanic, with an added mixture of blacks, Pacific Islanders, and some whites. Due to the citywide school busing policy, however, the school draws one-fifth of its children from Hays Valley, a predominantly black neighborhood, and nearly one-sixth of its students from Chinatown.

Ethnically, Hawthorne's 620 students are diverse. Nearly 40 percent are of Latino origin, 24 percent blacks, 23 percent Southeast Asians, 11 percent white, and the remaining belong to other ethnic groups. When Judith Kell was assigned to Hawthorne Elementary School, it was her first principalship. Kell, a veteran teacher of the San Francisco Unified School District, vividly described the situation when she was appointed three years ago: "The school was in a state of ill repair. There were more windows boarded and broken than whole. The stench of urine when you entered the premises was probably the worst part of it. . . . It appeared that the greater part of the community didn't take pride in the school." The school facilities were, in fact, off bounds to the community. The playground was fenced and locked each day after school and on weekends. In spite of this, graffiti appeared regularly on the aging exterior of the 120-year-old structure.

Judith Kell and the school reading specialist, Danelle Mann, agreed that many of the parents did not truly believe that school would make a difference for their children in the future. They did not have expectations for their children that included college. Parents were living at a subsistence level, which precluded supporting their children's educational experience in some of the most basic ways such as assuring that children get to school promptly in the morning and attend school on a regular basis. Many of the children had few aspirations for their future, and they lacked positive role models. When the school staff conducted a fifth-grade career survey, none of the responses included the professions.

Continued

BOX 3.1 *Continued*

Creating a New Vision

After one week on the site, Kell decided to work with a team of teachers to draw up some goals for the school year. Four of the eight goals related directly to improving the school facility and its utilization, whereas two others focused on developing parent ownership and community pride in and respect for the school. The goals, shared with and endorsed by the faculty, pointed the direction toward a set of common activities to which the entire staff felt committed. Then the arduous (and ongoing) effort to build parental and community support for Hawthorne began.

Creating a New Image

Improving the exterior and interior appearance of the school building was the first announcement to the community that Hawthorne was changing. With seed money from the San Francisco Education Fund and the parent club membership drive, a lively mural — painted by community artists — was designed on the exterior wall facing the school playground, which was also highly visible from the busy street on the school's east side. The community was invited to the dedication ceremony. Even as the mural was painted, graffiti art continued to appear on the adjacent walls. Rather than purge the graffiti, the principal and some students went knocking on doors in the neighborhood after school to try to discover the perpetrator's identity. Eventually, the young artist — a high-school student — came forward. Kell immediately enlisted his energy to extend the graffiti art, with the agreement that the subject matter have some relevance for the children. Now the school adornments, including a portrait of Martin Luther King, have been recognized as a unique combination of mural and graffiti, and the school site is included on the San Francisco Mural Art Tour.

Building Trust and Commitment

The majority of Hawthorne's students come from distant San Francisco neighborhoods. Children who live in the community leave early in the morning for other schools and return only after the neighborhood school is already closed. In order to bring the school closer to the neighborhood children who attend other schools, Kell moved to hire a playground director for after school and Saturday recreation. Hawthorne soccer and baseball teams emerged from the recreation program, drawing children from the neighborhood as well as the school. At the same time, the school building became available to community groups for ongoing as well as hoc meetings. For example, a Girl Scout troop, a recreation department art class, and the Mission Education Program (a community-based tutorial group) meet regularly during after-school hours.

Reaching Out to Parents

One of the difficulties faced by school principals is that of responding to the conflicting demands voiced by competing constituencies. On the one hand, the school board and superintendent issue district directives and demand adherence to rules and regulations. On the other hand, teachers seek professional and material support, validation, feedback, and materials and supplies. Meanwhile, parents' demands and needs are diverse and variable. Some are angry and see the school as a representative of a hostile and alien culture. Others view the school as an agency that will socialize their child in the norms for success, and yet another group of parents expect traditional academic learning. Clearly, the complexities of dealing with such a diverse clientele is an enormous challenge.

During her first year, Judith Kell attempted to meet this challenge by first reaching out to parents and bringing them into the school building. However, a large number, particularly those who lived in other neighborhoods, failed to respond to this overture. In the second year, she became convinced that the school had to do more to reach out to the parents of children who did not reside in the neighborhood. Together with several teachers, she held bimonthly parent outreach meetings during after-school hours at various locations in Hawthorne's key catchment communities. Where appropriate, these meetings were conducted in the native language of the community. Meetings focused on the parents as partners in the educational effort. Because many of the parents are recent immigrants, limited or non-English speakers, and low-income earners, the importance of parent training is recognized. Workshops were initiated for training parents in how to help their children with schoolwork, and the Latino Parent Empowerment Program, funded by the Zellerbach Foundation, emphasizes parents as responsible decision makers.

Besides the traditional school open house and community-based parent meetings, in the current year there is stress on written communication with student families. Parents are provided with Curriculum Newsletters to help their children at home with learning activities in reading and mathematics. Parents are reminded in writing of the importance of notifying the school of plans to leave the school. Written progress reports (in three languages) go home to parents on a biweekly or as-needed

Continued

BOX 3.1 *Continued*

basis—in some cases as often as every week. Progress reports provide space for parent feedback. Sample feedback indicates that parents are increasing two-way communication. The school also maintains a log of parent activities organized in three areas: parents as learners, parents as supporters, and parents as advocates.

The revival of Hawthorne Elementary School is built on a new and dynamic vision as well as a strategy of building trust through working closely with the community and making strides in involving parents in a broad range of school activities. This is consistent with the findings of research on effective schools, which indicates that a key ingredient of success is leadership to invoke community support. Hawthorne is reaching out to its constituents to cement a new relationship.

Building Trust

Culbert and McDonough (1985) see trust as the fundamental cement that binds an organization together, facilitating good communication, rectifying badly timed actions, making goal attainment possible, and creating the conditions for organizational success.

> *Without trust, everyday misunderstandings are taken as betrayals; simple directions become strident expressions; the best conceived plans fail. Without trust, individuals overpersonalize criticism and seek to hide the weak spots in their performance. Without trust, communications become wordy and defensive as individuals fight on issues that need to be openmindedly discussed if the organization is to be effective. Without trust, risk taking, innovation and creativity are stifled. (Culbert and McDonough, 1985, pp. 17–18)*

The relationship between leaders and followers is complex and reciprocal. Research on leadership confirms the reciprocal aspect of leader-constituent interaction. Good constituents, if given the opportunity, will generally select good leaders and hold them to high standards of performance. Conversely, good leaders build on the best positive impulses of their followers (Gardiner, 1989).

In rigid educational bureaucracies, however, there is often

little room for flexibility and maneuverability between leaders or constituents. It is not uncommon for teachers to refuse to accept their principal or superintendent as their leader. John Gardiner, former Secretary of Health Education and Welfare, writes:

> *The assumption by line executives, that given their rank and authority, they can lead without being leaders is one reason bureaucracies stagnate. Executives are given subordinates but they cannot be given a following. Surprisingly many of them don't even know they are not leading. They mistake the exercise of authority for leadership, and as long as they persist in that mistake, they will never learn the art of turning subordinates into followers. (1986, p. 6)*

The heart of effective leader-constituent interaction is effective communication between leaders and their constituency. Leaders need to be reliable, predictable, and fair in their dealings. Finally, leaders build trust by building their constituents' power. There is much to be gained in working to develop an effective style of constituent relationships. "Leaders who strengthen their people and have a gift for institution building may create a legacy that will last for a very long time" (Gardiner, 1986, p. 24).

Utilizing Schoolwide Expertise

Identifying and building on the expertise of others is a salient characteristic of participative leaders. The literature on school principals is no exception to this generalization. Glatthorn and Newberg (1984) argue persuasively for a team approach to instructional leadership at the secondary school level. They reason that since the principal is likely to have less expertise than a number of specialized teachers, team leadership (i.e., delegation of the instructional leadership role to members of the leadership team) enables the principal to focus attention on the areas in which he or she has a strong comparative advantage. Glatthorn and Newberg support the findings of others (Gersten, Carnine, and Green, 1982) who identify four critical instructional leadership functions: giving feedback about instruction, providing incentives for implementing programs, demonstrating a visible commitment to the program, and monitoring the progress of all students through the curriculum. It is not important who performs the instructional leadership roles—the principal, the teacher supervisor, or curriculum specialists—as long as they are performed.

Glatthorn and Newberg cite a convincing example in support of their views:

> *One of the most effective instructional leaders in the school we studied was the reading/language arts chairperson. Because a perceptive principal had recognized her talents and had legitimized her expertise, she was able almost single-handedly to improve the quality of teaching throughout the school by conducting staff workshops, developing and sharing materials, and encouraging colleagues to believe in the abilities of low income children. (1984, p. 62)*

The field studies of effective leaders have lent support to these perceptions. In their detailed study of eight principals who were identified by colleagues and university faculty members as effective, Blumberg and Greenfield (1980) observed several characteristics. First, effective leaders have a propensity to set clear goals that serve as a continuous source of motivation. Second, these individuals possess a high degree of self-confidence and openness toward others and a tolerance for ambiguity and ambiguous situations. In addition, Blumberg and Greenfield mention that effective school leaders continuously challenge existing assumptions and processes. They exhibit a tendency to test the limits of systems, both interpersonal and organizational. Principal Judith Kell (see Box 3.1) is fond of saying, "It's easier to ask forgiveness than permission."

The Florida State Department of Education's study of 31 principals supported these findings and added two additional items for attention. They found that the most effective principals (measured by student outcome assessment as well as selection by superintendents) used a participatory style of management and were not content to maintain the status quo (Blumberg and Greenfield, 1980).

In one of the more comprehensive analyses of the instructional role of the principal leader, de Bevoise (1984) sees five major support functions for educational leadership: implement programs, monitor student performance, provide incentives to teachers, evaluate teachers' performance, and demonstrate a pervading visible commitment. Leadership is not just the province of a single role in the school. When more people are involved, the chances for success of a particular program are considerably enhanced. "Ultimately, the provision of instructional leadership can be viewed as a responsibility that is shared by a community of people both within and outside the school. Principals initiate, encourage and facilitate the accomplishment of improvement according to their own abilities, styles and contextual circumstances" (de Bevoise, 1984, p. 20).

Developing the Team

Development is a primary dimension of a participative management style. The leader/developer has been described extensively in management literature. This approach to leadership calls for the leader/developer to work toward developing a team of key subordinates who are jointly responsible for the department's or school's success. A major emphasis of leadership is on the teaching role since the leader "must help develop the subordinates' abilities to share management of the unit's performance" (Bradford and Cohen, 1984, p. 61).

The team model of leadership rests on three cornerstones: (1) creation of a shared responsibility team, (2) continuous development of individual skills, and (3) determining and building a departmental vision. Bradford and Cohen (1984) add, "A whole new array of options open up when the leader's orientation becomes: 'How can each problem be solved in a way that further develops my subordinates' commitment and capabilities?' " (pp. 62–63). They claim further that the leader/developer approach increases the chance that tasks will be accomplished and accomplished with quality as associates seize new opportunities, share their knowledge, uncover problems before they become crises, and feel committed to carrying out decisions. The manager-as-developer approach leads to higher levels of motivation. In addition, there may be reduced difficulties with regard to leadership succession, continuity, and group cohesiveness. The participative leadership style emphasizes people-oriented activities without sacrificing a strong commitment to task accomplishment.

One of the classic studies of leadership took place under the direction of Rensis Likert of the University of Michigan's Survey Research Center. Likert sought to determine whether high-producing leaders behave in ways that are distinct from low-producing leaders. The Michigan studies concluded that the most effective managers are primarily "employee centered" rather than "task centered" in their approach. "Superiors with the best records of performance focus their primary attention on the human aspects of their subordinates' problems and on endeavoring to build effective work groups with high performance goals" (Likert, 1961). The study identified four aspects of participative leadership:

1. *Support.* Exhibit behavior that contributes to the subordinates' feelings of self-worth and value.
2. *Goal emphasis.* Exhibit behavior that stimulates enthusiasm for getting the work done.
3. *Work facilitation.* Remove roadblocks and obstacles in order to help staff get their work done.
4. *Interaction facilitation.* Exhibit behavior that helps to build the staff into a work team.

Blake, Mouton, and Williams (1981) examined the nature of leadership in higher education. They argue that the optimal style of management in educational settings is one that combines a concern for production with a concern for people. They contrast ineffective styles of management, which they label "Caretaker Administration" (characterized by a minimum attention to institutional development with bare caretaking of people concerns) and "Authority-Obedience Administration" (characterized by a high concern for institutional performance combined with a low concern for people), with an optimal style called "Team Administration." This most effective leadership style is achieved by placing emphasis on integrating institutional and individual goals by building a high-performance team (Blake, Mouton, and Williams, 1981).

In their comprehensive study of excellent principals, Blumberg and Greenfield (1980) cite an example of Ed, whose emphasis is on building an educational community with a strong human orientation. Ed states, "I'm interested in instruction and curriculum as well as developing a climate where children feel good about being here and teachers feel good about working here. I'm very much interested in human relations" (p. 79). Ed sees his leadership role as helping his team of teachers to create a climate in which the sixth-graders feel as bubbly and excited about learning as the kindergartners. Part of Ed's approach involves leading the staff to take responsibility for their environment and to develop the school as a community. Early in the first year, he began a process of communication.

*In our before-school-starts faculty meeting, I started out by
reading a statement about myself and about kids. That
made them know where I was and I think it made an impact on them. Then I asked them to do two things. First, to
write down what they thought was the worst thing that
could happen. Second, I asked them to write down what
resources they wanted from our community. . . .*

*We put it all down in newsprint, examined it, and
processed it together and then I put all the information on
ditto. It's all in the teachers' room now. We have an "I
want" board and an "I have" board. (p. 84)*

Ed's leadership style views teachers as adults, who can identify problems, make decisions, and act to solve their own problems. These issues are treated in more detail in the next two
chapters.

Leaders of schools report several distinct characteristics
when describing their work. As a result of the "loosely coupled"
nature of school organizations (Weick, 1976; see Chapter Two),
they report a sense of ambiguity and isolation with regard to other
leaders and they report feeling powerless (Blumberg and Greenfield, 1980). Participative leaders confront the isolation and power-
lessness by building teams. The effective educational leader tends
to be more of a coordinator and facilitator (Cohen and Harrison,
1979). These skills count importantly in team building. Box 3.2
summarizes five ways by which instructional leaders can act to be
effective.

In his work on the leadership styles of principals and student
achievement, Andrews finds that the educational leaders who are
most effective are those who "know how to empower people and
yell 'Charge!' " (Brandt, 1987). Andrews's research is based on
student achievement in one hundred schools. The research points
to the importance of a leadership team, which works closely together and guides the entire staff. The team leader empowers the
entire staff. Andrews provides us with a cogent example:

*In the case of the new principal who made such a differ-
ence, if you talk to teachers in the school, some will say
that the new principal didn't do anything: they did it all
themselves. Others will say they were trying to do it themselves before, but they couldn't pull it off. What was
needed was for the right principal to provide that facilita-
tive force. (Brandt, 1987, pp. 13–14)*

BOX 3.2 • *Rate Your Instructional Leadership by Identifying Your Strengths*

- *Defines mission.* You take advantage of any opportunity to discuss school goals, purposes, and mission with staff, students, and parents by making yourself visible in the school building, recognizing good teaching and student accomplishments at formal school ceremonies, and communicating excitement about future possibilities.

- *Manages curriculum.* You provide information and support teachers' needs for curriculum planning, innovation, and development. Further, you work to ensure a good fit between curriculum objectives and achievement testing, and you seek to increase your knowledge of instructional methods so that you can make valid and useful suggestions for, and critiques of, your staff's work.

- *Supervises teaching.* You spend time working on teaching with teachers, observing classes, and encouraging staff to try to their best. You coach and counsel teachers in a supportive manner, encouraging them to set goals for their own growth. When providing a critique for staff improvement, you play a mentor rather than evaluator role.

- *Monitors student progress.* You review student performance data with teachers and use student assessment information to gauge progress toward school goals. Further, you provide teachers with easy and timely access to student assessment information, and you use this information to help determine the strengths and weaknesses of the instructional program.

- *Promotes instructional climate.* You encourage teachers to try out new ideas, praise and recognize them for a job well done, and ask parents and students to do the same. You reinforce high expectations for academic achievement, and you establish and enforce clear guidelines for school policies and procedures.

Source: National Center for School Leadership, Leadership and Learning Newsletter, Vol. 1 (1) Spring 1989. Items from the Instructional Leadership Inventory are copyright © by MetriTech, Inc., 111 N. Market St., Champaign, IL. (217) 398-4868. Reproduced by permission.

The "right principal" is the one who acts to expand the leadership team. It is the principal who "whenever the spark of leadership emerges within their teachers they see it and nurture it" (Brandt, 1987, p. 15). This is accomplished in two ways: by encouraging teacher leadership within the classroom and by "using their creative ideas, their experience and their enthusiasm to bring the larger organization to its ultimate level of efficiency" (p. 15). The benefits inherent in this model of leadership, according to Andrews's research, are not insignificant. Quite the contrary, Andrews is led by his research to conclude that teachers' perceptions of the quality of principal leadership may be the single greatest predictor of incremental growth in student achievement.

In California's Hawthorne Elementary School the principal, Judith Kell, was able to develop a leadership team that performed all of the vital leadership functions (see Box 3.1). By expanding the leadership team and including classroom teachers as instructional leaders, class scheduling coordinators, and resource leaders in staff development, Kell was able to begin a process of comprehensive school improvement. By serving as coach and cheerleader for her staff instead of the often familiar police officer, she was able to gain her staff's assistance in meeting the complexities of her task. A key element in her communicating and cheerleading role was to work with her team to project a new vision of the future.

Summary

Leadership is a highly complex phenomenon. There are distinct theories as to what constitutes a leader, as well as a continuum of leadership styles ranging from the heroic, centralizing approach at one extreme to a laissez-faire style at another extreme. Between these two extremes is the participative leadership style. Research on effective educational leadership indicates four key dimensions of the participative style: creating and communicating a vision, building trust among colleagues, identifying and building upon expertise within the organization, and developing individuals and leadership teams within the organization to maximize performance and job satisfaction.

The first dimension, vision, is the ability to project a positive view of the future. The view serves as an inspiration to colleagues. The connection between this initial dimension and the remaining three, which together constitute the basis of empowerment, is critical. The effective leader empowers a group of colleagues or subordinates by allowing them to participate in the creation of their own vision. The participative leadership style empowers and transforms both leaders and their constituents.

Case Study

School District in Transition

(Authors' Note: Dr. Kenneth Hill, Superintendent of Redwood City (California) School District, describes a process in organizational change he initiated in the late 1970s. As the district's CEO, Hill's leadership style is distinct from that of his predecessor. In reading this case it is interesting to reflect on the type of leadership Hill brought to the district and the extent to which his leadership built vision, trust, expertise, and a "developing people" orientation to district policy. To what extent would it be necessary to have this type of central leadership, including the school board, in order to change leadership style at the school-site level? How many degrees of freedom are available to site managers? What are some of the obstacles to changing one's leadership style once a pattern has already been established?)

The Setting

The Redwood City School District is located on the San Francisco Peninsula, a sprawling suburban area that stretches between San Francisco and San Jose. The District has 7,000 students, kindergarten through eighth grade, housed in 14 elementary schools. Even though it is surrounded by affluent homogeneous communities, the Redwood City School District is composed of a heterogeneous student population, which is actually a microcosm of California's projected demography in the year 2000. The school population is 54 percent minority, with the Hispanic group making up 44 percent of the enrollment. The majority of these Hispanics have immigrated to California from one area of rural Mexico and most have limited formal education and little sophistication. The socioeconomic status of the Redwood City School District population ranges across a spectrum from the very wealthy to the very poor.

Historical Background

At the conclusion of the 1978–79 school year, the district posted a budget deficit of about $300,000. The business manager resigned, there was no director of instruction, and other central office administrators functioned in authoritarian roles as they tried to maintain the status quo. School-site administrators were expected to support the existing program and not rock the boat. For the most part, members of the administrative staff of the district were products of the system and most of them had held their positions for many years. Communication in the district was ineffective, and a climate of distrust was pervasive.

The restrictive organizational climate in the district was intensified by some serious economic setbacks during the decade of the seventies. The school revenue limit legislation of 1972, declining enrollment, and the fallout from California's Proposition 13, which curbed government spending severely and restricted program development, were all factors that contributed to the dismal picture. In 1979, the superintendent resigned rather quickly and the board began the process of filling the position.

A New Superintendent and His Goals: 1978–79

The favored replacement for the superintendent was the assistant superintendent for personnel, who had worked in the district for about nine years and was respected by most of the board members. The board hurriedly called an executive session to consider his appointment to the superintendency. The agenda for that meeting addressed what the candidate had to offer the district and how to make plans for the changing leadership. The board members, at various times, had discussed the need for restructuring the district's program and were looking for a type of management that would create vitality in the system. It recognized the need for better serving a growing minority population and it had ideas about creating change. The charge to the prospective superintendent was, How do you propose to develop a relevant educational program for a district in transition? In response to this question, the assistant superintendent presented six imperatives for revitalizing the district.

1. Increasing communication at all levels and all segments of the community

2. Providing more direct service to classroom teachers
3. Expanding efforts to identify employees who are not working to expectancy and providing remediation
4. Increasing efficiency of the central office staff
5. Expanding articulation with other agencies that support the district's function
6. Developing an organizational climate that increases productivity

In order to accomplish the stated imperatives, attention would be focused on the following goals:

- Establish a centrally coordinated management philosophy with a strong orientation to serving the schools. Through a centrally coordinated approach, strengthen districtwide programs in staff development, bilingual education, textbook selection, federal programs, special education, budget procedures, and policy development.
- Institute a Superintendent's Advisory Council with broad-based involvement of administrators to collaborate in solving some of the immediate district problems.
- Define a management communication policy that emphasizes effective listening, focusing on issues not personalities, respecting the feelings of others, being objective, eliminating the use of threats to accomplish goals, and treating people with respect, dignity, and concern.
- Encourage broad participation and involvement in activities that are youth oriented and community focused.
- Implement a leadership training program that encourages principals and their staffs to develop programs that are appropriate to the needs of students in their individual schools.

The assistant superintendent was selected as superintendent, with four board members voting for appointing him and one against. After the appointment, one central office administrator left the district and another retired from the system. The central office required a complete revamping.

The new superintendent immediately contracted the services of a consultant who was an expert in school budgets to audit the financial situation of the district. Meanwhile, the personnel position was filled by an Hispanic administrator, and three of the district's best principals were brought into the central office. One of these successful administrators was designated to restructure the federal program office, another was to develop the curriculum office, and the third was to assist in policy development and other matters relating to the administrative organization. In addition, an expert in bilingual education was also brought on board. Team building then began.

A Vision of Management: 1979–83

During that first summer, the total district administrative staff met at an offsite location to establish the goals for the year and to define an operational philosophy. The team-building exercise was done "in-house" by using the organizational development skills that some of the administrators had obtained during their graduate work. The grassroots approach to organizational change during that first summer was followed by a new districtwide spirit supported by an energized central office staff. This was an abrupt departure from the controlled climate of the previous central administration. Concurrently, a crusty old business official with a profound understanding of the process of education and a reputation for organizing school district business offices was employed to straighten out the business affairs of the district.

As the school district moved through the change process, new board members were elected. By 1982, the board had four new members, with only one remaining from the original five who appointed the superintendent. With this new board, a spirit of meaningful board involvement in the district's development emerged. With an active board and a vital central staff, the superintendent felt secure in taking prudent risks and could place more emphasis on organizational development. By the fall of 1982, just a little over two years after the beginning of this change episode, the district had a strong central organization, a defined set of operational procedures, a forthright business and accounting system, a well-defined bilingual education program, a set of curriculum standards for the major subjects, an emerging staff development program, and an entrepreneurial spirit.

In August of 1983, through a consensus process, the board and the total management team developed a document that contained the guiding tenets of organizational development in the district. This document, entitled "Principles of Governance for the Redwood City School District," outlined 10 principles for the operation and governance of the district. They focused on such issues as shared decision making, trust development, team spirit, appropriate instructional behaviors, and ongoing planning processes. This was a home-grown declaration of direction. The principles were reviewed constantly and communicated frequently to the staff.

Climate for Change

Three major thrusts were established during the academic year of 1983–84: developing a long-range plan, intensifying management training, and revitalizing the teaching staff. The long-range plan was written around some existing major priorities that had been identified by the board, the superintendent, and his staff. These priorities included the following:

Revitalization of the middle schools

Development of a state-of-the-art certified evaluation program

Unification of the school district

Development of a long-range plan

Continuation of participative curriculum development

Task forces, including teachers, administrators, board members, and community members, were established to study each of these areas of interest. Plans and subplans were developed by the task forces with the long-range planning group, which coordinated the recommendations into a unified plan. This plan then defined the district's thrust in the program improvement process for a period of three to four years.

Emphasis in the second area, management training, was accomplished through a grant that was received from a local corporation. The district contracted the services of an expert in school organizational development from the University of Oregon. The management staff met for an extended period during August of that year and reserved one Saturday a month for sessions with a consultant. Organizational development activities, which promoted trust building, communication skills, decision-making capabilities, and competence in problem solving, were major topics in these workshops.

During the latter part of that year, staff revitalization was addressed by instituting an early retirement program that had multiple options and was more radical than retirement incentive plans normally associated with public institutions. About one-third of the district's teachers decided to retire, and several administrators decided to leave their jobs. The characteristics of the district were beginning to change. There were new administrators coming to the district and school staffs were being rejuvenated by teachers who were more responsive to the changing student population.

During 1983–84, the reorganization of the district was in high gear, but financial resources were scarce. Due to quirks in state-funding formulas, the district received much less in state revenues than neighboring districts. The board realized that additional resources must be garnered through creative endeavors because the district could not rely on assistance from the state for renewing programs. Frustration with limited resources gave impetus to the formation of a small group devoted to seeking program-improvement money from foundations and corporations. This ad hoc group, consisting of the board president, the superintendent, a vice principal, and several teachers, met on a periodic basis to discuss ideas, write proposals, and solicit foundation funds for implementing these ideas. The grant-seeking group enlarged as new ideas emerged and more foundation funds were received. It finally evolved into a group comprised mostly of teachers who knew they had the support of the district leadership in their improvement endeavors. About $300,000 to $400,000 a year was obtained by the district through the grant-seeking program. These action-research projects supported the overall district shift in emphasis from a centrally coordinated operation to a more school-based approach to program development. Even though the district had constantly encouraged program development at local schools, only two schools had implemented unique programs. One of these schools was an "open alternative" and the other used a whole-language approach to teaching literacy. The grant-seeking process was the catalyst for establishing a cooperative learning program at a third school and opened the door for several other broad-based instructional improvement programs in schools of the district.

Decentralization and the Participatory Spirit: 1984–87

During the second year of implementing the long-range plan, the board and superintendent attended a year-long Saturday morning course on strategic planning offered at a local university. This activity initiated a new generation of planning in the district.

The development of the Redwood City School District Plan was accomplished through a participatory process that included the board, central administration, union representatives, and principals. Constant feedback and validation were given by the district management team and teachers as the district moved through the planning process.

The strategic planning group looked at societal trends that were affecting education. A scenario that described the world of the future was developed and possible responses to those dynamics were organized into a coherent approach to educational planning. Finally, a mission statement with goals and objectives was formulated and specific educational plans were promulgated for meeting the challenges of the future. The plan emphasized partnerships, school staffs, parents, and community members working together to develop relevant school programs. The spirit embedded in the goals of this districtwide plan moved the dynamics of decision making closer to classrooms and reaffirmed the district's interest in empowering parents and teachers in local school decision making.

In the early stages of strengthening the planning process, a new era in union negotiations began. The teachers' association became dissatisfied with the adversarial approach to collective bargaining and the board and administration considered the traditional negotiation approach contradictory to the Principles of Governance. The leadership of the association, the board president, and the superintendent met to discuss the question, How can the negotiation process be modified to serve its purposes, but be consistent with the district's Principles of Governance? This small committee suggested a process that began with a climate-setting meeting with the board, the superintendent's staff, the two negotiating teams, and the executive board of the association in February of each year. The meeting was designed to reaffirm the belief that the parties involved in the negotiating process would not directly or indirectly take advantage of each other. During that meeting, a schedule for the negotiation meetings was established and the teams meet through the spring. Each year during late May or early June, the total group meets again to review the process or to celebrate the conclusion of the negotiations. These negotiation procedures are now used by the other bargaining units in the district.

Another spinoff from the meetings with the teachers' association was the development of a District Advisory Council. The council was formed to improve communication with teachers through regular meetings of a representative body consisting of two board members, central office administrators, several principals, and a teacher from each school. The purposes of the council were to review districtwide problems as defined by the council, study them, and advise the board about how they could be solved. Eventually the District Advisory Council was expanded to include representatives from noncertified support services.

By 1986–87, the district had evolved into a vital, responsible organization. Genuine and open communication was encouraged, a strong central value system based on democratic approaches to governance was established, a staff development program that nurtured the district goals was in place, program development was encouraged at individual schools, and the district began shifting its resources from more central priorities to the classrooms of the district. The shifting of resources took the form of allocating discretionary money to school sites for program development. The condition for funding required an active school-site council with elected parent and staff representatives. The school-site council was to be the major decision-making body, with a school improvement plan submitted to the district board for its approval and monitoring. The emphasis on local site participation in the decision-making process rounded out the partnership between school staffs, local parents, and the board of education.

Another chapter in the organizational change program was written in the spring of 1988. The district received a foundation grant for developing a collegial evaluation model that would mitigate the traditional subordinate-supervisor roles associated with one-on-one evaluations of teachers by principals. The propositions guiding the proposal were that intimacy is required between teachers and their principals if genuine individual professional growth is to occur and that the traditional civil service type of evaluation is contradictory to the district's Principles of Governance. The grant called for developing a model that advocates professional growth of teachers through a collegial process.

Summary and Outlook: 1990 and Beyond

The process of change in the district has its roots in some defined beliefs. Most of those tenets were from industrial models of organizational development articulated by experts such as Warren Bennis, Douglas McGregor, Rensis Likert, Chris Argyris, William Ouchi, Robert Waterman and Tom Peters, Terrance Deal and A. A.

Kennedy, and George Ordione. The key elements of restructuring management included an initial understanding of organizational development among those planning the change process. Second, there was a commitment to encouraging people to express points of view, experiment, take risks, and criticize. Third, there was a central value system projecting the mission of the organization and developing in people the responsibility that goes with accomplishing the mission. Last, but not least, there was an ethos that applauds group work and broad participation in decision making.

The change process and all the elements associated with it are becoming institutionalized in the district. The importance of empowering schools to develop under the aegis of a dynamic district plan is firmly established. The success of the organization no longer depends on the leadership of a few people—adaptability to changing circumstances has become the culture of the system.

This case was prepared by Kenneth Hill, Superintendent, Redwood City School District, California.

Endnote

1. The term *leader* first appears in the English language as early as 1300, although *leadership* was first used only at the beginning of the nineteenth century (Stogdill, 1974).

References

Blake, R.; Mouton, J.; and Williams, M. S. *The Academic Administrator Grid.* San Francisco: Jossey-Bass, 1981.

Blumberg, A., and Greenfield, W. *The Effective Principal.* Boston: Allyn and Bacon, 1980.

Bradford, D., and Cohen, A. *Managing for Excellence.* New York: Wiley and Sons, 1984.

Brandt, R. "On Principal Leadership and School Achievement: A Conversation with Richard Andrews." *Educational Leadership* (September 1987):9–16.

Bridges, E. *Educational Administration: The Developing Decades.* Berkeley: McCutchan, 1977, pp. 202–230.

Carlyle, T. "Heroes and Hero Worship." In R. Stogdill (Ed.), *Handbook of Leadership.* New York: Free Press, 1974.

Certo, S. C. *Principles of Modern Management,* 4th ed. Boston: Allyn and Bacon, 1989.

Cohen, D., and Harrison, M. "Curriculum Decision Making in Australian Education: What Decisions Are Made Within Schools?" *Journal of Curriculum Studies II* (July–September 1979):257–262.

Culbert, S., and McDonough, J. *Radical Management*. New York: Free Press, 1985.

De Bevoise, W. "Synthesis of Research on the Principal as Instructional Leader." *Educational Leadership* (February 1984): 14–20.

Fiedler, F. E. "How Do you Make Leaders More Effective? New Answers to an Old Puzzle." *Organizational Dynamics* (Autumn 1972):3–18.

Fiedler, F. E. "Personality and Situational Determinants of Leadership Effectiveness." In D. Cartwright and A. Zander (Eds.), *Group Dynamics: Research and Theory*. New York: Harper and Row, 1968.

French, J. R., and Raven, B. H. "The Bases of Social Power." In D. Cartwright (Ed.), *Studies in Social Power*. Ann Arbor: University of Michigan Press, 1959.

Gardiner, J. *The Heart of the Matter: Leader-Constituent Interaction*. Washington, D. C.: Independent Sector, June 1986.

Gardiner, J. *On Leadership*. New York: Free Press, 1989.

Gersten, R.; Carnine, D.; and Green, S. "Administrative Supervisory Support Functions for the Implementation of Effective Educational Programs for Low Income Students." Paper presented to AERA Annual Meeting, New York, March 1982.

Glatthorn, A., and Newberg, N. "A Team Approach to Instructional Leadership." *Educational Leadership* (February 1984):60–63.

Hickman, C., and Silva, M. *Creating Excellence*. New York: New York Library, 1984.

House, R. J. "A Path-Goal Theory of Leader Effectiveness." *American Science Quarterly* 6 (1971):321–338.

Kouzes, J. M., and Posner, B. Z. *The Leadership Challenge*. San Francisco, Jossey-Bass, 1987.

Likert, R. *New Patterns of Management*. New York: MacGraw-Hill, 1961.

Manasse, L. A. "Principals as Leaders of High-Performing Systems." *Educational Leadership* (February 1984):42–46.

March, J. "American Public School Administration: A Short Analysis." *School Review* 86 (February 1978):217–250.

Mumford, E. *The Origins of Leadership*. Chicago: University of Chicago Press, 1909.

Murphey, A. J. "A Survey of the Leadership Process." *American Sociological Review* 6 (1941):674–687.

Powers, D. R., and Powers, M. F. *Making Participatory Management Work*. San Francisco: Jossey-Bass, 1983.

Stogdill, R. *Handbook of Leadership*. New York: Free Press, 1974.

Vaill, P. "Notes on Spirit and Spirituality." Mimeo, George Washington University, 1987.

Weick, K. E. "Educational Organizations as Loosely Coupled Systems." *American Educator* (Spring):23–25, 47–48.

CHAPTER FOUR

Motivation

Introduction

George Winston took over as the third principal in four years of Whitter High School, a large urban multiracial school. The school's reputation had been sliding for nearly a decade. Discipline problems were rampant, ranging from extremely high rates of cutting class and student absenteeism to dealing drugs and physical violence erupting on a regular basis on the schoolgrounds. Of the 180 staff members, 80 percent had been at the school for over 10 years and nearly half had completed more than 20 years of services. Although acutely aware of the school's problems, the dominant attitude among the teaching staff was to turn a blind eye to the situation. One teacher remarked that after having pursued a young male student in the girls' bathroom twice and being shoved against the wall by the student, she was not about to stick her neck out again. Other teachers complained that so many students cut classes on a regular basis that they didn't really have the time to contact all the parents regarding the problem.

Student discipline was not the school's only problem. George Winston had already started to receive a steady stream of complaints regarding some of the veteran teachers. One parent had called to report that his daughter's social studies teacher was routinely 20 minutes late for a 45-minute class period and was apparently receiving and making telephone calls in the classroom during class time. Another parent complained that her son's history teacher was also routinely late for the first period class, which begins at 7:45 A.M.

During the past three years some of the school's most highly praised teachers had chosen to leave the district to take teaching positions elsewhere, sacrificing loss of seniority and pay. Winston had known that teacher, parent, and community morale were lagging when he assumed the post. But the lack of motivation among the staff to deal with the deteriorated situation was extremely disturbing.

Motivation is the push or pull that stimulates people to act and excel. It unlocks the door to quality performance in any situation—on the job, in a leisure activity, as well as in personal and social life. Understanding the general dynamics of motivation is fundamental to effective management. If a school hopes for the best possible quality work from its staff, the key manager—its principal—must understand and be able to apply the basic principles of human motivation. This chapter focuses on three interrelated topics: (1) motivational issues in school settings, (2) prominent theories of human motivation as they have been studied and applied in school environments, and (3) the role of participatory management as a potential motivator for school-site personnel.

Motivation in the School Setting

Motivation functions in organizational settings at three levels: the individual, the immediate workgroup, and the entire organization. Likewise, factors affecting the motivation of individual employees are present at each level. In a school, low teacher motivation may be the consequence of a personal problem off the job, a specific situation associated with the job such as a particularly difficult group of students, burnout from too many years spent in a high-intensity situation, boredom from a lack of variety or new challenges, dissatisfaction with pay and benefits, or demoralization because the school district is facing financial difficulties.

Certain characteristics of the contemporary teaching force and the teaching profession itself, as presently constituted, present motivational challenges that are specific to schools. Many teachers currently in the system have reached the top of their district salary scales, and many districts do not have differentiated staffing patterns or career ladders that permit continued professional growth and achievement. The fact that the staff composition of many schools has not changed significantly in more than 10 to 15 years can have a significant impact on staff motivation in general. Low motivation of individual teachers or small groups of teachers can affect the overall school climate. This may create motivational problems at the workgroup and organizational levels as well for individual employees.

Other motivational roadblocks emanate from the particular characteristics of the school as a workplace. Limited time for collegial interaction and team efforts can be a motivational deflater for teachers, especially for new entrants into the profession (Little, 1982). The absence of well-defined measures of professional performance and feedback also plagues the teaching profession. Lack of monetary rewards and upward mobility denies teachers the sense of opportunity and professional progress (Kanter, 1981).

Each of these features of schools and teaching have important implications for motivation.

1. *The aging teaching force* may affect employee motivation. A 20-year followup study (Kottkamp, Provenzo, and Cohn, 1986) of Lortie's classic study of school teachers in Dade County, Florida (1964) revealed that teachers are both older and more experienced than they were two decades ago. In 1984, more than 50 percent of the teachers in the Dade County district were over 40 years old and 70 percent had more than 10 years' teaching experience. By contrast, only 40 percent of the teachers in 1964 were 40 or more years old and over 70 percent had less than 10 years' teaching experience. These demographic features are not unique to Dade County, Florida. They are indicative of a nationwide demographic profile of the teaching force (U.S. Department of Education, 1989).

Two important implications arise from this demographic picture. The first is how to motivate seasoned teachers to continue to grow professionally and strive for excellence, many of whom anticipate between 5 and 15 more years of classroom teaching prior to retirement. The second is how to attract and retain a high caliber of new university graduates in the teaching profession. Studies of teacher motivation and sources of job satisfaction among teachers provide key data in the proposal of solutions to these questions. These are discussed later in this chapter.

2. *The structure of the teaching profession* creates a set of motivational problems uncommon to other professions. These derive from the lack of a clearly defined career ladder, which can serve as a motivator for improved performance and validation of achievement (Kanter, 1981). Increasing domains of responsibility with experience that serve to enrich the jobs of senior professionals tend to be absent in the teaching profession. Moreover, the ambiguous relationship between demonstrated professional performance and promotion vitiates career advancement as a motivator.

3. *The organization of schools* around self-contained classrooms promotes a climate of professional isolation. The stimulation gained from working collaboratively with experienced colleagues, a characteristic of many other professions (e.g., law, medicine, engineering, social work), is limited in most school settings (Little, 1982). This reduces yet another dimension of the potential motivational spectrum found in other service industries with high concentrations of professional employees.

Implicit Assumptions about Human Motivation

Most managers formulate their own theory of human motivation, either implicitly or explicitly. School administrators are no exception. McGregor (1960) develops the idea that there are two basic philosophies of human behavior that underlie two contrasting approaches to management. These are called Theories X and Y. Theory X integrates a set of assumptions about behavior, including beliefs that people are basically lazy, will avoid work if they can, and will take advantage of a situation if given the opportunity. In contrast, Theory Y views people as basically honest, wanting to do a good job in their work, seeking responsibility, and looking for opportunities to take initiative.

These contrasting perspectives on human behavior have quite different implications for managers and their approaches to employee motivation. Because the Theory X manager distrusts employees, he or she will tend to insist on tight controls and close supervision. Furthermore, this manager will lean toward centralized decision making and offer few opportunities to employees to make suggestions about how to improve the ways things are done in the organization. In order to keep people in line, the Theory X manager will rely heavily on economic rewards and sanctions to motivate employees. School administrators rarely have the freedom to use differential economic rewards, which are governed closely by collective bargaining agreements and civil service regulations. Instead, they may use rewards and sanctions within their control, such as allocation of students, space, and materials. By contrast, the Theory Y manager is more inclined to delegate authority and responsibility to others and allow the employees to participate in decision making.

Theory Y advocates may find the content theories of motivation (described in the next section) intuitively appealing, whereas Theory X proponents may be more attracted to process theories elaborated in conjunction with the case of merit pay. The use of participative management to motivate builds a bridge between the two schools of thought as they have and continue to be applied to employee motivation.

Figure 4.1 demonstrates how motivation affects behavior, regardless of a manager's implicit predilection toward Theory X or Theory Y. In this model, motivation is defined as the individual's inclination to engage in a specific activity. Performance has two

Figure 4.1 • *Motivation: The Contextual Determinants*

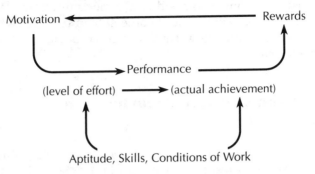

dimensions. First is the level of effort put forth by the individual in an activity or toward the realization of a specific goal. Second is the quality of the actual performance, independent of the effort put forth. This distinction is important, because sometimes an individual will try very hard to attain a goal or perform a task, without substantial success. That is, the effort may be great, but the quality of results is limited. This is because other factors intervene between motivation and performance. Three salient factors are predetermined aptitude for a specific activity, previously established skills relevant to performance of the activity, and conditions of work (including technology and support) that may assist in performing a given activity. These three intervening factors are especially important because they affect the quality of performance, just as motivation can affect the quality of performance. However, if an employee is lacking essential skills or does not have the proper technology to do the job, his or her lack of performance cannot be blamed on motivational factors.

A simple example should suffice to illustrate this point. A teacher with an aptitude for art will tend to be more motivated and to exhibit a stronger level of effort when it comes to engaging a group of students in an art project than a teacher with no aptitude for art. Drawing further on this example, the teacher who has formal training in art and the teaching of art may outperform the teacher with no training even when both are judged to be highly motivated. Finally, the teacher who has space and materials for art projects at her or his disposal may more successfully engage students in an art project than the teacher who has inadequate space and few materials.

According to the model, rewards are the directly perceived

consequences or feedback on performance. Most theories of motivation postulate that rewards do influence motivation. Where the theories differ from each other is precisely in terms of what constitutes a "reward" and how that reward impacts on motivational predispositions.

Process and Content Theories of Motivation

There is a wide spectrum of motivational theories. The applications of some theories have been studied in school settings over the past 35 years. In this section, we review several key theories of motivation and their implications for educational work environments: (1) the process approaches associated with expectancy theory, goal theory, and behaviorism/operant conditioning; and (2) the content approaches associated with hierarchy of needs and two-factor theory of motivation.

Process Theories

Three prominent process theories of motivation are *expectancy theory* (associated with Vroom), Locke's *goal theory,* and Skinner's *behaviorism.*

Expectancy Theory

Expectancy theory posits that there are three elements that determine motivation. The first element is known as the individual's *valence* for a particular outcome. The valence is essentially the attractiveness of a given outcome or reward that is likely to be forthcoming if the person acts. The theory's second element is termed the *instrumentality* of the individual for a possible reward or outcome. Instrumentality refers to the likelihood the individual attaches to receiving a particular reward if a goal is achieved. The third element of the theory is known as *expectancy.* Expectancy refers to the employee's perceptions of the probability that the desired goal will actually be attained.

The fundamentals of expectancy theory can be illustrated with the following example: In Valley Vista Elementary School, the principal has a policy that allows teachers to change grade level once every three years by choice and requires them to move once every five years. She believes that this type of change introduces challenge and professional growth into the teacher's job, in addition to giving each staff member a broader view of the school as a total organization. Ms. Keiffer would like to move to teaching sixth grade instead of fourth grade, where she has been teaching for the past three years, thus her *instrumentality* for motivation is high. However, she knows that the two sixth-grade teachers, one at the sixth-grade level for three years and the other for four, do not want to change. Therefore, she perceives very little possibility of changing unless one of the existing sixth-grade teachers can be made to move in the coming school year. Thus Keiffer's *expectancy* for being able to change is low. Therefore, she cannot bring up the possibility of change with either the principal or her colleagues, indicating a low *valence* for this reward. (It might also be added that she continues to teach fourth grade for the next two years with a limited amount of motivation and enthusiasm.)

Studies applying the expectancy theory of human motivation to schools find that motivation among teachers and administrators is clearly stronger when "desirable" organizational rewards are present. One study among secondary teachers indicated that motivation was related to job satisfaction and perceived performance (Miskel, Defrain, and Wilcox, 1980). Another study of teachers' motivation over a period of a school year showed that teachers were motivated by the degree of communication among colleagues as well as student achievement and specific attitudes of students and other teachers (Miskel, McDonald, and Bloom, 1983). The importance of expectancy theory is its concern with the motivational process: Are the rewards being offered as incentives really desirable to employees? What, if any, is the likelihood of reaching the level of performance needed for reward attainment? Will the reward really be forthcoming if the appropriate performance level is actually achieved?

Goal Theory

Goal theory, like expectancy theory, asserts that most human behavior is purposive and regulated by explicit goals. Postulating that the intention to achieve a specific objective is a primary motivator, goal theory links goal-directed motives to the level of individual effort expended on performance. Goals of the work environment are assumed to be explicitly understood by employees. Individuals will choose among alternative courses of action or goals to be pursued on the basis of personal value judgments. As in expectancy theory, individuals have varying instrumentalities with regard to the degree that they perceive behaviors to be linked to an actual reward.

Three generalizations emerge from the research based on goal theory. First, specific performance goals are stronger motivators and enhance achievement more than general performance goals. For example, Lockwood High School formulates the following goal: to increase the number of female and minority students taking advance placement mathematics and science courses in the next four years by providing counseling, special tutoring, and selective summer enrichment courses. John Dewey High School, by contrast, decides to try to improve school climate for minority students in the coming academic year. The first goal is highly specific, whereas the second goal—noble though it may be in conception—is diffuse and less likely to be either a motivator or realized unless the school specifies exactly what is meant by "improved school climate for minority students."

Second, goals that are more difficult to achieve, once they have been accepted by the employee(s), are better motivators than easily achieved goals—even when the goal is so difficult that no one can actually achieve it. For example, an inner-city urban high school may set a goal of reducing the dropout rate to zero in a three-year period. Although this goal may be unrealistic, if the school staff and administration are seriously committed to the goal, it may be a stronger motivator than simply settling for the goal of reducing dropouts by 50 percent.

Third, involvement of employees in setting work-related goals leads to greater employee satisfaction (Campbell and Pritchard, 1975; Garland, 1982; Latham and Yukl, 1975; Mento, Carledge, and Locke, 1980; Mitchell, 1979). The case of school-site planning teams used by the Vallejo Unified School District (see Chapter Two) illustrates the motivational impact of staff participation in goal setting for annual school improvement programs.

Goal theory presents possibilities and challenges when applied to schools. Among these is the importance of establishing specific goals shared by teachers, administrators, and other school personnel. Although goal theory does not explain how or why employees accept certain goals rather than others, it does imply that employees involved in establishing job-specific as well as organizational goals are more likely to be highly motivated and buy into the goals than those who do not. Teachers are accustomed to setting goals for themselves within the context of their classroom teaching (e.g., specifying instructional and learning objectives for themselves and students), but they must also be involved in generating broader organizational goals. Participative goal setting, described in Chapter Three, can be viewed as a motivator and as a tool for school improvement.

Behaviorism/Operant Conditioning

A third process theory of motivation is B. F. Skinner's behaviorist model, also referred to as *operant conditioning* (Skinner, 1953). Behaviorism incorporates three basic assumptions. First, humans generate action/behaviors. Second, these behaviors are determined and controlled in systematic ways by both genetic and environmental factors. Any behavior or action will elicit a consequence or response from the environment in which it occurs. This consequence will either positively reinforce the behavior, increasing the likelihood of repeating the same action, or negatively reinforce the behavior, decreasing the probability of another future occurrence. And third, environmental conditions are the fundamental determinants of internal processes (i.e., thoughts, feelings, and motives). Therefore, behavior is primarily the consequence of environmental conditioning rather than caused by inner drives as postulated by content theorists (see the next section of this chapter).

According to the behaviorist model, reinforcement is the key to influencing motivation. Behaviorists distinguish between reinforcements and rewards. All positive reinforcers can generally be referred to as rewards, but not all rewards are positive reinforcers (i.e., not all rewards will actually reinforce the desired behavior). One critical task of managers is to identify rewards that *do* reinforce desired employee behavior.

Kerr (1975) argues that many organizations create motivational forces that lead to unwanted and unintended consequences by rewarding behaviors that are not desired and by discouraging behaviors that are desired. Schools are no exception to this pattern. One of the particular dilemmas is the lack of close linkage between performance and rewards in school settings. *Currently, teachers do not tend to be rewarded for either specific teaching competencies or achievements.* This is due, in part, to (1) difficulties in gathering information and measurement of competence (see Chapter Six), (2) existing reward systems based on seniority, (3) salary increments linked to additional studies rather than job-specific training and job performance, and (4) the paucity of extrinsic rewards under the discretion of school-site managers.

Management applications of the behaviorist approach to motivation are incorporated in the MBO (management-by-objectives) method. In terms of motivation, MBO emphasizes setting specific objectives for performance that are mutually defined and understood by employees and management. An integral part of MBO involves the establishment of systematic feedback on performance vis-à-vis these objectives. When objectives are met, performance is reinforced through recognition and reward. When objectives are not met, the situation is jointly analyzed by management and employees; blockages are identified and a strategy to achieve the objective is agreed upon. Notice, however, that neither the MBO approach nor the behaviorist model call for punishment.

Punishment is frequently confused with negative reinforcement. Unlike negative reinforcement, punishment seeks to suppress or extinguish a behavior by introducing a sanction or by removing a positive reinforcer in response to the undesired action. Skinner argues strongly against the use of punishment to control behavior. The reason is based on observations that, although punishment can extinguish a behavior in the short term, when the punishment is withdrawn, the behavior is likely to recur. Negative reinforcement, on the other hand, involves the removal of a negative stimulus when the desired behavior is exhibited.

Take the example of Ms. Ryebock, described by the principal in the Wisconsin junior high school where she has been teaching math for the past 20 years. Although Ryebock thinks of herself as having a lot to offer as a teacher and is very enthusiastic and liked by her students, her instructional skills are weak. She has received several "marginal" performance evaluations, resulting in no salary advancement over the past three years. She has also received numerous parent complaints for not really teaching and challenging the students. Ryebock has been receiving negative reinforcements—poor evaluations and parent complaints—as well as punitive action—the lack of salary advance. The principal describes her as "very slow and deliberate in response to suggestions." What needs to be done to help Ms. Ryebock modify her behavior? First, one might ask, is she aware of some specific actions that she might take to change her "weak instructional skills"? Second, once she takes those actions, does she immediately receive some positive reinforcement for changes in her behavior? Third, do the negative reinforcements (i.e., the parent complaints and marginal evaluations) cease? From the behaviorist perspective, this sequence of conditions would need to take place in order to anticipate a change in Ryebock's teaching behaviors.

Content Theories

Two popular content theories of human motivation are the hierarchy of needs theory developed Abraham Maslow, one of the founders of humanistic psychology, and the two-factor theory of job motivation associated with Frederick Herzberg. These models are referred to as content theories because each focuses on the sources of motivation rather than the motivational process (i.e., interplay between motivation, performance, and rewards).

Needs Theory

The needs hierarchy model hypothesizes that human beings are motivated to satisfy the same set of universal needs. Maslow conceived of five fundamental needs, each of which rises in turn to dominate the individual and then recedes in response to being satisfied. The first need, on which all others are based, is the satisfaction of basic physiological demands (i.e., food, shelter, sleep, and sexual gratification). Beyond this baseline, humans are motivated to seek satisfaction for less tangible needs in an ascending order. These needs are centered around safety and security, social acceptance and recognition, self-esteem, and self-actualization. (See Figure 4.2 on page 106.)

Although the needs achievement model is widely cited, it has been difficult to verify empirically. The higher-order needs are complex concepts with multiple aspects and not easily measured (Miskel and Ogawa, 1988). Studies of needs satisfaction among school personnel show that the major needs deficiencies among teachers were in the areas of self-actualization, esteem, and autonomy (Trusty and Sergiovanni, 1966). Administrators, however, seem to exhibit fewer needs deficiencies than teachers on all five dimensions, with the greatest deficiency for both administrators and teachers being autonomy needs (Chisolm, Washington, and Thibodeaux, 1980). Autonomy, another need dimension identified by Porter (1961), is defined by concepts such as participation, authority, independent thought, and action. Research by Chisolm, Washington, and Thibodeaux (1980) found that administrators generally exhibited fewer deficiencies with respect to needs than did teachers. However, both groups had the highest deficiency level with regard to the need for autonomy. This research suggests that more opportunities for participation, as well as decentralization of decision making and taking initiative, would meet motivational needs of both teachers and administrators.

Two-Factor Theory

In the late 1950s psychologist Frederick Herzberg developed another content theory of motivation. Drawing on the ideas of Maslow's hierarchy of needs, Herzberg was especially interested in identifying motivational factors in the workplace. His study of technical/professional employees in a large engineering firm identified two groups of variables. One group of factors (called *motivators*), which included sense of achievement, recognition, the work itself, responsibility, and advancement, motivated employees toward high-quality performance.

Another set of factors included salary; interpersonal relations with peers, subordinates, and superordinates; status; company policy; and administrative practices such as possibility for professional growth, working conditions, job security, and personal life. These aspects (identified as *hygiene* factors) did not appear to contribute to employee motivation. Rather, they seemed only to cause dissatisfaction if the employees' expectations were not met. The presence of hygiene factors, however, was not sufficient to motivate employees or provide them with a sense of job satisfaction; their impact was, in fact, neutral. Herzberg concluded, therefore, that work satisfaction and dissatisfaction were not opposites, but were separate and distinct dimensions of an employee's orientation toward work (Miskel and Ogawa, 1988).

The two-factor theory has been studied in school settings. There are differences between teachers' and administrators' attitudes towards hygiene and motivating factors, with teachers tending to exhibit a greater desire for hygiene factors over motivators than do administrators. Administrators, by contrast, are more inclined to take risks, especially when linked to motivating factors like job advancement or increased prestige and power (Miskel, 1974). It is, of course, difficult to tell whether these tendencies are embedded in the respective jobs or that the respective jobs attract individuals with systematically different motivational inclinations. The two-factor theory, however, does give some insight into the distinction between necessary and sufficient conditions for motivating employees. What constitutes hygiene and motivating factors for one group of professionals may not necessarily be the same for another. However, there is some evidence that the type of factors that motivate teachers have remained rather stable over time (Kottkamp, Provenzo, and Cohn, 1986).

A 20-year followup of Daniel Lortie's study of the teaching profession in Dade County, Florida, showed that teachers are overwhelmingly more satisfied by intrinsic rewards than extrinsic, or

TABLE 4.1 • *Most Important Category of Rewards to Dade County Teachers*

Reward	1964 %	1984 %
Extrinsic		
The salary, respect received, and position of influence	11.9	11.3
Intrinsic		
The opportunities to study, plan, master classroom management, "reach" students, associate with colleagues and children	76.3	70.2
Ancillary		
The economic security, time, freedom from competition, and appropriateness for my capabilities	11.8	18.4

Source: R. B. Kottkamp, E. F. Provenzo, Jr., and M. M. Cohn, Table 16, "Stability and Change in a Profession: Two Decades of Teacher Attitudes, 1964–1984," *Phi Delta Kappan,* April 1986.

ancillary, rewards (Kottkamp, Provenzo, and Cohn, 1986). These data are illustrated in Table 4.1. Although extrinsic rewards correspond rather well with the motivating factors postulated by Herzberg, intrinsic and ancillary rewards both have characteristics of the hygiene cluster. However, the intrinsic rewards identified in this study are close to the type of expectations that professionals in general demand of their work. The lack of orientation toward traditional extrinsic rewards may be a reflection of resignation by teachers to the scarcity of these incentives in the teaching profession. Thus teachers place a premium on those rewards that can come from the work process itself. Their expectations for extrinsic rewards are low because they believe these are unlikely to be forthcoming.

Application of Motivation Theories

The array of motivational theories reviewed presents an eclectic picture of what stimulates employees to act in the work setting. What can the practitioner, the school-site manager, or even the organizational researcher hope to glean from these varied perspectives on human motivation as manifest in organizations, especially schools? Table 4.2 provides a visual comparison of the different theories as they relate to the three dimensions (motiva-

TABLE 4.2 • Theories of Motivation Compared

	Motive Generators	Performance	Reward
Process Theories			
Expectancy Theory	Valence (i.e., individual preference)	Expectation of being rewarded	Instrumentality (i.e., value placed on reward by the individual)
Goal Theory	Individually defined	Degree of difficulty of goal	Importance of goal to individual
Behaviorism	Positive reinforcement	Reinforcement schedule	Contextually determined
Content Theories			
Needs Hierarchy	Fixed human needs (physical, security, social, self-esteem, self-actualization)	Not explained	Needs satisfaction
Two-Factor Theory	Money, status, advancement	Not explained	Motivators rather than hygiene factors

tion, performance, and reward) of the motivational process described at the beginning of this chapter.

Content theories of motivation suggest that motivators are uniform for the population, whereas process theories imply that motivators can be quite specific to the individual or the given organizational environment. These are contrasting perspectives and each offers insights for the manager.

Process theories help the manager to understand how motivators influence performance and give some ideas about how rewards may be designed to stimulate motivation, leading to improved performance. Expectancy theory asserts that although finding out what motivates employees may be necessary, it is not a sufficient condition for stimulating quality performance. Performance will be stimulated to the extent that the employee judges there is a good possibility of obtaining the desired reward (expectancy). Thus it is not expedient for schools to introduce incentives that are impossible for a significant number to attain even though they may be valued by many teachers. Participation in identifying and choosing among reward options is a useful practice to establish.

The importance of establishing organizational goals and objectives for orienting employee effort in specific directions is a corollary of goal theory. Managers must work to bring individual and organizational goals into the closest possible alignment. Teacher participation in schoolwide goal setting and planning is one of the most obvious vehicles for achieving this alignment. In the Vallejo Unified School District (Chapter Two), the annual school team planning exercise, whereby one- and three-year goals are set by school administrators and teachers, jointly serves to unite site personnel around common objectives and motivates them to take specific actions to achieve those objectives.

Behaviorism suggests that it is especially important to link rewards with desired actions. There is not much use in rewarding actions that are not valued by the organization in terms of its overall effectiveness or in rewarding actions that have an ambiguous relationship to desired outcomes. One common practice in schools is to reward teachers financially for additional study. There is no proven link between taking additional university coursework and professional effectiveness of teachers (Levin, 1970). Teacher effectiveness depends on a host of other factors. Therefore, from the behavioral perspective, additional study should not be rewarded per se. From the behavioral perspective, what should be rewarded are activities or studies that result in improvements in effective teaching.

FIGURE 4.2 • *Unsatisfied Needs and Hypothesized Employee Behavior*

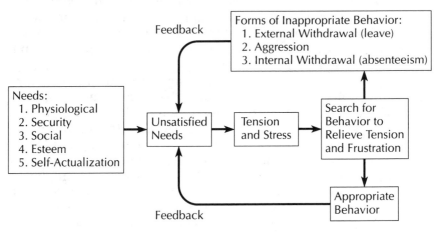

Source: Adapted from B. Kolasa, *Introduction to Behavioral Science in Business* (New York: Wiley, 1969), p. 256.

Content theories suggest clusters of factors that may be important motivators in specific contexts. Figure 4.2 illustrates an hypothesized set of outcomes in the workplace as a result of unsatisfied needs. Employee behavior may move in the direction of undesirable ("inappropriate") behaviors or appropriate behaviors, depending on how the situation is handled. Research shows that schools are weak in providing opportunities for self-actualization and autonomy among teachers and administrators. Although these may not be universally important to all school-site personnel, they have been demonstrated to be motivators for many. Schools would do well to consider these factors as key components of organization and job redesign efforts. More opportunities for teachers to share school power and increase their scope of professional responsibilities, especially where these impact on their abilities to "reach" students, are potentially strong motivators.

The Question of Incentives

Motivation theories raise a number of questions regarding the role of incentives in the practice of management. When is it appropriate to use incentives as motivators? Toward whom should incentives be directed? Are there any dangers in embarking on an incentives program in an effort to stimulate motivation? Who should be responsible for establishing incentives policies and implementing an incentives program in practice?

When Are Incentives Appropriate?

Consider the following problem profiles presented by an experienced school principal.

Teacher A Profile:

- 67 years old, 32 years' experience in district
- Teaches science and math
- Stays to self
- Very proud; thinks of self as good teacher
- Highly frustrated with misbehavior of students
- Received satisfactory evaluations most of career, but recent evaluations indicate weak instructional skills
- Blames lack of student achievement on parents
- Currently experiencing serious discipline problems in math classes

School Staff (20 Teachers) Profile:

- 80 percent have been teaching 20 years or more
- Most have spent their entire career either at current school or in district
- Most have participated in curriculum development projects either within district or with teachers from neighboring districts
- There is a general familiarity with current educational trends
- Most of the women socialize in the staff room
- Most of the men (five) and one woman socialize in the custodian's room
- Many teachers do joint planning in departments
- A few teachers stay to themselves both professionally and socially
- Teachers are vocal as individuals but passive in staff meetings
- Student absenteeism and cutting classes has grown over the past three years
- Student performance on statewide standardized tests has declined slightly but staff does not seem concerned

The administrator describing these two scenarios is confronted with a complex set of issues. In the first profile a veteran teacher, past the age of retirement, is experiencing difficulties. In the second profile, there are indications that the morale of an experienced and well-trained staff is flagging. Motivation may be a critical factor in both cases. Could the right incentives help to motivate the teachers concerned to change certain professional behaviors?

The site manager must assess each situation in terms of the potential to change factors influencing each individual's behavior. In the former case, there may be very little in terms of incentives that a site-level administrator could offer the veteran teacher: He or she is at the top of the career ladder and has maximum benefits, maximum salary, and only two years before mandatory retirement. Situations like this may require district support to devise an incentive such as an immediate retirement bonus, or to offer a counseling program for teachers approaching retirement age that deals with some of the personal and professional issues confronting individuals as the end of their career approaches.

In the latter case, the administrator is confronted with the need to identify incentives that might revitalize the staff's motivation to tackle specific problems such as declining student attendance and increases in cutting classes. Because the staff is composed of well-established professionals who probably have realized most of the existing monetary incentives the district offers, the administrator will probably have to explore other types of incentives to stimulate a change.

Toward Whom Should Incentives Be Directed?

Discovering the link between incentives and staff motivation can be exhilarating for any manager. However, incentive programs have the potential to introduce divisiveness and increase competition among employees where more cooperation and team effort is needed to tackle a particular organizational problem. Consider the problem of declining attendance and increased student cutting of classes in the second profile. An incentive program that gives bonuses to the four teachers with the best student attendance records during a semester has the potential to foster divisiveness. Therefore, when considering incentives, a careful analysis needs to be made regarding the desired changes and who should make them.

When incentives are directed at individuals, expectancy theory asserts that their motivation is more than a function of the desirability of the incentive. It is also a function of the perceived possibility of receiving the award. Zero-sum incentives, which do not allow all staff the opportunity to earn the reward if their performance meets a specified criterion, have the danger of backfiring as incentives if the goal is to raise the general motivational level of employees. Thus incentives for the top performers may lower a staff's general proclivity to pursue the desired goal.

A recent study of an incentive program designed to reduce teacher absenteeism in a New York state school district proved to be highly effective in its first year. Not only did the median number of days the teachers were absent decline by 50 percent but the number of teachers with a perfect attendance record increased from 8 to 34 percent of the district personnel. The incentive program was designed so that any teacher could draw one share from a fixed bonus pool ($72,822) for each day absent less than seven (which was the mean number of teacher absences in the year prior to initiation of the program). In theory, this meant that each teacher would be eligible for the entire pool. In actuality, some 1,274 shares were claimed, each worth $57.16. A full-time teacher with perfect attendance earned a bonus of $400.12, or slightly more than 1 percent of the average teacher paycheck. This is an instance of a win-win incentive program whereby all employees are eligible for the reward if they meet the criterion (Jacobson, 1988).

Most merit pay plans have been organized on zero-sum principles, but recent analyses suggest that schoolwide merit pay plans may be better motivators and more effective in producing behavioral changes that enhance the school's performance as an organization (see Box 4.1).

Although incentives to motivate employee performance are of immediate concern to the school-site manager, in the organizational context of schools, principals have neither the authority or the resources to establish monetary incentives. Nonmonetary incentives are more within the control of site administrators, but these are most commonly used as rewards for individual teachers rather than as part of staffwide incentive plans. Participation has a potentially important role to play in employee motivation (discussed in the subsequent section).

Meanwhile, one cannot ignore the role of the district and the state educational authorities in helping to establish meaningful and workable incentive programs to stimulate teacher motivation.

BOX 4.1 • *The Quality Incentives Program—*
How It Works

With the passage of legislation providing financial rewards for "merit" schools, the Dade County Public Schools and United Teachers of Dade (UTD) negotiated a plan now known as the Quality Instruction Incentives Program (QUIP). QUIP is designed to recognize significant improvements in student achievement, both academic and physical.

Each school, as well as each teacher, votes on participation in the program. When QUIP was first introduced, more than 75 percent of schools chose to participate, with the approval of at least a two-thirds majority of all faculty members. Of the 243 schools then eligible for the program, all but 11 chose to join.

Each individual school's plan, developed by a council of school employees, is evaluated and approved by a QUIP Committee made up of equal numbers of UTD and Dade County Public Schools representatives. The committee, co-chaired by a member of each organization, also administers the program on a daily basis. The State Department of Education grants final approval.

In developing plans, schools are free to focus on whatever areas they determine should have a high priority, based on that school's special needs. In elementary schools, most plans focus on basic skills, especially communication. Geography and culture have been targeted in junior high schools. In senior high schools, efforts are concentrated on reading skills, geography, writing, and math.

At the end of the school year, the results of each school's efforts are evaluated to determine the gains in student achievement since the previous year, based on Stanford Achievement Tests results. Because the focus is on both intellectual and physical development, students also must have a participation rate of at least 80 percent in the Presidential Fitness Test and must have maintained or exceeded the participation rate of the previous year.

Selection of schools is a two-step process. Schools that show a dramatic improvement in student achievement are selected in the first "Quality" round. Of these schools, those schools that have developed the most outstanding projects to improve student achievement are selected as "Educational Excellence" schools. A panel of prominent Dade County citizens judges the special projects, selecting those that have had the most impact on students.

The School Board has also approved funds for a companion program—QUIP-SC, for "special centers." These schools are ineligible for QUIP because they don't compile the required test data on which QUIP criteria are based, such as alternative schools, exceptional educational centers, and vocational, adult, and community schools.

Awards are made "Academy Award-style" each October at a special luncheon attended by members of the school administration, union, and community and business groups. The entire school staff has a share in the financial rewards—teachers, administrators, aides, secretaries, cafeteria workers, and custodians.

Apart from the improvement in the school's instructional programs, QUIP has resulted in other benefits. Morale has increased among teachers and administrators, as well as among the nonprofessional staff who have been made to feel they are part of the program and can share in the financial rewards.

During the 1987–88 school year, more than 69 schools participated in QUIP. Employees received a share (up to $1,400) of the $3.2 million set aside for Dade County by the state legislature. Since the program began, employees of Dade County Public Schools have shared more than $16.9 million in QUIP funds.

Source: *Labor Management Cooperation Brief,* June 1989.

Under current conditions, this is most likely to proceed within as well as beyond, in certain instances, the collective bargaining process (see Chapter Ten). Clearly, teachers' associations along with educational management must work together to develop more site-level and districtwide incentive programs with both material and nonmaterial components.

Motivation and Participation

Our theme is participation as a management principle and tool. Therefore, we close this chapter with several suggestions regarding the use of participation in school-site management as a motivator. Participation is a means as well as an end in management. In previous chapters, we have emphasized the application of participatory approaches to leadership, goal setting, problem solving, and decision making. Applied to each of the essential organizational processes, we have argued that involving teachers at the site level will serve to enhance the general operating effectiveness of the school. In considering employee motivation, we now examine participation from another viewpoint—as an end in and of itself.

When properly orchestrated, participation has the potential to be both its own reward and a stimulant for greater professionalism.

Commitment and Participation

Seeing work as their calling or commitment is one characteristic that distinguishes professionals from other types of workers (Benveniste, 1987). Teachers are not exceptions; school management must find ways to enlist their commitment if a high level of motivation is to be forthcoming. Meaningful participation enlists commitment. It draws the group together around common professional concerns; utilizes its joint skills, knowledge, and experience to solve work-related problems; and creates an organizational agenda within which each professional can situate his or her work. Without participation, some teachers do indeed retain a sense of professionalism; however, many begin to drift as they sense a lack of esprit de corps. And sometimes they develop an adversarial attitude toward the very organization in which they work.

Professional Goals and Participation

The goals of a profession are supraorganizational; that is, they transcend any particular organizational setting in which the professional might find himself or herself. Sometimes the goals of an organization and the goals of the professional may coincide; in other instances, they may conflict. Participation in organizational goal setting, problem solving, and decision making help to bring the wider goals of teachers as professionals into conformity with the goals of the schools where they work. This process of adjustment is bidirectional. Teachers need to fit into the specific goals and objectives of the schools where they teach, but schools also need to build those goals and objectives around their stock of professional capabilities. It is a process of mutual stretching and shrinking. Nothing motivates the professional more highly than the experience of an organization taking advice from its own experts.

Collegiality and Participation

Another characteristic of professionals is collegiality—the sense of belonging to a group of like-qualified, if not like-minded, peers. Schools have been criticized greatly for not fostering collegiality among their faculties (Little, 1987). The sense of belonging to a group of professional peers develops in organizations where colleagues have the time and opportunities to plan, discuss, and work together on projects and activities of common professional interest. A collegial atmosphere can be a great motivator. It heightens professional and organizational commitment along with professional identity. It also increases the possibility of professional exchange and learning. Participation in common professional activities, including curriculum planning, team teaching, performance evaluation, and staff development, increases collegial relations among teachers. Teachers who work at schools with high staff morale will be more motivated than their counterparts working in low-morale settings.

Visibility

Kanter (1981) suggests that visibility is one of the power-related rewards that professionals seek. Visibility means being seen by others in the profession for one's deed well done. It is different from scrutiny, where work is under continual surveillance. Schools need to enhance the visibility of their teachers as professionals. In a Newark, California, elementary school, one principal who wanted to foster greater participation from the faculty started by using one of the monthly faculty meetings to visit the room of each teacher. During that visit, the teacher shared aspects of his or her teaching program with colleagues. This served several ends. It gave each teacher professional visibility with their colleagues and it initiated a dialogue among the teachers around specific teaching techniques and aspects of the elementary school curriculum. It also motivated teachers to organize themselves, reflect on the meaning of their work as it might appear to colleagues, and put their best foot forward for their peers.

Summary

Although motivation is intangible, effective schools seem to abound with highly motivated teachers. Theories X and Y of management make implicit assumptions about human motivation. It is significant that content and process theories of motivation developed by psychologists can be used to support Theory Y, but there is little support for Theory X. In organizations, like schools, where the problem is to motivate professionals with very few extrinsic rewards available and where collective bargaining agreements limit managers in their degrees of freedom, one would do best to identify and foster the intrinsic motivators that appeal to teachers. Greater participation in key areas of concern to teachers can also be a powerful motivator. Motivation is at the core of a quality working environment. Without it, teachers cannot really teach, students cannot learn, and schools cannot be effective.

Case Study

Daniel Webster Elementary School

(Authors' Note: This case presents a problem that many site administrators commonly encounter: A staff member who has been a strong, reliable professional gradually or sometimes even suddenly exhibits a changed pattern of behavior. In this case, a new, committed principal finds herself at odds with an older experienced and respected teacher. Readers may want to consider the problem in terms of the theories of motivation examined in this chapter. How might content theories help the principal understand a change in the teacher's behavior? What could the principal draw upon from process theories that might help to rekindle the teacher's dedication? What other factors besides motivation issues are at play in this situation? What resources are available within the school setting to help the principal in relationship to this particular teacher?)

This was Ms. Mendosa's third year as principal at Daniel Webster, a midsized elementary school in the heart of San Antonio, Texas. It was 3:10 P.M. and Ms. Mendosa was finishing her review of the first semester report cards to be sent home the following day. Momentarily her thoughts strayed to the differences between Daniel Webster and Bedford, the school where she had earlier spent four years as principal. With its enrollment of 525 students and 28 teachers, Daniel Webster was considerably larger than the previous small suburban site of 250 students and 12 faculty. This, of course, had both advantages and disadvantages. On the plus side for Daniel Webster was the greater variety of competencies among the teachers. If she needed a teacher to organize a musical event she could turn to Mr. Harris, for the science fair there was Mrs.

Padilla, and for a dramatic production Ms. Roebuck had boundless enthusiasm.

Mendosa had moved quickly to expand and improve the quality of the bilingual teaching, making it the heart of the language arts curriculum in kindergarten through third grade. She felt both justified and extremely confident of her position: 65 percent of the students were native Spanish speakers and all but a handful were bilingual. Having just completed her doctorate in bilingual education, she was conversant with educational research demonstrating that children learn to read more readily in their maternal language and then later transfer basic skills to a second language. She had also studied several particularly effective programs in the southwestern states for her thesis.

Fortunately, she had been able to identify a core of teachers on the staff who had bilingual language competency and an interest in developing the program. Of the eight teachers in the K–2 grade level, five were Anglo and three were of Latino descent. Her proposal for two bilingual classrooms of the three at each grade level, K–2, had been enthusiastically received by the eight grade-level teachers. All wanted to participate. However, the principal felt that it was necessary to maintain at least one regular classroom at each grade level, both as a control to see how the program worked vis-à-vis the traditional approach and to give parents a choice for an all-English environment if they felt strongly in this regard.

Selecting the bilingual teachers had proved to be problematic. Ironically, three of the most qualified were teachers of Anglo origin who had specialized training in bilingual education and spoke fluent Spanish. Among the teachers of Latino background, three were native Spanish speakers and two had only a moderate command of the language. None of the Latino teachers had any special training in bilingual teaching techniques. All, however, wished to be part of the program. Mendosa assigned the six teachers with fluent Spanish language capability to the initial program. At the same time, she told the remaining two Latino teachers who had wanted to be included that they could be rotated into the program in the future, providing they improved their Spanish language capabilities and acquired some bilingual teacher training, which she was willing to support as their principal.

By the middle of the program's second year, the bilingual program seemed to be working exceptionally well. However, the behavior of Mrs. Garcia, an extremely meticulous, usually restrained second-grade teacher who had not been included in the program, had begun to change. She had called in sick six times during the first semester—after a 10-year perfect attendance record. Her attention to detail, though still acceptable, had declined from its prior impeccable quality. This semester's report cards were late, and upon examining them, Mendosa noted that Mrs. Garcia's usual thoughtful and often lengthy notes to parents were missing.

At the last staff meeting, Garcia, usually quiet, had argued forcefully that the bilingual program was severely limiting the students' learning of English, which she felt was absolutely fundamental to their future success educationally and otherwise. She complained that although her students were advancing in their Spanish language reading skills, their acquisition of English language vocabulary was lagging, and she noted that the tendency to speak Spanish among themselves was increasing since the program's initiation. Although Mendosa thought she saw signs of nonverbal support among some other members of the staff for Garcia's position, the other teachers in the bilingual program had strongly defended the program—both conceptually and in practice. Toward the end of the discussion, the principal observed that Mrs. Garcia had become silent, assuming a sullen expression. The following day, Mrs. Garcia called in sick.

If Mrs. Garcia been a less dedicated and respected teacher among her colleagues, Mendosa might have been able to dismiss her opposition more easily. However, knowing that this teacher had 20 years' experience at the school, had received highly positive evaluations, and had refused numerous offers of promotion in order to remain in the classroom, which she described as her "mission in life," gave Mendosa pause.

Examining her own feelings, she was perplexed as to why Garcia, originally enthusiastic about the program, had become so resistant. Although she had wanted to have a heart-to-heart talk with her for sometime now, Mendosa could not bring herself to do so. Perhaps it was because she just did not understand the reasons behind Garcia's tenacious dislike for the program.

References

Benveniste, G. *Professionalizing the Organization.* San Francisco: Jossey-Bass, 1987.

Campbell, J. P., and Pritchard, R. D. "Motivational Theory in Industrial and Organizational Psychology." In M. D. Dunnette (Ed.), *Handbook of Industrial and Organizational Psychology.* Chicago: Rand McNally, 1975, pp. 63–130.

Certo, S. C. *Principles of Modern Management*, 4th ed. Boston: Allyn and Bacon, 1989.

Chisolm, G. B., Washington, R.; and Thibodeaux, M. "Job Motivation and the Need Fulfillment Deficiencies of Educators." Paper presented at the Annual Meeting of the American Educational Research Association, Boston, 1980.

Garland, H. "Goal Levels and Task Performance: A Compelling Replication of Some Compelling Results." *Journal of Applied Psychology* 67 (1982):245–248.

Herzberg, F. "The Motivation-Hygiene Theory." In V. H. Vroom and E. L. Deci (Eds.), *Management and Motivation*. New York: Penguin Books, 1970.

Jacobson, S. L. "The Effects of Pay Incentives on Teacher Absenteeism." *The Journal of Human Resources* 24 (1988):280–286.

Kanter, R. M. "Career Growth and Organization Power: Issues for Educational Management in the 1980s." *Teachers College Record* 82 (Summer 1981):553–566.

Kerr, S. "The Folly of Rewarding A, While Hoping for B." *Academy of Management Journal* 18 (1975):769–783.

Kottkamp, R. B.; Provenzo, E. F. Jr.; and Cohn, M. M. "Stability and Change in a Profession: Two Decades of Teacher Attitudes, 1964–1984." *Phi Delta Kappan* (April 1986):559–567.

Latham, G. P., and Yukl, G. A. "A Review of Research on the Application of Goal Setting in Organizations." *Academic of Management Journal* 18 (1975):824–845.

Levin, H. M. "A New Model of School Effectiveness." In *Do Teachers Make a Difference?* U.S. Department of Health, Education, and Welfare, Office of Education, Washington, DC: U.S. Government Printing Office, 1970.

Little, J. W. "Norms of Collegiality and Experimentation: Workplace Conditions of School Success." *American Educational Research Journal* 19 (1982):325–340.

Little, J. W. "Teachers as Colleagues." In V. Richardson-Koehler (Ed.), *Educators' Handbook: A Research Perspective*. New York: Longman, 1987.

Lortie, D. *Schoolteacher: A Sociological Study*. Chicago: University of Chicago Press, 1975.

Maslow, A. "A Theory of Human Motivation." In V. H. Vroom and E. L. Deci (Eds.), *Management and Motivation*. New York: Penguin Books, 1970.

McGregor, D. M. *The Human Side of Enterprise*. New York: McGraw-Hill, 1960.

Mento, A. J.; Carledge, N. D.; and Locke, E. A. "Maryland vs. Michigan vs. Minnesota: Another Look at the Relationship of Expectancy and Goal Difficulty to Task Performance." *Organizational Behavior and Human Performance* 25 (1980):419–440.

Miskel, C. G.; Defrain, J. A.; and Wilcox, K. "A Test of Expectancy Motivation in Educational Organizations." *Educational Administration Quarterly* 15–16 (1980):70–92.

Miskel, C. G.; McDonald, D.; and Bloom, S. "Structural and Expectancy Linkages Within Schools and Organizational Effectiveness." *Educational Administration Quarterly* 19–20 (1983):49–82.

Miskel, C. G., and Ogawa, R. "Work Motivation, Job Satisfaction, and Climate." In N. J. Boyan (Ed.), *Handbook of Research on Educational Administration*. New York: Longman, 1988, pp. 279–304.

Mitchell, T. R. "Organization Behavior." *Annual Review of Psychology* 30 (1979):243–281.

Porter, L. W. "A Study of Perceived Need Satisfactions in Bottom and Middle Management Jobs." *Journal of Applied Psychology* 45 (1961):1–10.

St. John, D. "A Unique Labor-Management Partnership Has Made Dade County Public Schools a Model in Educational Reform." U.S. Department of Labor, Bureau of Labor-Management Relations and Cooperative Programs. No. 16, June 1989 Labor Management Brief.

Skinner, B. F. *Science and Human Behavior.* New York: Free Press, 1953.

Trusty, F. M., and Sergiovanni, T. J. "Perceived Need Deficiencies of Teachers and Administrators: A Proposal for Restructuring Teachers Roles." *Educational Administration Quarterly* 2 (1966):168–180.

U.S. Department of Education. *Digest of Educational Statistics, 1988.* Washington, DC: Government Printing Office, 1989.

CHAPTER FIVE

Solving Problems and Making Decisions

Introduction

Between 1980 and 1984, John Muir School experienced a decline in its school reading scores. During 1985, in the course of preparing for a state-mandated program quality review, the teaching staff became aware of the seriousness of the problem. The principal convened a team to diagnose and make recommendations about what the school could do.

Using the nominal group technique (see Box 5.1), the principal was able to elicit a number of possible causes. One member of the committee felt that the decline was a result of uninteresting reading materials and a lack of connection to writing. Another member saw the problem as related to the school's low average attendance rate. A third member argued that too little time was devoted to practicing reading and writing in comparison with previous years. Yet another committee member noted a lack of connection between reading and other curricular areas.

The committee decided to form a quality circle to study the problem and examine these and other possible causes. At the next meeting the committee prepared a fishbone distinction diagram (see Figure 5.6) to help them identify causes of the problem. They then brainstormed possible solutions using the Synectics creative problem-solving approach (see Box 5.2).

The principal selected several recommendations for implementation: (1) An action plan was developed that called for each teacher to attend staff development workshops on reading curriculum over the next three years. (2) A computerized attendance program was installed and staffed with parent volunteers who called parents of absent students. (3) Parent volunteers were trained to assist in implementing the new reading curriculum.

These actions were implemented over the course of the next three years. Problems that arose during implementation, such as how to deal with "at-risk" students, were solved by the team of teachers working with the principal. The next program quality review concluded, "It is obvious that the staff has a strong commitment to a quality schoolwide written language program for all students. Students write daily and writing is integrated into other curricular areas. A variety of strategies are used and there is a clear progression of sophistication in reading and writing skills."

Many school personnel encounter frustrations, impediments, and problems in the course of their work. When we discuss problems with principals and teachers they enumerate a litany of problems:

What can we do to keep "at-risk" students from dropping out?

What can we do to reduce the quantity of litter following our lunch period?

How can we ensure that our winter holiday program is not a disaster?

What can we do about uninspired and burnt-out teachers?

What can we do about parents who have unrealistic expectations for their children and the school?

How can I get new teachers involved in our school?

Solving problems and making decisions is at the heart of school management. We have chosen to focus on problem solving since we see decision making as part of the problem-solving process. Some theorists argue that management consists of only two basic functions: (1) sequential functions of planning, staffing, organizing, and controlling; and (2) continuous functions of solving problems and making decisions (MacKenzie, 1969). Research shows that effective administrators are those who are competent in both areas—they are flexible thinkers, who see problems as opportunities and who can make decisions (Brightman and Urban, 1978).

Theory suggests that a structured and orderly approach is needed when solving problems. Without a structured approach one might become overwhelmed by the sheer enormity of the task. Problem solving requires data, observations, potential solutions or hypotheses, and a method for sorting the information or data. However, recent research suggests that merely following a logical sequence or method is not enough. Leadership style can have a dramatic effect on the quality of problem solving and decision making (Vroom and Yetton, 1973). Broad participation in the problem-solving process is beginning to be recognized as the sine qua non of effective decision making.

This chapter examines the process of problem solving and decision making. It begins with a problem typology and a discussion of the relationship between problem solving and decision making. We then survey several models of problem solving and approaches to decision making: behaviorist, organizational process, bargaining, experiential, and rational. We review the constraints that problem solvers face and suggest several techniques for overcoming them. In discussing the methods for diagnosing and solving problems, we discuss several participative approaches, including the nominal group technique, synectics, and quality circles.

What Is a Problem?

Generalissimo Francisco Franco, former Spanish dictator, had a curious method for handling problems that required his decision. He would sort them into two heaps. In one, he placed those problems that were so difficult and complex only God could solve them. In the other, he placed those problems that, if ignored long enough, the passage of time would resolve. A *problem* may be defined as a discrepancy between a present situation and a more preferred state of affairs. It is more than a frustration. Teachers and principals may experience many frustrations in the course of their work. They may be frustrated by the regimented structure of the school day or by the onerous reporting and record keeping required by state authorities. However, unless they are motivated to specify a more desirable condition and propose alternatives to change the current situation, they have not yet conceived and consequently are not yet ready to solve a problem. The mark of a problem begins with an awareness of an unsettled question or an undesirable situation that one is willing to act to change by visualizing alternatives and taking action.

Problems may be classified along several dimensions. To begin, problems may be operational or strategic. *Operational* problems are immediate. The shortage of paper in the supply room is an operational problem. *Strategic* problems are long term in nature and affect organizational goals. A projected budgetary shortfall due to decline in the school district's tax base is a strategic problem.

Problems may also be classified according to degree of *structure.* Is the problem well-defined (i.e., repetitive, routine, or easily defined)? Or is it ill-defined, ambiguous, poorly understood, novel, or elusive? Well-structured problems generally have a single cause and are amenable to standardized diagnosis and solutions. On the other hand, ill-structured problems, which tend to abound in educational environments, may have multiple causes and require great attention just to diagnose and define. Today's paper shortage is most likely a well-structured problem. Paper was in the supply cabinet yesterday, it's not there today; the range of alternative explanations is likely to be limited and mutually exclusive. (However, this is not necessarily certain; for example, the storeroom clerk may not have done his or her job because of interpersonal problems that are ill-structured.) The matter of declining reading test scores is more likely to be ill-defined. The range of potential explanations is broad and solutions are generally not likely to be mutually exclusive (Brightman, 1980).

Finally, problems can be viewed as crises or opportunities. *Crises* are like a fire in the building; they demand quick reactions and require immediate solutions. Opportunity-related problems pertain to future conditions; to solve them requires proactive behavior, involving taking action or making decisions in anticipation of an impending problem. Thus not all problems are alike. A clear understanding of the nature and type of problem is important to perceiving how it may best be approached.

Models of Problem Solving

Which models exist to describe or provide guidance in solving problems? In this section we examine several models of problem solving. Each of the models emphasizes theories of how people perceive and analyze problems. Three of the models are descriptive, whereas two are prescriptive or normative.

Descriptive Models

Descriptive models attempt to explain the reality of how individuals go about solving problems. They are derived from observations of people in the act of problem solving.

Behaviorist Model
Based on E. L. Thorndike's pioneering studies of problem-solving behavior of cats, the behaviorist model views problem solving as a combination of trial and error and a hierarchy of learned

solutions (Thorndike, 1965). According to the model, if a person solves a problem and is rewarded, the problem-solving behavior is apt to be employed in similar problem situations. The problem is the stimulus, the solution is the reward. Solutions that have worked in the past are ordered in a hierarchy. The individual selects the first solution in the hierarchy and continues down the hierarchy until the problem is solved and the behavior is rewarded. Although this model may explain human problem solving in simple and repetitive tasks, its scope is limited since real-world problems are rarely repetitive and well structured. Moreover, it does not account for abstract reasoning, which might be exemplified by skipped stages or combined solutions (Brightman, 1980).

Organizational Process Model
Problem-solving behavior may under certain circumstances be a function of operating procedures and processes. This model suggests that "to explain an organization's decision at time *t*, we need only examine their standard operating procedure at time *t* − 1" (Brightman, 1980, p. 16). This approach views all problems as programmable and the organization's policies as the program for their resolution. Problems are solved as regular patterns of behavior. Decision rules involve finding out what is the policy or what has been done in the past rather than what is the best way of dealing with this particular issue. Thus problem solving is a function of organizational tradition, structure, and procedure.

Bargaining Model
The bargaining model views decision making as the result of power struggles among different groups or individuals, each with different objectives and bases of authority. Rather than a logical sequenced approach following clearly defined steps, problems are solved through a process of negotiation. To a large extent, the solution will be a function of the distribution of power and the negotiating skills of the different proponents. This model is commonly observed in many personnel problems and labor disputes. Its implications are discussed in greater detail in Chapter Ten.

Normative Models

Normative models build on what has been learned from observing problem solving but synthesize that learning to a recommended strategy for problem solving.

Experiential Model

The experiential approach, first proposed by John Dewey, was based on Dewey's interpretation of the process followed by successful problem solvers at work (Dewey, 1933). Dewey observed that problem solving seemed to be comprised of three stages: diagnosis, analysis, and solution. In the *diagnosis* phase one begins with a sometimes vague, sometimes concrete notion that something is wrong. The diagnosis phase is critical because problem solvers frequently attempt to solve problems before they understand them and consequently solve the wrong problem (Brightman, 1980). The *analysis* stage is concerned with identifying working hypotheses and reaching for potential solutions by way of further observation and testing. The *solution* stage builds on the experience, knowledge, and deductive abilities of the problem solver to predict which solution is optimal or in closest conformity with experience and observation.

Rational Model

The rational model builds on the experiential approach. The model calls for a decision maker or group to carry out a series of specific steps, indicated in Figure 5.1. The approach is normative in that it suggests that decision makers should follow this procedure to solve problems and make decisions. The model distinguishes between problem solving and decision making. Decision making is an integral part of problem solving. It is those steps taken in selecting among alternatives or choosing an alternative course of action. Problem solving emphasizes diagnosing a situation, gathering data, and analyzing information, whereas decision making stresses assigning priorities and choosing among optional courses of action. The relationship between problem solving and decision making is illustrated in Figure 5.1.

Constraints to Problem Solving

The organizational culture and structure can be either a catalyst or a barrier to effective problem solving. These factors affect the performance of the individual within the organization, either acting to promote or restrain creative thinking, willingness to experiment or take risks, and the ability of the decision maker to survey and include information and expertise from throughout the organization. There are three main categories of constraints to problem solving: structural, contextual, and attitudinal.

FIGURE 5.1 • *The Rational Model of Problem Solving and Decision Making*

1. Problem Awareness—What is wrong?
2. Problem Diagnosis—What evidence supports this view?
3. Define the Problem and Decision Objectives—What do we wish to achieve? What are the goals?
4. Generate Alternatives—What options or alternatives exist?
5. Predict Consequences of Actions on Decision Objectives—Test the alternatives; what effect will each alternative have?
6. Select among Alternatives—Which is the best or optimal option?
7. Develop an Action Plan—What are the next steps? What specific action would be taken? Who should do what and when should they do it?
8. Communicate the Plan to Staff—What do others need to know in order to implement the solution?
9. Implement the Action Plan—Take the actions indicated in step 7.
10. Monitor, Evaluate, and Revise—Did everything go as planned? What went wrong? What changes in the diagnosis or solution of the problem should be made?

Problem Solving

Decision Making

Structural Constraints

Structural constraints include the degree of formalization and hierarchical differentiation in the school or organization. For example, where bureaucratic structures prevail, the dominant mode may be the organizational model. It is not that such a model is necessarily limiting but it will be clear that it is not appropriate to deal with all types of problems. Schools that are tightly structured into differentiated departments may find that "functional myopia" inhibits crossing departmental barriers to search for interdisciplinary solutions. Formalization, or reliance on rules and procedures, stifle innovative solutions, whereas informal organizations permit a degree of openness, which is a necessary condition for creative problem solving (Shepard, 1967).

Centralized structures may inhibit creative solutions since problem solvers must spend time gaining permission from those higher up on the organization's ladder, dampening enthusiasm and spontaneity, as well as leaving less time for creative search for solutions. Decentralization sponsors greater autonomy and initiative. However, once a potential solution has been identified and is ready for implementation, centralized organizations appear to be more effective (Brightman, 1980).

Contextual Constraints

How an organization reacts to a problem may constrain its problem-solving behavior independent of the structure of the organization. Under certain conditions schools may react poorly and reach premature consensus or fall victim to *groupthink*, the loss of willingness and ability of group members to evaluate one another's ideas critically, thereby producing a deterioration of a group's problem-solving ability (Janis, 1972). These behaviors may cause incorrect diagnosis of what the problem really is, which may result in solving the wrong problem, rejecting a correct course of action, accepting and implementing an incorrect solution, or solving the right problem too late (Smart and Vertinsky, 1977). Group members develop a type of ethnocentric view, which causes them to fail to consider possible negative consequences of a solution and results in premature fixation on a "group" solution without critical consideration of other alternatives. Symptoms of groupthink are identified in Figure 5.2.

Groupthink can be avoided by participative leadership, encouraging a sharing of viewpoints on all matters facing the group. Several methods can be used to avoid groupthink: (1) create subgroups to work on the same problem and then share their alternative solutions; (2) discuss problems with outsiders, or assign one member to play the "devil's advocate"; and (3) hold a "second-chance meeting" after a consensus has been reached to test a consensus (Schermerhorn, 1984).

Attitudinal Constraints

The attitudes of individual problem solvers can also constrain decision making. When individuals lack a questioning attitude or are intimidated by their peers or superiors, they may fail to ask the questions needed to reveal the source of the problem. Teachers are familiar with this in the form of the student who nods his or her head in agreement but doesn't have the faintest idea what is being discussed.

FIGURE 5.2 • Symptoms of Groupthink

Illusions of group invulnerability: Members of the group feel it is basically beyond criticism or attack.

Rationalizing unpleasant and discomforting data: Refusal to accept thoroughly.

Belief in inherent group morality: Members of the group feel it is "right" and above reproach from outsiders.

Stereotyping competitors as weak, evil, and stupid: Refusal to look realistically at other groups.

Applying direct pressure to deviants to conform to group wishes: Refusal to tolerate a member who suggests the group may be wrong.

Self-censorship by members: Refusal by members to communicate personal concerns to the group as a whole.

Illusions of unanimity: Accepting consensus prematurely, without testing its completeness.

Mind guarding: Members of the group protect the group from hearing disturbing ideas or viewpoints from outsiders.

Source: John Schermerhorn, *Managing for Productivity* (New York: Wiley, 1989), p. 398. Copyright 1989, John Wiley & Sons, Inc.

Participation in Problem Solving and Decision Making

The vignette about John Muir School (presented earlier in this chapter) illustrates several features of participatory problem solving. The team approach to problem identification contributed to a broad and comprehensive diagnosis of possible causes. The committee analyzed those factors that might have produced the decline in student performance. They collectively surveyed the views of other teachers to collect additional data. Next they generated alternative solutions and made recommendations to the principal. Then the team stayed with the problem through the process of implementation and actively worked to gain the commitment of the entire school staff.

This approach to problem solving helped to ensure a careful diagnosis as well as coordination and commitment by the entire school to the recommended actions. The result of the subsequent performance review indicated that the broad-based buy-in by the staff played a major role in the program's success. Table 5.1 illustrates the multiple benefits that accrue from participation in problem solving at each step of the process.

TABLE 5.1 • *Benefits of Participation in Problem Solving*

Step	Role of Participation
1. Problem Awareness	Helps to focus attention on existence of a problem. Where avenues of communication are not open, problems may not be brought into the open for solution and may fester.
2. Problem Diagnosis	Brings in other views to ensure that the problem is correctly diagnosed. Expands the data-gathering network. Helps to obtain a range of practical observations on the nature of the problem.
3. Problem Definition	Helps to gain acceptance and buy in to problem solving by those who have a stake. Participation and consultation at this stage help speed implementation of the solution.
4. Generate Alternatives	Recognizes and incorporates professional knowledge of teachers in school-level decision making and principals in school-district decisions.
5. Test Alternatives	Same as 4.
6. Select among Alternatives	Helps to ensure that there is commitment to selected alternative. Also helps to minimize sabotage of selected decision.
7. Develop an Action Plan	Gains the commitment of those who must implement and undertake tasks.
8. Communicate the Plan	Helps to facilitate the understanding of how the decision may impact on those outside of the unit and to reduce inadvertent sabotage.
9. Implement the Action Plan	Helps to ensure a coordinated team effort provided there was adequate participation in prior steps.
10. Monitor, Evaluate, and Revise	Helps to ensure adequate feedback on successes as well as glitches by those directly affected.

Forming participative problem-solving and decision-making structures not only may facilitate making better decisions but it can also encourage teachers to assume greater responsibility for what goes on in the school. March and Simon (1958) argue that expanding the influence of those at lower organizational echelons not only increases the efficacy of those members but allows organizational leaders to participate more fully. Tannenbaum (1968) calls this the "polyarchic organization"; when more people exert influence, then the degree to which they are influenced by others tends to increase. A loosely coupled organization has difficulty in securing commitment and accountability. Polyarchism provides a way of addressing this drawback. Thus when educational leaders are having difficulty in getting others to comply with their decisions, this theory suggests that if principals allow teachers to exert more influence over decisions, teachers will be likely to accept leadership over a broad range of decisions.

The studies on educational problem solving and decision making exhibit a remarkable consistency. Chase (1952) studied 1,800 teachers in 216 systems located in 43 states. He found that teachers who had an opportunity to participate "regularly and actively" in making school policies were far more likely to exhibit enthusiasm and support for their system than teachers who reported limited opportunities to participate. Bridges (1964) found, not surprisingly, that teachers preferred principals who involved the staff in decision making. And Flannery (1980), in a study of the relationship between teacher involvement in decision making and job satisfaction in 22 Wisconsin high schools, found that those teachers who had the highest levels of expertise were particularly interested in working for schools where they could participate in school-level decision making. Flannery concluded that teacher job satisfaction was "positively and significantly" related to participation in school-level decision making.

One highly successful experiment in teacher involvement, carried out from 1974 to 1977, was funded by the National Institute on Education of the U.S. Department of Health, Education and Welfare's program on local problem solving (Crockenberg and Clark, 1979). The goals of the project were to train classroom teachers to participate along with their principals in identifying and solving school-site problems. A critical element of the program's success was a joint agreement between the teachers' bargaining agent, the California Teachers' Association, and the San Jose Unified School District. The project identified some 13 areas and five levels of teacher involvement in decision making (see Figures 5.3 and 5.4).

A critical element was the use of training sessions that focused on specific needs and problems of district schools. In addition, there was clear specification of precisely who had legitimate authority to make specific decisions within the joint decision structure. Nevertheless, two years after the demonstration project's end, it was seen to be "thriving" in only 6 of the original 12 schools. The reason for a breakdown was attributed to budget reduction as a result of California's Proposition 13, which drastically reduced educational resources throughout the state. These reductions forced layoffs and caused teachers and administrators to retreat behind the barriers of an adversarial form of collective bargaining (Crockenberg and Clark, 1979).

Nevertheless, despite the general tenor of this research, several questions remain. Should a principal involve teachers routinely in all decisions? If not, then in which decisions or under what conditions should the principal seek to share decision mak-

FIGURE 5.3 • *Possible Areas for Teacher Involvement in Decision Making*

1. School Budget and Expenditures
   Policy for instructional accountability in purchase of new equipment and materials
   Procedures for supplying all classrooms with necessary basic supplies
   Procedure for planning and obtaining faculty input on learning resources purchases
   Allocation of school budget to program areas
   Petty cash instructional funds for each teacher
2. Inservice Training and Faculty Meetings
   Mandatory inservice requirements (i.e., advance notice of program and content, released time)
   Teacher role in determining scheduling, program, content
   Assessment of teacher training needs (e.g., use of aides and paraprofessionals)
   Teacher-designed inservice training for teachers with appropriate resources
3. Principal/Teacher Relations
   Policies defining equitable, consistent and effective personnel management practices
   Development of guidelines for acting on parent concerns regarding teachers
   Guidelines for grievance procedures at the school level
   Reciprocal accountability

Continued

FIGURE 5.3 *Continued*

Guidelines for principal consultation with all related teachers prior to action requested by a parent

4. Certificated Support Personnel
   Guidelines for staffing of school special programs and projects
   Parameters for use of specialist re: ongoing programs
   Clarification of job responsibilities for counselors, vice principals, nurse, psychologist, etc.

5. Teacher/Parent Relationships
   Guidelines for teachers to select their own representatives to parent/community organizations and service clubs
   Policies for appointments and visitations
   Consultation with involved teacher prior to action at other levels
   Teacher involvement in design of special programs, open houses, fairs, expositions, etc.

6. Teacher Personnel Policies
   Equitable policy for distribution of extra-duty assignments
   Procedure for changes in level and combination of personnel or subject in teaching assignments
   Policy for involvement of teachers in decisions relating to school assignments and programs
   Environment and conditions enabling teachers to instruct in style best suited to them
   Policy to accommodate individual differences and teaching styles of certificated personnel

7. Student Personnel Policies
   Equitable student personnel and discipline policies
   Fair assignment and transfer policies based on individual student needs and differences
   Instructional resource options to accommodate individual student learning styles
   Scheduling procedures sensitive to student socioeconomic and ethnic needs
   Policy regarding psychological referrals and their impact on other students and teachers

8. Evaluation
   Procedure for open information feedback to staff on both positive and negative outcomes of continuing projects/programs
   Preevaluation consultation with staff to avoid duplication of effort and needless data collection
   Coordination of 127 project objectives and Stull objectives to meet *minimum* standards
   Reciprocal evaluation

9. Curriculum Content and Philosophy
   Policies for teacher involvement in developing innovative programs and discontinuing existing programs
   Teacher role in defining curriculum and educational philosophy (open education, modular scheduling, team teaching, etc.)
   Method of articulation between and among programs

Time and opportunity to study results of potential new programs and projects within and outside the district
Coordination of school rules and curriculum emphasis with recreation and other after-school programs
10. Instructional Materials
Procedure for allocating instructional resources
Evaluating and obtaining complete curricular packages for full instructional benefit
Equitable policies for student use of library/media materials
11. Instructional Methods and Grouping
Policies for teacher load, staffing patterns, class composition, scheduling patterns
Options for implementation of a variety of teaching and learning styles
12. School Procedures
Guidelines to limit classroom interruptions
Guidelines for messages and referrals
Methods for obtaining assistance in proposal writing
Methods of obtaining teacher and parent input for proposal writing
Distribution of association mail
13. School Priorities
Procedure of setting priorities
Teacher participation in generating items for priority setting

Source: Vincent Crockenberg and Woodrow W. Clark, "Teacher Participation in School Decisionmaking: The San Jose Teacher Involvement Project," *Phi Delta Kappan* (October 1979). Reprinted with permission.

FIGURE 5.4 • *Levels of Involvement*

1. *Recommendation:* The faculty or staff council would act in an advisory capacity to the principal, suggesting policies and ideas.
2. *Information:* The council would be informed of the principal's decisions and in turn inform the rest of the faculty of these decisions and what they required of the teachers by way of action and implementation.
3. *Consultation:* The council would be consulted by the principal for its recommendations before the principal took action.
4. *Approval:* The council would be consulted about decisions and have the right to alter, approve, or reject decisions of the principal.
5. *Authorization:* The council would initiate decision making, with the principal offering ideas and suggestions to the council and carrying out the decisions of the council.

ing? And what role should the principal play in order to encourage effective group problem solving?

Let us begin with the first issue: Should teachers be involved in solving all types of problems and making all manner of decisions? The research findings on this question are clear. Teachers do not want to participate in making *all* decisions. Some teachers will want to participate extensively; others will not want to participate at all. Generally, teachers exhibit what some researchers call "zones of indifference" (i.e., broad areas over which the school administrator's decisions will be accepted without question (Alutto and Belasco, 1972). When teachers are asked to participate in problem solving and decision making about issues that they regard as either trivial or outside their areas of expertise, the result is resentment and complaints of excessive meetings (Bridges, 1964).

This necessarily begs the next question: Over which issues should the principal consult and involve teachers? Bridges (1967) offers three guidelines: First, involve teachers in solving problems and making decisions over those issues where the teachers' personal stakes are high. Empirical research indicates that teachers desire a high degree of participation in (1) textbook selection, (2) determining instructional methods, (3) appointment of new staff, (4) resolving pupil problems, (5) budget preparation, (6) building and site plans, and (7) determining work schedules (Conway, 1978). If the principal attempts to make unilateral decisions in any of these areas, such decisions are likely to be met with resistance and alienation of the staff.

A second test is expertise. Teachers are unlikely to be interested in making decisions on matters outside their scope of experience or expertise. For example, teachers are usually disinterested in decisions surrounding administrative staff matters such as hiring a new janitor or the vendor of school equipment.

Third, although many decisions will fit into one of the above categories, certain decisions in which the staff has little stake will, for practical reasons, merit teacher involvement (Bridges, 1967). For example, in determining attendance policies and procedures, it is advisable to involve teachers in discussing and thinking through the issues since their acceptance is essential for effective implementation.

One further issue involves the makeup of a problem-solving and decision-making group. Should the principal be a member? The answer depends to a large extent on the leadership style of the principal (see Chapter Three). When the principal has good staff, rapport, and limited status differential, the results of group decision making are apt to be best. Why? An experimental study of 20 groups of school decision makers found that in those groups without the principal present, there was a greater degree of risk taking and the analyses were more productive and efficient. These findings parallel those of a milestone study of decision making among

B-26 combat crews. In that study the suggestions of lower status crew members were often ignored and passed over despite the fact that they had many more correct solutions (Bridges, 1967).

Approaches to Participatory Problem Solving

Where does the educational administrator begin when he or she is faced with a problem to be solved or a decision to be made? Certain technical problems can be solved by using a variety of computer programs for scheduling facility use, projecting student populations and enrollments, or computing the costs of contracts. Yet a wide range of problems are not simply technical, for example, decisions about new curricular approaches or issues related to performance evaluation. In this section we discuss several methods for handling problems. Each of these techniques has particular strengths; each is appropriate for particular types of problems. Some are better suited to problem diagnosis, whereas others are more appropriate for decision making. However, each of these approaches begins from the premise that consultation, involvement, and group decision making are generally superior to individual decision making.

The methods discussed include the nominal group technique, the Synectics approach, and quality circles. In addition, some ancillary methods are described in Box 5.1. Table 5.2 contrasts the problem-solving techniques discussed in this chapter with regard to (1) whether the focus is on decision making (D/M)or problem solving (P/S); (2) the degree of training required; (3) the suitability for handling ill-defined problems; and (4) the role of the principal in the process. Each approach has advantages and each uses different methods to focus group activity in order to ensure creative and productive problem solving. Quality circles require extensive training; the others do not (see Table 5.2 on page 138). All are designed to utilize a group climate. Each seeks to bring out valuable ideas without creating confusion or wasting time.

Nominal Group Technique

The nominal group technique (NGT) is a flexible method that is valuable for identifying problems, finding solutions, and planning programs. The essence of the NGT is anonymous and silent

---

BOX 5.1 • *Some Techniques for Problem Solving*

Nominal Group Technique

The NGT is a flexible method for identifying problems and finding solutions. The procedure begins with silent and anonymous responses to a question or group task, for example, "What can we do to improve the performance of minority students on the academic achievement test?" Each individual writes his or her ideas, which are collected and listed with anonymity preserved. Then each item is discussed to clarify its meaning. Then and only then are the ideas finally discussed and evaluated. Following discussion, the group then ranks the solutions and decides on a course of action.

Synectics Approach

Similar to the nominal group technique, this approach begins with a problem statement identifying the precise nature of the problem to be solved. The group then undertakes goal wishing or identifying desirable outcomes. An excursion is used to generate lateral thinking about proposed solutions. Then a force fit of the ideas to the problem at hand shifts the focus back to the specific problem. Concerns and critical comments are then handled in an itemized response. Following the evaluation of the proposed solutions, a possible solution is identified.

Force Field Analysis

This is a method for classifying and analyzing the nature of forces that may affect the resolution of a problem. It is also valuable as a method for finding ways to decrease resistance and opposition and build support for a group solution to a problem. First, state the problem as clearly as possible and a desired outcome. Then identify the "supporting" and "restraining" forces in the field (i.e., those factors that facilitate movement toward the solution and those that restrain movement toward a solution). The group then brainstorms suggestions for decreasing resistance and opposition and for increasing the supporting forces.

Proposal Weight Analysis

Once a number of solutions have been identified, the issue becomes how to decide among them. This method provides guidance to selecting the "best" solutions. First, determine whether the problem has a multiple solution or an alternative solution. A multiple-solution problem has a large array of solutions, each of which contributes to a total solution. For instance, a team analyzing the problem of the low proportion of girls attending school in Nepal identified a number of potential solutions, including changing social attitudes, providing small financial stipends to families who sent their daughters to school, and building daycare centers so that families would not have to rely on their school-age children for this job could all contribute to a solution. Alternative-solution problems require a choice between two or more possible ways of solving the problem. For example, "Will we choose curriculum package A or package B?" To weigh proposals, identify the criteria by which the group proposes to decide among the proposals. Form a matrix by listing the proposals on the left side and the criteria along the top. Then evaluate each proposal by each criteria. Score each proposal by the following scale:

+ + Very good
+ Good
0 Neutral or inapplicable
− Not so good
− − Very poor

By totaling the scores, the picture will become clearer. Group members might wish to accord greater weight to some criteria. Those proposals with the most + + signs are marked with an asterisk (*). The group may then suggest ways to reduce the weak points of the outstanding proposals.

Quality Circles

These are regular problem-solving groups composed of teachers (and principals) that meet regularly to identify and solve problems. The group normally consists of 7 to 10 members and one leader. All participation is voluntary and meetings are regular, usually once a week. Formal training in problem solving is usually a part of the circle meetings. The group applies statistical and "fishbone" techniques to analyze identified problems.

---

group response to a well-defined question. The procedure begins with silent and anonymous responses to a question or group task, for example, "What can we do to improve the performance of minority students on the state's mathematics test?" Each individual writes his or her ideas on a piece of paper. At the end of 10 to 20 minutes the ideas are listed, usually anonymously. This nominal process creates a list of potential solutions that is generally not subject to the degree of self-censorship or groupthink of conventional group discussions. At this point the group discusses each

TABLE 5.2 • *A Comparison of Problem-Solving Techniques*

Method	Focus	Degree of Training Required	Suitable for Ill-Defined Problems	Role of Principal
NGT	D/M	Minimal	No	Participant
Synectics	D/M	Minimal	Possibly	Participant/ client
Quality Circle	P/S	Extensive	Yes	Client

item on the master list to clarify its meaning. Then and only then are the ideas finally discussed and evaluated by the group. By deferring the evaluation until this stage, brainstorming or the uninhibited generation of ideas is facilitated. Deferred judgment improves both the quantity and the quality of ideas. Following discussion, the group then ranks the solutions or decides on a course of action.

The Synectics Approach

Similar to the nominal group technique is the Synectics approach, developed and popularized by the Synectics Consulting Group. (A visual presentation showing the application of this method by a problem-solving group at Bell Telephone is illustrated in the film, "Problem Solving Strategies: The Synectics Approach.") This approach begins with a problem statement *identifying* the precise nature of the problem to be solve. The problem-solving group discusses and agrees on the definition of the problem (see Box 5.2). Then the group begins a step called *goal wishing.* This is a process in which group members identify or wish for desirable outcomes. For example, if the problem is defined as "poor reading skills among third-grade students," then one group might wish for a situation in which students prefer reading books to taking their recess. Or if the problem is "student discipline interferes with teaching," one might wish for a situation in which all students sit in their seats and pay attention.

The next step, *excursion,* is a strategy for generating ideas. Taking the characteristics of the solution from the goal-wishing stage, group members are asked to participate in developing and volunteering ideas that exhibit the characteristic from other areas.

BOX 5.2 • *The Synectics Problem-Solving Approach*

The seven steps to group problem solving developed by the Synectics Corporation are summarized below. The group facilitator guides the problem-solving group through each of the steps to move toward possible solutions.

Step 1
Identify the problem. Get a clear, concise understanding of the problem shared among all members of the group.

Step 2
Goal wishing. Every member of the group identifies desired outcomes. For example, if the problem is poor reading skills among third-grade students, then one group member might wish for a situation where students would prefer reading books to playing at recess.

Step 3
The excursion. Group members generate ideas that exhibit characteristics of the problem from other areas. For example, if a goal wish is "joyful learning," then illustrations of joyful learning from an unrelated field such as sports, cooking, or travel might be generated.

Step 4
Force fit. Group members begin to generate possible solutions that come from the Excursion phase (e.g., a reading marathon, read and feast parties, a read your way around the world excursion).

Step 5
Itemized response. Each of the possible solutions generated is assessed in terms of its good features and possible concerns. (e.g., Read and feast parties sound like a way to motivate poor readers, but how can I do cooking in my own classroom?)

Step 6
Recommendations. For each concern, recommendations are solicited on how the concern might be handled.

Step 7
Identifying feasible solutions. The individuals with the problem are asked to indicate in their view whether or not the solutions presented are feasible avenues for dealing with the problem.

For example, if a characteristic of the outcome is "joyful learning," then illustrations of joyful learning from an unrelated field such as sports might be sought. The purpose at this stage is to encourage lateral thinking and expand the potential idea pool.

The fourth step is called the *force fit.* In this phase, ideas from the excursion stage are reintroduced to generate possible solutions of the designated problem. This, of course, is one of the great strengths of the group problem-solving methods—the ability to have a vast and expansive idea pool and to build on the ideas of the entire group. Only after solutions are force-fitted does any critical evaluation begin. The reason for this is that to introduce negativity at an earlier stage would have the likely consequence of inhibiting the flow of suggestions, creative ideas, and contributions by group members. The supportive and participative environment is vital to the generation of creative ideas from which solutions may be crafted. Evaluation of the ideas follows a process termed an *itemized response.* This procedure starts not from the premise of finding what is wrong with each idea, an approach inherently detrimental to group process, but rather by itemizing the good features of each idea followed by an enumeration of "concerns." Once the group identifies the concerns, *recommendations* are sought on how each concern might be handled. At this point the group leader is asked to respond with regard to which of the enumerated solutions represent *feasible solutions.*

Quality Circles

Several school districts located throughout the United States have begun using quality circles to more effectively utilize the intelligence, skills, and creativity of teachers in problem solving. The quality circle is a small group (usually between 6 and 12) that meets voluntarily on a regular basis to identify, examine, and solve problems within the department or organization. Quality circle members are trained in group process and problem-solving techniques.

The quality circle concept was developed in Japan following World War II. During this period Japan faced economic problems due to the poor quality of its merchandise. Today, quality circles are widely recognized as a major source of Japan's resurgence and they have been widely introduced in many U.S. companies (Crocker, 1984). Where successfully implemented, they have increased employee job satisfaction and improved communication and labor relations.

The quality circle process differs from the typical committee or task force in that circle members receive careful training (usually about 15 hours) in specific techniques and procedures. Training assistance may be provided by one of the many quality circle volunteers located in various parts of the United States. The circle begins by identifying problems it is presently facing and that are affecting group members. For example, at Oregon City High School three circles were formed. For one hour a week, a math circle examined the distribution and loss of textbooks, a language arts circle focused on excessive classroom interruptions and administrators' awareness of the state of the art of teaching English, and a clerical staff circle dealt with the problem of communication with immediate supervisors (Hawley, 1984).

The quality circle uses a range of essential problem-solving techniques, as indicated in Figure 5.5. Members receive training on each step or problem-solving tool or technique. These techniques include:

1. *Brainstorming.* This is used to identify problems, causes, and solutions. Each member voices, in turn, one idea until all members decline to present a new idea. Criticism is not permitted.
2. *Multivote clarification.* In order to narrow the focus to the best ideas, the group members vote to indicate which ideas from the brainstorming session merit further consideration. Members may vote as many times as they wish; ideas are ranked by the number of votes they receive.
3. *Consensus.* Individuals discuss each proposal to explain and understand each one. Voting then proceeds with a limited number of votes for each member.
4. *Fishbone distinction.* This technique is also referred to as the *Ishikawa* technique after its originator. Circle members fill in a fishbone diagram, which includes space for four categories of possible causes: materials, methods, people, and equipment. Figure 5.6 further explains this method.
5. *Data collection and analysis.* Members use a variety of techniques—checklists, surveys, interviews, and simple statistical methods—to gather data and explore problems.
6. *Is/Is-not analysis.* Also known as the *Kepner-Tregoe* system,

FIGURE 5.5 • *Quality Team Problem-Solving Framework*

Topics	Steps	Tools	Results
I. Problem Finding	1. Identify Problem 2. Select Problem	1. Brainstorm, Process Flow 2. Multivote, Clarification, Consensus	Problem Statement
II. Problem Analyzing	3. Specify Problem 4. Identify Causes 5. Verify Causes	3. Is/Is-Not Analysis 4. Brainstorm, Fishbone Distinction 5. Data Collection, Is/Is-Not Analysis	Cause Statement(s)
III. Decision Making	6. Decide on Objectives 7. Generate Solutions 8. Evaluate Solutions 9. Make a Decision	6. Musts/Wants 7. Brainstorm, Data Collection 8. Compare to Musts/Wants 9. Consensus	Solution Statement(s)
IV. Implementation	10. Develop Implementation Plan 11. Anticipate Problems 12. Implementation Approval 13. Implement Solutions 14. Postevaluation of Implementation	10. Brainstorm, Data Collection 11. What If? Brainstorm Effects 12. Project Summary, Informal Review 13. Use Plan Developed 14. Collect and Analyze Data	Successful Implementation of Solution

Courtesy of Hewlett-Packard Company.

FIGURE 5.6 • *Fishbone Distinctions*

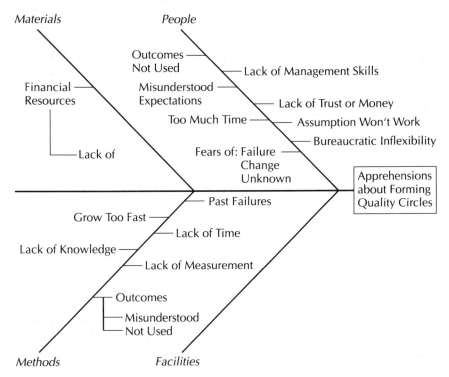

Source: David Hawley, "Quality Circles," *Oregon School Study Council Bulletin,* 28(1) (September 1984).

    this technique is used to differentiate what, where, when, and to what extent a problem *is* or *is not.*

7. *Musts/Wants.* Used to evaluate and decide among potential solutions, this method distinguishes the critical and essential features of the solution from only those that are desirable.

8. *What if? analysis.* This method is used to speculate about what could occur in implementing a solution if the worst case happened. For example, consider: "What if we required students to replace lost textbooks or face expulsion and a parent filed a lawsuit?"

    The results reported by schools that have used quality circles are mixed. The Oregon City School District reported a number of positive outcomes (Hawley, 1984). One teacher reported, "It made me see that policy and management decisions aren't cast in stone. Changes can be made by people who have an interest in the change, if they use available channels." Another stated, "People who are affected by decisions have a chance to help make them" (p. 17).

On the other hand, the Oregon District, San Francisco District, and a Baltimore school all indicated several limitations. The first issue was time. The detailed methods used by the circles take a great deal of time both in the group as well as outside collecting data and interviewing others. In addition, where management makes a slow or ineffective response to the group's effort, frustration can develop, as occurred in a San Francisco high school when a year's work by a circle was dismissed by the new principal as unworthy. Thus there is the issue of the role of the principal; without the principal's support, the circle cannot function.

Summary

Considerable evidence suggests that teachers do want to participate and become involved in resolving school-site problems and in making decisions. However, the evidence also indicates that teachers are wary of doing so because in a number of instances they found that they benefited little and they questioned whether their involvement had made any difference (Duke, Showers, and Imber, 1980). Teachers wish their involvement to be meaningful, to have weight, or be efficacious. Mohrman, Cooke, and Mohrman (1978) found a desire by teachers to become involved in several critical areas: issues pertaining to the administrative or organizational structure of the school, procedures for evaluation of teacher performance, selection of department heads or unit leaders, hiring of new faculty, and evaluation of the effectiveness of a department or subject team. In most instances, teachers are not satisfied with present levels of decision involvement. In a review of eight studies of teacher involvement in decision making, Schneider (1986) concluded that the factor of greatest significance was that in each study less than 5 percent of the respondents indicated that they were satisfied with their degree of decision involvement.

What should a school administrator do and where should he or she begin? First, assess the teachers' actual versus desired degree of involvement in decision making. Second, become aware of the psychological importance of decision involvement for the job satisfaction and ultimate productivity of teachers. Discuss with the teachers and reach agreement with them regarding their views on what constitutes decision involvement and what it ought to be.

Then begin involving the interested individuals in planning, delegating responsibility to others with full trust that it will be done and giving direction or support where requested. Provide training in the use of problem-solving and decision-making techniques as needed and as requested. Provide the staff with the resources they need and let them know that they have the administration's confidence and support. Then find ways to acknowledge and reward the problem-solving team's accomplishments.

The avenues available for participation in school-site problem solving and decision making are numerous and varied. A structured approach to problem solving is helpful in diagnosing, analyzing, and solving problems. In addition, there are numerous benefits to be derived from participation at each step of the process. The detailed discussion in this chapter of problem-solving methods provides further understanding of how to use several of these techniques.

Case Study _____

The Quality Circle

(Authors' Note: Introducing participative problem solving is not always as easy as it might seem. Read Part A and list the vice-principal's options. What did he do wrong? Then read Part B. How could he have avoided the situation in Part A? Will the new approach resolve the situation?)

Part A

John Collins, vice-principal of Grant High School, became interested in using quality circles to improve problem solving at his school after attending a district-sponsored management conference. Some other districts were using this method and reported improved labor relations and employee satisfaction as some of the related benefits. He had read several books on the topic and the slogan "None of us is as smart as all of us" stuck in his mind.

Collins reread the training material, reviewing the sections on how to train quality circle members, the description of what group leaders should do during the quality circle sessions, and how to measure quality circle progress. The next week he decided that he would seek the approval of his principal and initiate a quality circle the following month.

After gaining the principal's approval, Collins selected seven of his most effective teachers and sent them a note asking them to participate in the school's new quality circle. He instructed them to begin by discussing the problem of excessive absenteeism and tardiness of Grant's teachers.

When he arrived at the scheduled meeting, Collins met with the teachers and gave them an orientation about the nature of quality circles and told them that he had the principal's authority to implement any worthwhile solutions that they could identify. He thanked them for their willingness to participate and left the room.

Two months later the group called Collins to inform him that they were ready with their recommendations. Collins expected them to present him with a list of suggestions from which the administration could review and make a selection. Instead, he received a laundry list of outstanding complaints about the school's workload, excessive meetings, unrequested assignments, and aloofness of the administration. Feelings of confusion, anger, and betrayal welled the vice-principal's mind. Before responding, he wisely asked for a coffee break to give himself time to consider his options.

Part B

After thinking through the situation, Collins decided that implementation of the quality circle had lacked the necessary groundwork to ensure acceptance and commitment from the teachers. He realized that he should have met with small groups of teachers and discussed the problems of staff attendance with them, exchanged information, and laid the groundwork for the quality circle by providing some training for the teachers. However, it was too late to do that now.

He decided to ask the group to adjourn the present meeting so that he could consult with the administration about the group's concerns. At the next meeting he decided he would bring in an outside consultant to share some ideas with all of the teachers and staff members on quality circles and how they might help the school deal with some of the problem areas identified by the group. Collins could then ask for *volunteers* for a school quality circle. The school would have to establish a commitment to provide training and support to the quality circle. The circle could deal with a variety of problems and the teachers and staff and even parents might be involved in selecting the problems to be treated.

On discussing his experience with a colleague from another school that had a successful quality circle in operation, Collins realized that the quality circle is a process and not a panacea.

References

Alluto, J., and Belasco, J. "A Typology for Participation in Organizational Decision Making." *Administrative Science Quarterly* (1972): 117–125.

Bridges, E. M. "Teacher Participation in Decision Making." *Administrator's Notebook* 12 (1964):1–4.

Bridges, E. M. "A Model for Shared Decisionmaking in the School Principalship." *Education Administration Quarterly* 3 (Winter 1967):49–61.

Brightman, H. *Problem Solving: A Logical and Creative Approach.* Atlanta: Business Publishing Division, Georgia State University, 1980.

Brightman, H. J., and Urban, T. "Problem Solving and Managerial Performance." *Atlanta Economic Review* (July–August 1978):23–26.

Chase, F. S. "The Teacher and Policy Making." *Administrator's Notebook* I (May 1952):1–4.

Choing-Do, H., and Lindquist, R. "The 1952 Steel Seizure Revisited: A Systematic Study in Presidential Decisionmaking." *Administrative Science Quarterly* (December 1975):587–605.

Conway, J. A. "Power and Participatory Decision Making in Selected English Schools." *Journal of Educational Administration* 16 (May 1978):80–96.

Crockenberg, V., and Clark, W. W. "Teacher Participation in School Decisionmaking: The San Jose Teacher Involvement Project." *Phi Delta Kappan* (October 1979):115–118.

Crocker, O. et al. *Quality Circles.* New York: American Library, 1984.

Dewey, J. *How We Think: A Restatement of the Relation of Reflective Thinking to the Educative Process.* New York: D.C. Heath, 1933.

Duke D. L.; Showers, B. K.; and Imber, M. "Teachers and Shared Decisionmaking: The Costs and Benefits of Involvement." *Educational Administration Quarterly* 16 (1980):93–106.

Flannery, D. F. *Teacher Decision Involvement and Job Satisfaction in Wisconsin High Schools.* Ph.D. dissertation, University of Wisconsin-Madison, 1980.

Hawley, D. "Quality Circles." *Oregon School Study Council Bulletin* 28 (September 1984).

Janis, I. *Victims of Groupthink.* Boston: Houghton Mifflin, 1972.

MacKenzie, R. A. "The 3-D Process of Management." *Harvard Business Review* 69 (November–December 1969):80–87.

March, J., and Simon, H. *Organizations.* New York: Wiley, 1958.

Mohrman, A. M.; Cooke, R. A.; and Mohrman, S. A. "Participation in Decisionmaking: A Multidimensional Perspective." *Educational Administration Quarterly* 14 (Winter 1978):13–19.

Schermerhorn, J. *Management for Productivity.* New York: Wiley & Sons, 1984.

Schneider, G. T. "The Myth of Curvilinearity: Analysis of Decisionmaking Involvement and Job Satisfaction." *Planning and Changing* 17 (Fall 1986):146–158.

Shepard, H. A. "Innovation Resisting and Innovation Sponsoring Organizations." *Journal of Business* (October 1967):470–477.

Smart, C., and Vertinsky, I. "Designs for Crisis Decision Units." *Administrative Science Quarterly* (December 1977):640–657.

Tannenbaum, A. *Control in Organizations.* New York: McGraw-Hill, 1968.

Thorndike, E. L. *Animal Behavior: Experimental Studies.* New York: Hafner, 1965.

Vroom, V., and Yetton, P. *Leadership and Decisionmaking.* Pittsburgh: University of Pittsburgh Press, 1973.

CHAPTER SIX

Planning and Managing School Finance

Introduction

Principal Robert Wagner opened the meeting of the newly
formed Lakeland Junior High School budget committee
with these words, "As I'm sure you all know, funding of
education is not an easy matter. Education should be our
society's number-one priority. However, it appears that the
voters are not willing to pay for quality education. Despite a
tremendous effort by our parents' association, tax initiative
J, which would have increased our budget by the 10 percent we needed to reduce class size and save our extracurricular programs, failed. Frankly, I just don't know where
we will get the money we need to maintain our music program, support our school librarian, pay for our intrascholas-
tic athletics, or pay for the new instructional aides that our
teachers identified as essential for our at-risk reading program."

The budget committee was comprised of five teachers
and two parent representatives in addition to the principal
and vice-principal. Jeanette Hart was the newly appointed
head of the English department. Her hopes for developing a
model reading program rested on getting those new materials. Her department had spent the last year developing
ideas, researching curriculum, and participating in in-
service training in preparation for the at-risk reading program. In five minutes these hopes were dashed. She
realized that she would have to find out more about the
school's and district's budget so she could find an answer.

Like all other organizations, schools require financial resources to pay for their operations. What do educational managers
need to know in order to secure and allocate resources in order to
accomplish the objectives established by the managerial team?
How will alteration of the institutional structure facilitate improved financial performance? This chapter deals with issues of
school finance, including the relationship between plans and finance, the nature of educational costs, how to budget resources,
how to finance projects, and how to control costs. For school-based
management to be truly effective, teachers need to be involved in
the budgetary process for the reason that so many of a school's
decisions hinge on the allocation of available resources. When
teachers share ownership and responsibility for the use of resources, they are able to assist the administration in developing

workable methods of economizing on scarce resources while ensuring that educational necessities are not overlooked. When the entire school community feels a sense of responsibility for the financial resources of the school, greater care will be evidenced in financial decision making in most instances, which will result in better decisions.

However, in order for teachers to be effective participants in the budgetary process, it will be important for them to learn something about school finance and school budgeting.

The Content of Educational Finance

In 1989–90, the total investment in K–12 education in the United States was estimated at $212 billion. The average cost of educating each elementary and secondary school student is $5,246. Over the past decade, expenditure on education has grown by 110 percent. This expenditure was used to support a nationwide school system with some singular characteristics. Most of the nation's schools are nonprofit organizations. They provide a range of services to society, but those services are not sold. Instead, they are financed largely through tax revenues that are allocated to the school system by way of the political system (see Table 6.1). Schooling is provided to the users free of charge. There is little competition among providers of education at the precollegiate level; a family that chooses not to send its children to a public school must pay for the full cost of schooling. This has been related to problems with regard to equity, since the ability to choose an alternative school is directly related to a family's income.

Meanwhile, the school board plays an ambiguous role. On the one hand, it is a buyer of education, representing the interests of the public. School boards, as selected representatives, must re-

TABLE 6.1 • *K–12 Revenue, 1967–1987 ($ billion)*

	1986–87		1976–77		1967–68	
Total Revenue	158.8		75.3		31.9	
Federal	10.1	(6.4%)	6.6	(8.8%)	2.8	(8.8%)
State	79.0	(49.8%)	32.7	(43.4%)	12.3	(38.5%)
Local	69.7	(43.9%)	36.0	(47.8%)	16.8	(52.7%)

Source: U.S. Department of Education Center for Educational Statistics, *Digest of Educational Statistics, 1988* (Washington, DC: U.S. Government Printing Office, 1989).

view the supply and quality of educational service with the public interest in mind. On the other hand, it is a supplier/operator of the school system. It must carry out the managerial functions of organizing and controlling the school system to achieve public policy objectives.

At the same time, the perceptions and priorities of the electorate determine the availability of funding for education. This is true at three levels: Congress allocates federal funding for categorical programs (such as special education) in response to concerns of the electorate; the state assemblies are the major source of funding for education in each of the states; and local property taxes and school bond issues are a further source of funding as determined by the local electorate.

Within the school district decisions are made in response to program needs and priorities. Recently, a good bit of public concern has shifted toward issues of productivity and accountability for funds received. Presently, revenues are appropriated on the basis of student attendance, enrollments, or programmatic offerings. Yet this approach to school finance leaves two questions unanswered: Is the money allocated for educational purposes well spent? Is there evidence of efficient and effective management of the financial resources? Some researchers have pointed to evidence that there is no strong empirical relationship between school expenditures and student performance. In a thorough review of two decades of educational research, Hanushek (1989) concluded that expenditures are not systematically related to student achievement. According to Hanushek, expenditure increases within the current institutional structure are likely to be dissipated into such areas as growing administrative overheads, with the result that the growth in costs will exceed gains in student performance. Finn (1987) has interpreted this to suggest that what public schools need is a dose of market-driven competition. These views suggest that much thought needs to be given to the allocation and use of educational resources.

Planning and the Budget

Instructional expenditures normally comprise about two-thirds of the educational budget. The number of students, teachers' salaries, and average class size determine instructional expenditures. Teachers' salaries in turn are determined by teacher experience, teacher education, whether teachers are unionized, and the strength of the teacher bargaining unit (see Chapter Ten).

The fundamental activity that occurs in any well-managed organization is planning. It is the activity that translates ideas into actions. The purpose of a plan is to facilitate the accomplishment of institutional objectives. Policies and procedures are the framework for programs, which in turn are the building blocks of any organization's actions. For example, administrators and teachers in the Vallejo Unified School District meet each year to prepare a district educational plan (see Figure 6.1). The plan is comprised of school-site plans prepared by a team of school administrators, teachers, and parents from each school in the district.

The budget is the financial plan that underlies the action plan, translating ideas and intentions into a resource allocation that reflects the institution's priorities. Ideally, the budget is a financial plan that forecasts how money will be spent in order to

FIGURE 6.1 • *Guidelines for Developing a School-Site Plan: Vallejo Unified School District*

I. School Philosophy and Goals

The school philosophy and goals statement should include:

- A brief written description of the vision or underlying philosophy of the staff about education at the school (a belief statement)
- A few brief statements of the global outcomes the school hopes to achieve:
  —academic outcomes
  —effective/social outcomes
- References to how your school is addressing the goals in the *Five-Year Instructional Improvement Plan*

II. Establishing Goals and Incorporating a Schoolwide Vision

Any comprehensive planning process will need a point of departure that planners can use to focus and unify the effort over the length of the planning cycle. Establishing broad goals that represent the mutually supported aspirations of the school and community will serve as a common starting point for the process and help planners identify the desired and agreed-upon outcomes that will affect student learning. These broad goals constitute a shared vision of the school's fundamental purpose and allow the members of the school community to reach a consensus as they set targets for improvement. A vision of the school contains elements that unify all aspects of change and tie the efforts of individual staff members to one coordinated whole.

These goals or outcomes represent the global concepts of the educational system and should not be confused with specific learning objectives. Here, the emphasis is on identifying those aspects of learning and child development that are endorsed by the entire school community and constitute the school's primary mission. Expressing these goals in terms of student outcomes or benefits and

Continued

FIGURE 6.1   *Continued*

obtaining consensus among the school community will set the tone and direction for subsequent planning activities.

In developing goals, it is helpful to limit the scope to the essential functions of the school to resist the temptation to include superfluous detail. Typically, planning groups will focus on a half-dozen basic concepts and express them in simple and concise terms. When well drafted, these concepts generally will fit on a single page. In this form the concepts are readily communicable to all participants, students, and members of the school community.

As program development activities continue, the unifying goals may be repeatedly referenced and will help to maintain a clear vision of the collective aspirations of all those working to improve educational experiences for students.

III. Description of the School

Please include a one-page description of the school including such data as:

- Geographic information
- Demographic information (e.g.)
  - Number of students
  - Ethnic and racial composition of student body
  - Types of programs at the school
  - Staffing
  - AFDC count
- General information about the curriculum
- General information about instructional approaches
- General information about staff development

IV. Describing the School

The description of the school and its current programs provides a context for the planning effort and the improvement strategies that will follow. Typically, the description will include basic geographic and demographic information, as well as pertinent general information on the curriculum, instructional approaches, staff development, and program development at the site. Constraints also affect the improvement activities the school planners wish to undertake and should be addressed in this description. Elements that may help to set the stage for school improvement may include staff seniority or turnover, parent participation or volunteerism, and availability of school and community resources. Additional support and technical assistance will come from the district, neighboring schools, program review consortia, and county offices of education.

V. Component:_____ Funding Source:_____

Current Conditions	Objectives
An analysis of needs and strengths based on sources of data such as: • PQR criteria • Model curriculum standards "Performance Report of California Schools" • PQR and self-review findings • Proficiency standards and test results • Attendance records • Behavior records • Attitude surveys • Needs surveys • WASC reports	• Establish priorities and focus efforts • Based on needs/strengths • Specify level of achievement • Specify time frame • Specify means of measuring achievement

VI. Component:_____ Funding Source:_____

Activities

• Strategies for reaching improvement goal
• Describe what staff wants to change, do differently, or continue
• Focus on specific approaches
• Some activities may be suggested by PQR criteria

Approaches may include:
—Curriculum strategies
—Instructional strategies
—Staff development activities
—Acquisition and use of materials

Time Line	Responsibility	Evaluation
• When will the activity occur?	• Who has primary responsibility for seeing that the activity occurs?	Data sources may include • PQR or self-review results • Post-tests, surveys, etc. • Review of school records • Review of state and local test data

Used with permission from Vallejo Unified School District.

achieve the organization's programmed objectives. Budgeting, then, is the formulation of program plans in terms of financial costs.

Budgetary Conflicts and Potential Pitfalls

The budget can be a source of conflict and a problematic focal point in any organization. When there is intense competition for limited resources, the budget allocation can result in heightened tensions, pitting groups of employees against one another. Leaving key employee groupings out of the budgeting process can become a source of institutional paranoia. If the budget is inflexible or unalterable, it can become a straightjacket as opposed to a vehicle for facilitating goal accomplishment. If budgetary goals are allowed to supersede educational goals, the mission of the school may become obscured.

What Schools Produce

Schools provide social services. They train students in basic academic as well as job-related skills. (Chapter One presents a more complete discussion on the role of schooling.) Schools also socialize students into society's values, cultures, and norms. One strand of educational theory questions whether the aims and objectives of such socialization are indeed benign. Critical theorists are apt to view the role of the school system in terms of an institution designed to reproduce the existing social class structure—schooling the middle and upper segment of society for success and advancement and schooling the underclass for failure (Spring, 1972; Carnoy, 1972; Illich, 1970). In any event, one should be clear regarding the role and mission of the school system and whether it is serving the true interests of all pupils.

The Concept of Costs

Costing is the art of measuring the consumption of resources in financial terms. However, not all costs are immediately financial. For example, wear and tear on a physical facility or conflict among staff members are two types of costs that may not be evident until much later. The former will eventually lead to expenses for replacement or repairs, whereas the latter may lead to a loss in teacher time from teaching (which may not be immediately apparent).

Costs such as teacher salaries or purchase of art supplies are concrete and easy to comprehend; other costs are more subtle, however. *Opportunity costs,* a term frequently used by economists, measures the cost of the foregone next best alternative. For example, an administrator is faced with a choice between hiring a reading specialist or a music teacher, and chooses the reading specialist. The opportunity cost of hiring the reading specialist in lieu of the music teacher is the benefit to the school and children that would have resulted from hiring the music teacher.

Controllable and Uncontrollable Costs

Another subtlety of costing is the distinction between controllable and uncontrollable costs. These are expenses over which the district or school cannot control or influence. Public school principals, as well as many superintendents and school boards, typically encounter a situation in which they are able to exercise control over very few of their costs. Some budget items, such as per capita allowances or reimbursements for average daily attendance, will be mandated by the state; others, such as teachers' salaries, will have been negotiated by the school district. One reason behind the limited controllability is the fact that schooling is highly labor-intensive. Normally, between 60 and 75 percent of the education budget goes for the payment of personnel.

Schools are subject to extensive legislation with regard to every aspect of school life; laws are often developed with little regard for their budgetary impact. For example, recent legislation requiring asbestos removal from schools has had a substantial and adverse impact on the budgets of many districts. And the legislation of the late 1960s and 1970s, which sought to curb the pernicious effects of school segregation by busing, resulted in substantial increases in the transportation line item for many school districts.

Finally, the nature of the school calendar contributes to high and uncontrollable costs. Schools are costly to construct, yet they are not utilized for the entire portion of the year, adding to the cost of schooling.

Financial Decision Making

In making financial decisions, several concepts are useful. These are the notion of unit costs, average costs, marginal costs, benefit-cost and cost-effectiveness. *Unit costs* are useful for gaining insight into the comparability of items. For example, if one was interested in the cost of educating each student in a special education program in a particular district, one might be interested in either (1) the cost per pupil per year, (2) the cost per pupil per school week, (3) the cost per pupil per day, or (4) the cost per pupil per 45-minute period. Alternatively a principal may be interested in the daily cost of operating the school or the cost of educating one class of students for each 45-minute period. In each instance the cost refers to the *average cost*, which is calculated by dividing the total figure by the appropriate number of students.

The *marginal cost* is the cost of, say, adding one more student to the program. In this case, one would not need to add another classroom or hire another teacher. One might need only to purchase an incremental amount of school supplies. Hence the marginal cost of an additional student might be very small. In contrast, for a school that is operating at capacity and encounters the need to add another class, the marginal cost might be very high if it means building a new classroom.

Benefit-Cost and Cost-Effectiveness Analyses

Benefit-cost and cost-effectiveness analyses have been used increasingly by educational decision makers in recent years. These methods have been developed to compare the costs of a program or activity with the outcomes or benefits that it produces. *Benefit-cost analysis* is used to compare costs and benefits of alternatives when the outcomes can be expressed in monetary terms. It provides an indication of the relative efficiency of using resources in different programs. When outcomes are not easily measurable or are converted to monetary terms, cost-effectiveness analysis may be used (Levin, 1983).

In undertaking a benefit-cost analysis, the educational decision maker will begin by attempting to identify all of the costs of a program or activity. Then each of the benefits will be enumerated and a value will be placed on each benefit. Normally costs and benefits will occur over a period of several years. Consequently, both costs and benefits will have to be adjusted or discounted by the time value of money (i.e., the interest rate) in order to determine the present value (i.e., to convert the value of future anticipated benefits into current dollars). The ratio of benefits (B) to costs (C) may be expressed in the following formula:

$$B_0 + \frac{B_1}{(1 + i)} + \frac{B_2}{(1 + i)^2} + \cdots \frac{B_n}{(1 + i)^n} \div$$

$$C_0 + \frac{C_1}{(1 + i)} + \frac{C_2}{(1 + i)^2} + \cdots \frac{C_n}{(1 + i)^n} = B/C$$

where:
i = interest rate
subscripts refer to years

In this formula, a B/C is the benefit-cost ratio. A ratio greater than 1 indicates a program for which the benefits are greater than the costs, which generally indicates a worthy investment. For example, in a study of the costs and benefits of a vocational training program it was estimated that current value of the future benefits to society and the students involved totaled $3.2 million, whereas the cost of the program totaled $2.1 million. In this case the benefit-cost ratio was 3.2/2.1 (Useem and Girling, 1985).

Cost-effectiveness is another related technique. Frequently one is unable to identify specific benefits of a program. Yet there may be several alternative ways of accomplishing the same objective. For example, in seeking to improve student math performance, the decision maker may be considering two options: (1) hiring a math specialist and (2) purchasing a computer-assisted learning package. If both are rated as equally effective, then the option that is the least expensive will exhibit the higher cost-effectiveness ratio (C/E).

Making the Money Go Around

These techniques and others can be employed in making decisions about typical financial problems such as: What is the present state of resource use and availability for each of the school's or district's programs? Which areas are served well and which are served poorly? What are the priorities? What level of resources does each program area need?

Among the approaches that can be employed are (1) benevolent despotism, (2) a percentage formula, (3) creeping incrementalism, (4) open market, and (5) a combination. Each of these approaches has its advantages and disadvantages. *Benevolent despotism* is perhaps the method most commonly practiced by principals and superintendents. It involves an individual, independent decision based on the administrator's knowledge and familiarity with a wide range of issues and needs. Its main advantage is that it is quick. However, it suffers from the disadvantage of a limited information base; not all issues may be adequately considered, and it may reflect the decision maker's biases rather than full factual information.

The use of a *percentage formula* is also common: If the chemistry department has 10 percent of the student enrollment, then it deserves 10 percent of the budget. This method is also quick and it has the added advantage of relying on an objective basis rather than on subjective feelings. However, since some subjects such as laboratory sciences are clearly more costly to operate than others, it may not be a valid decision rule. Moreover, it permits little opportunity for input from those who operate or are affected by the program.

Creeping incrementalism avoids the mindless methodism of a formula. According to this decision rule, the prior year's budget for each program is augmented by the same overall proportion, say 5 percent. In this way, programmatic cost differences are reflected. However, this approach, too, fails to include the input of those involved in or affected by the program.

The *open-market* method provides a more systematic and thorough approach to making budgetary decisions than any of the preceding techniques. It involves each unit preparing a request for funds and providing a written justification for that request. For example, the chemistry department would prepare a "pro forma" or desired budget and the rationale for the projected costs. The appropriate administrator or administrative committee would review each such request and make overall determinations based on these submissions.This approach has the advantage of securing the input of teachers and interested parties who are close to the program, thereby ensuring that relevant information is considered. Nevertheless, this is a time-consuming process and it may lead to inflation of estimated costs in anticipation of receiving a reduced allocation from limited resources.

Resource Compendium

One method for getting a sense of the resource priorities in the school or district is to prepare a resource compendium. This is a listing of the status or condition of the school's or district's available resources. Each cost item is itemized on a list and categorized according to a five-point rating scale in which 1 indicates very good and 5 indicates poor conditions or availabilities. Simply reviewing the list of resources can assist the decision makers in iden-

FIGURE 6.2 • *Resource Compendium*

Cost Item	1	2	3	4	5
Books		2			
Audiovisual equipment				4	

1 = Very Good. All essential items/needs are provided in good condition and many inessentials are present.

2 = Good. All essential items/needs are provided in reasonable condition and a range of inessentials are present.

3 = Adequate. All essentials are provided; some are in poor condition or inadequate numbers, including some inessentials.

4 = Inadequate. Insufficient number of textbooks and equipment to allow necessary classroom activities to occur. Few inessential items are present.

5 = Poor. Essential items are unavailable.

Source: Adapted from Brian Knight, *Managing School Finance* (London: Heinemann, 1983).

tifying the items most in need of improvement. This method is illustrated in Figure 6.2.

Types of Budgets

The budget plays several roles. First, the budget serves as a contract, identifying just how resources are to be allocated. Second, in that managers must stay within their budgets, it provides a basis for managerial control over programs. Finally, it may be used as a mechanism for evaluation when the performance of program managers is compared with their program budget objectives. Although there is considerable interest in program budgeting, it is unlikely that many educational institutions or districts will be managed in this fashion.

Line-Item Budget

The most common type of budget is a list of functions or item classifications. This is known as a *line-item budget.* One specifies the things needed to be purchased. Once these are included in the approved budget, the administrator is free to go ahead and spend the designated amounts to acquire the indicated resources. However, there are several problems with line-item budgets. First, they tend to focus on itemized expenditures, such as the purchase of paper clips or basal readers, as opposed to outcomes or benefits from an expenditure (e.g., improved reading skills). Also, line-item budgets do not invite consideration as to whether a specified activity should be done at all and they do not relate the resources requested to performance. Finally, line-item budgets tend to be static and inflexible, unable to readily accommodate changing conditions. This undercuts the authority of the implementing agency to make responsible decisions at the site. A site administrator should be able to choose resources that best meet the needs of the situation and the time. An example of a school district's line-item budget appears in Table 6.2.

Program Performance Budget

The essential idea behind a program performance budget is that the budget is organized in terms of end products, such as math proficiency as opposed to personnel, supplies, and equipment. The implementation-level administrator would be given the budget and the flexibility to work within it, hiring or purchasing resources to achieve program objectives. The line-item budget has as its focus the identification and the auditability of what was purchased; the program budget is concerned with accountability for broad program objectives.

Program performance budgets drive the allocation of resources to the areas of greatest need. For example, inadequate performance in sixth-grade mathematics would result in the design and funding of programs to address that portion of the school curricula. It might result in the recruitment of high-quality teachers in this area of high priority.

School Finance and Teacher Working Conditions

One of the most crucial areas of financial decision making concerns the recruitment and salary levels of teachers. Setting attractive salary levels is important, but it may be just as important to ensure good working conditions. Indeed, in some instances it may be far more important. The benefits derived from school improvement programs can have substantial financial payoffs in retaining highly skilled teachers. In Utah, for example, some districts have provided new opportunities for teachers by devising

TABLE 6.2 • *1987–88 General Fund Budget (Less External Funding): San Diego City School District*

Income by Source

State: Continuing Educational Support	$217,783,945	48.47%
State: Lottery	9,354,000	2.08%
Local Taxes—Revenue Limit	163,882,696	36.47%
Local Taxes—Debt Service	10,585,572	2.36%
Miscellaneous Local Sources	5,458,987	1.21%
Federal	5,569,000	1.24%
Carryover Balance including Lottery Carryover	36,688,147	8.17%
Total	*$449,322,347*	*100%*

Appropriations by Expenditure Classification

Employees' Salaries and Benefits	$372,634,323	83%
Books and Supplies	16,525,409	4%
Contracted Services and Other Operating Expenses (insurance, utilities, elections, etc.)	27,122,454	6%
Capital Purchases/Improvements and Equipment Replacement	12,768,246	3%
Other Outgo, Transfers, Tuition, Contingencies, and Ending Balance	20,271,915	4%
Total	*$449,322,347*	*100%*

Appropriations by Program

General and Special Education Instructional Programs	$262,526,830	59%
Instructional Support	60,479,262	14%
Pupil Services	22,951,160	5%
District Administration	14,297,404	3%
Maintenance	8,015,670	2%
Operations (utilities, custodians, and gardeners)	30,682,086	7%
School Policy Services	1,849,699	—
Transportation	19,831,269	4%
Stores, Receiving, and Distribution	668,563	—
Community Services	248,967	—
Food Services	50,115	—
Facility Acquisition and Construction	7,377,651	2%
Fringe Benefits/Retired Persons	71,756	—
Other Outgo	19,037,540	4%
Reserves	—	—
Net Ending Balances	1,234,375	—
Total General Fund (Less External Funding)	*$449,322,347*	*100%*

new jobs that increased teacher collaboration and involved teachers in schoolwide planning and development. Such programs provide a relatively low-cost method of improving teacher satisfaction and teacher retention under conditions in which schools are unable to compete financially with other employers. This approach can also prove useful when retrenchment is necessary. Setting aside resources for teacher involvement in planning and school improvement may be the most effective way to deal with flat or declining revenues (McDonnell, 1983; Odden, 1985).

Finding Resources

Rarely does an administrator find that the financial resources are adequate to perform the many tasks that he or she would like to accomplish. A popular cartoon in the late 1970s, taking its inspiration from John Lennon's song "Imagine," depicted a group of army generals holding a bake sale. The caption read, "That will be the day, when the schools have all the money they need and the military has to hold a bake sale!" Unfortunately, for those in educational management, we are not yet there. And since most of the educational administrator's budget is earmarked for salaries and other uncontrolled costs, one of the few avenues through which to obtain a degree of budgetary flexibility is fund raising and grant writing.

There are many sources of finance for schools. Clearly, the major source of funding will come from flat grants that are channeled to the school district on a per student or classroom basis. A majority of states use an equalizing plan to ensure that minimum funding levels are achieved by all districts. When a significant source of funding is property taxes, state aid may match local district expenditure on a sliding scale. For districts with low revenue levels, state-matching grants may provide a large percentage of local costs, while providing little or no funds for high revenue districts.

In California, nearly two-thirds (66 percent) of the $15 billion of state, local, and federal funds for K–12 education in 1984–85 came from the state budget, mainly from sales and income taxes. Nearly one-fifth, or 19 percent, came from property taxes, only 7 percent from federal sources, and a remaining 8 percent from miscellaneous local sources. In 1984, California voters approved a state lottery to fund supplemental activities, which was projected to provide about 3 percent of the educational budget by 1988 (California Coalition on Fair School Finance, 1985).

However, the degree of variability regarding state financing for schools is wide. In some states, such as New Hampshire, state aid is less than 10 percent of total revenues, with local taxes providing the bulk of the educational budget. In Hawaii, the major source of financing is provided by the state; local revenues provide nothing (Cohn, 1979). In general, the federal role in financing K–12 education remains quite limited, with less than 10 percent of elementary and secondary expenditures coming from federal sources. Federal funds are limited to special purpose programs such as aid for children of poor families, aid to schools located in "federally impacted areas" (i.e., where large federal installations are located) and "categorical" aid for programs such as vocational education, special education, and drop-out prevention (Cohn, 1979).

Involving Teachers and the Community

School-Based Fund Raising

Based on our observations, effective administrators spend a good bit of their time writing grants or providing support and encouragement to teachers to write grants, working with the parents and community to identify sources of financial support, and organizing fund-raising benefits and activities. This area in particular illustrates the benefits that can flow from a team environment with teachers and administrators working together to generate additional educational resources. The reasons why such approaches tend to be effective is that teachers come to understand the financial issues and problems that administrators face daily. No longer are these issues solely the problems of "management"; instead, they have become the problems of the school team. In addition, when hard choices must be made, teachers can provide some important guidance regarding the likely consequences. The team environment also provides teachers with the opportunity to comprehend more fully some of the limitations associated with certain types of categorical funds. Openness in the budget process can result in significant gains as teachers come forth with their ideas for cost effectiveness and as inherent suspicion and bad feelings are overcome. However, there are risks. Teachers may find inequities between administrative and teaching salaries or identify sources of administrative "waste," which could provoke disagreements that would have to be worked through. Nevertheless, on balance, a candid approach is nearly always the best guide for action.

A key to the success of Kensington Hilltop Elementary School has been the active efforts of Barbara Chriss to generate supplementary funding to pay for elective programs. (See the case study at the end of this chapter.) Supplemental funds provided by parent groups have provided funding for an enrichment program that has been the centerpiece of the school's renewal. Essential to such a program are the catalytic efforts of the principal, teachers, and parents working together (see Chapter Nine).

There are many potential sources of finance besides federal, state, and local sources: Pupils can raise funds for specific activities by way of a sponsored walk or raffle; staff members may sponsor a fund-raising event such as an auction of donated items; and local firms, banks, and wealthy individuals can be approached In addition, the school can submit grant proposals for the funding of specific projects or programs.

Grant Writing

When considering a grant proposal, it is essential to be very specific in identifying what it is that is being proposed. The individual(s) should learn everything possible about the foundation or granting agency, speaking with them to understand their priorities and criteria, and finding out who will make the decision and what they are looking for. The individual(s) seeking the grant should then prepare a concise proposal, identifying (1) the specific goals and educational benefits, (2) the activities that are proposed to be undertaken, (3) any supplemental sources of funds, and (4) any potential savings that will make the project cost-effective.

What can principals do to involve their staff in garnering resources for the schools? Here are some possible options:

1. Hold a grant-writing workshop for teachers. Invite representatives of local foundations or university grant offices to attend and give presentations.
2. Find a sponsor for small grants ($300) for teachers to prepare grant proposals.
3. Meet local business people and ask them about their concerns and interests in public education and what sorts of programs they would like to see happen at community schools. When they respond, ask them for suggestions about how to finance their ideas.

4. Create an academic advisory board for the school. Select well-connected community members and retired teachers to serve on the board. Ask them to advise the school on programs and fund raising. (This may need to be cleared with the Board of Education.)
5. Mount an educational tax incentive. In 1987, the citizens of Berkeley, California, facing deteriorating facilities and a spiraling class size in the schools, put together a tax initiative campaign for a parcel tax earmarked for reducing class size. Placed on a ballot, Measure H won the required 75 percent voter approval. A citizen panel is charged with implementing the provisions of the law.
6. Form an educational foundation. Several states have made strides in establishing educational foundations that provide supplementary resources for schools, meeting a range of needs that cannot be met within the structures of the typical budget. Such foundations provide teachers with incentives and funding to pursue and develop new ideas and programs that enrich the educational environment. Stimulated in part by seed money from the Ford Foundation, some 110 such foundations were initiated in California between 1980 and 1986 and provided supplemental resources of between $1 and $400 per student (Torrance, 1988).

Schools as Responsibility Centers

Chester E. Finn, Former Assistant Secretary for Educational Research, argued in a recent article that in order to enable public schools to operate more productively, each school should be responsible for its own key educational management decisions. "We need to treat the school as the unit of production and cede to it internal resource allocation, personnel, scheduling and curriculum" (Finn, 1987, p. 67). At present, principals and teachers have far too little control over the school district's educational budget. There is little opportunity for school leaders to provide financial rewards to effective departments and educational programs.

Decentralizing some financial management to the school would permit vital decisions about how teachers apply their time and how money and other resources are to be used in a new and more collegial way by the principal, teachers, and parents. At present, educational decision making is far too centralized to encourage effective participation by those closest to the students. Devolving fiscal responsibility to the school level encourages better use of resources. Just how would this work? At Berkwood-Hedge School in Berkeley, California, teachers are responsible for managing the school's budget. As a result, the teachers look after the resources very carefully since the money is theirs and any savings can be used to pay for the programs they want.

One way to accomplish this effectively is the formation of a school budget committee. At one school the budget committee consisted of representatives from each department, in addition to administrators. The establishment of this committee called for management to relinquish their right to exercise power through budgetary allocations and to take an important step toward fostering a campuswide sense of trust.

San Diego's superintendent, Tom Payzant, inherited a school system with an inefficient and overstaffed central district office. In an effort to conserve resources and restructure the central administration, he foresees an eventual change in which central-district departments would offer their services to schools on a fee-for-service basis. (See the case study at the end of Chapter Eleven.) Schools that needed assistance in meeting affirmative action goals might contract with the district to provide program-planning and grant-writing assistance and purchase this with the school's annual budget. Nonessential central-district departments offering services that failed to attract purchasers would have to change their service or face loss of employment.

Summary

School finance is an issue critical to the success of any school or district. One of the quickest ways for a principal or district to run into difficulty is to fail to manage its finances prudently. This chapter reviewed some of the central components in planning the budget and making decisions. The participation of teachers in the budget process is an element that can contribute to cost savings and better use of educational resources.

Case Study _____

Kensington-Hilltop Elementary School

(Authors' Note: Many schools, faced with limited financial resources, have taken an increasing interest in the resource gener-

ation and resource allocation process. Readers may want to consider the factors that were instrumental in Kensington-Hilltop's efforts to acquire and deploy additional funds for a math/science specialty program. What, if any, is the relationship between program planning and the acquisition of resources? Does this case illustrate how greater involvement in site-level program planning can begin to generate more involvement in the generation and allocation of resources? What advantages do you think Kensington-Hilltop might have over other schools in the same district when it comes to actually spending the additional funds the school is receiving for the specialty program?)

Kensington-Hilltop Elementary School commands a panoramic view of the northern San Francisco Bay, Marin headlands, Golden Gate Bridge, and the city of San Francisco. Nestled in a well-groomed, upper-middle class neighborhood of a medium-sized, urban unified school district, Kensington-Hilltop has the reputation of being isolated—geographically, educationally, and administratively. Since 1987, the enrollment has doubled from 275 to 575 students. Approximately 30 percent of the children come from minority ethnic groups: about 20 percent black, and the remaining 10 percent from Asian, Hispanic, and Pacific Islander backgrounds. Until 1987, Kensington-Hilltop was a neighborhood school. But with a changed district policy of open enrollment, designed to provide students and their families with a choice among different curriculum models, Kensington-Hilltop has been designated as a school offering a gifted and talented specialty program. As a result, students from outside the neighborhood have been applying in large numbers.

Limited Financial Support

Kensington-Hilltop receives an annual basic site allocation from the Richmond Unified School District. That allocation is limited in several respects: Most of the monies are encumbered to cover personnel costs, which are fixed. The nonsalaried items are not adequate to cover the actual costs to the school if it desires to meet more than minimal operating needs.

Nonsalaried Items	*Per Student Allocation*
Classroom Supplies	$12.89
Office Supplies	.42

Textbooks (replacements and additions)	2.97
Library Books	4.10
Health Supplies	.17
Custodial Supplies	3.47
Test Supplies	1.00

Barbara Chriss, principal since 1984, comments that the allocation for classroom supplies is about 25 percent of the actual needs to support a quality program, the office supply allocation is generally spent by the first month of the school year, the health supply allocation does not even cover a year's supply of bandages, and the custodial budget is far from sufficient. At present there is no allocation for the purchase of nonconsumable instructional materials and equipment.

Because Kensington-Hilltop is a relatively "privileged" school in a district where two-thirds of the students come from minority groups and families at or below the poverty line, the school receives only bare-bones funding from the district and less than $5,000 in categorical funding. Schools in more depressed neighborhoods with lower test scores are eligible for entitlement funding from the state and federal governments, which can be used to buy more materials as well as to reduce class size by hiring resource teachers and/or teacher aides.

Faced with these constraints and a burning desire to run an exceptional educational program at the school, Chriss boldly used nearly all of the annual site allocation for classroom supplies that directly support student learning and the instructional process, while aggressively seeking money from other sources to fill the shortfall. Two successful tactics have been to seek support in the form of grants and to stimulate parents to organize themselves in several fund-raising arms for the school.

The school won one grant from the state to support staff-development activities as part of a school improvement plan that focused on the teaching of mathematics. This grant provides resources for paid staff release time. Another complimentary technology grant brought in funds that made possible capital purchases ranging from math manipulatives to computers.

In addition to seeking grants, the school has worked with four parent groups in resource-generating activities. Together, these groups form the Kensington-Hilltop Parent Organization, including the PTA, the Dads' Club, the School Site Council, and the Kensington Elementary Foundation (KEF). The KEF is a tax-exempt, nonprofit organization allowed to seek grant funding for the school as well as make direct solicitations to the parents and members of the community for financial contributions.

The Kensington Elementary Foundation has been especially successful in raising supplemental resources. Founded in 1986, the foundation currently generates $48,000 to $50,000 each year. Along with money raised through other parent organizations, most of this is allocated directly to classroom activities. Each classroom teacher receives a discretionary supplies budget. Classroom size has been reduced by providing part-time specialists for enriched classes in art, music, science, and physical education. Specialized academic classes for smaller groups of 12 to 15 students means that the regular classroom teachers' pupil load is typically reduced from 31 to 33 students to 12 to 15 for nearly half of the school day.

Money raised through parent organizations has also provided for certain schoolwide inputs, including photocopy equipment; extensive climbing/play structures on the school yard, in response to a survey asking students what they would like in their playground; and the Young Audience Program, which presents a variety of cultural/multicultural programs each year for schoolwide assemblies.

Allocation Resources: Plans and Decisions

As already mentioned, these resource-generation efforts were originally inspired by a specific program to improve the quality of mathematics teaching and learning at school. Some years ago, the principal had noted that even though students were performing relatively well on statewide standardized measures of mathematics achievement, their attitude toward mathematics were very poor. Chriss stated, "Most of our students responded to the state student attitude survey that they did not like math. I noticed this among our test results and brought the issue to the staff. From this starting point, we developed a school plan that focused on mathematics. It included staff development (the inspiration for our grant applications) as well as greater investment in classroom tools and technology for mathematics learning."

The math program provided a basic format for implementing the schoolwide Gifted and Talented specialty program. The specialty program was built around the idea that even young elementary school students can choose special subjects in which they are motivated to excel, and elementary teachers should be given the option to choose to teach in special areas if they so desire.

This move toward a more diversified and specialized curriculum—starting with the mathematics orientation—generated a demand for more resources. The principal and teaching staff prepared a program and plans to respond to the demand. From the program and plan, resource-generating activities, and eventually a permanent resource agency, the Kensington Elementary Foundation (KEF) arose.

Decisions regarding the allocation of incremental resources have gone relatively smoothly. Barbara Chriss reports that she works together with the School Site Council, composed of 10 elected members, 5 parents, and 5 teachers, to develop the budget requests that the school puts to the Foundation. She believes this process works well because the school has a well-formulated plan with specific program objectives.

Ironically, the resource constraints that originally motivated the school and parents to seek new sources of budgetary support is beginning to abate. Kensington-Hilltop currently finds itself on the crest of a major districtwide restructuring wave. A plan to configure an array of specialized magnet schools with different focuses has been mandated by a new superintendent, Dr. Walter Marks, with backing from the school board. In 1989, the district was selected as one of the five regional sites for a nationwide conference on choice in education. This means that the specialized Gifted and Talented program at Kensington-Hilltop is being greatly expanded and resources are forthcoming to support the changes, many of which had already been initiated by the school's faculty and administration. For the 1989–90 school year, the school received a $150,000 supplemental allocation from the district to support the implementation of a schoolwide elective program. "In the past, we have raised the money for this program on our own, so now we are more than ready to spend what the district is giving us," Chriss states with confidence.

References

California Coalition on Fair School Finance (CCFCF). *California's K–12 School Finance System.* Menlo Park, CA, 1985.

Carnoy, M. *Schooling in a Corporate Society.* New York: David McKay, 1972.

Cohn, E. *The Economics of Education* (rev. ed.). Cambridge, MA: Ballinger, 1979.

Ewing, D. *The Managerial Mind*. Riverside, NJ: Free Press, 1964.

Finn, C. E. "Education that Works: Make the Schools Compete." *Harvard Business Review* (September–October 1987):63–68.

Hanushek, E. A. "The Economics of Schooling: Production and Efficiency in Public Schools." *Journal of Economic Literature* (September 1986).

Hanushek, E. A. "The Impact of Differential Expenditures on School Performance." *Educational Researcher* (May 1989):45–51.

Illich, I. *Deschooling Society*. New York: Harper and Row, 1970.

Knight, B. *Managing School Finance*. London: Heinemann, 1983.

Kolderie, T. "Education that Works: The Right Role for Business." *Harvard Business Review* (September–October 1987):56–62.

Levin, H. *Cost Effectiveness: A Primer*. Beverly Hills, CA: Sage, 1983.

McDonnell, L. "School Improvement and Fiscal Retrenchment: How to Improve Education When Resources are Declining." In A. Odden and D. Webb (Eds.), *School Finance and School Improvement: Linkage for the 1980s*. Cambridge, MA: Ballinger, 1983.

McLaughlin, C. *The Management of Nonprofit Organizations*. New York: Wiley and Sons, 1986.

Odden, A. "The State Finance of State Policies Designed to Enhance the Teaching Profession." Mimeo, California Commission on the Teaching Profession, May 1985.

Spring, J. H. *Education and the Rise of the Corporate State*. Boston: Beacon Press, 1972.

Torrance, A. "California's Educational Foundations." Ph.D. Position Paper. School of Education, University of California, Berkeley, 1988.

U.S. Department of Education Center for Educational Statistics. *Digest of Educational Statistics, 1988*. Washington, DC: U.S. Government Printing Office, 1989.

"U.S. Schools Called Costly and Inefficient" *San Francisco Chronicle*, August 24, 1989, p. A19.

Useem, M., and Girling, R. *Evaluation of the Regional Nonformal Skills Training Program*. USAID, Caribbean Regional Development Office, Barbados, 1985.

CHAPTER SEVEN

Professional Growth and Staff Development

Introduction

In 1986 Petaluma schools launched an experimental process to change staff development districtwide. Previously,
staff development activities were decided by an administrator in the district's central office. Poor attendance at the
district-sponsored programs was an indication of teacher
dissatisfaction. The experiment involves a trust agreement
between the teachers' association (AFT) and the district
administration. Under the terms of this agreement, a staff
development team, composed of teachers, site administrators, and representation from the central administration,
now decide jointly what will take place during the four days
of negotiated in-service training for district teachers.

Thus far, the staff development team has made a number of decisions that mark a departure from the previous
practices. Teacher experts are substituted for outside workshop leaders, and activities are designed across grade levels
and schools—when appropriate—rather than limiting opportunities to a single subject, grade, or school. This allows
teachers the chance to interact with colleagues on a districtwide basis and choose from a variety of professional
development offerings rather than a single district-selected
offering. To date, teachers and district management agree
that these changes would not have occurred without involving teachers in determining professional development
options.

In the case of Petaluma, the district has been able to move
away from a centrally defined and executed process that carried
little verve and received minimal enthusiasm. Petaluma is experimenting with a new management system for staff development.
Some districts and schools are considering new staff development
designs and techniques, such as coaching and mentoring,
whereas others are redefining the scope of activities and concerns
that constitute staff development.

Dissatisfaction with staff development practices is commonly
expressed by teachers. Experienced teachers complain that workshops do not address their most immediate concerns; they are frequently impractical, and they are conducted by specialists or
administrators who are disconnected from the realities of classroom and school settings. The teachers' union and the district ad-

ministration in Petaluma were able to recognize jointly that the absence of teacher involvement in determining staff development needs, as well as designing and executing staff development activities, constituted a serious flaw in their program. The realization has been taken seriously, and the district is immersed in an experimental process to redesign their staff development management system.

There are at least three prominent reasons for reexamining existing staff development practices with an eye to restructuring their scope, management, and design and execution. These reasons include the real potential for teachers' professional growth vis-à-vis staff development, the motivational role staff development can play, and the contribution staff development can make to the organizational climate in the schools and on a districtwide basis.

Staff development has been surprisingly neglected in the field of educational management and administration. It need not be. Educators should take care to distinguish between traditional practices and what could and should be accomplished. In this chapter we will examine the key reasons for placing a high priority on staff development. Following this discussion, an analytic framework for understanding the variety of staff development needs in any complex organizational system is presented and discussed in reference to school districts. Finally, we turn to the questions of the design and execution of staff development programs. During the past decade, considerable research on staff development has provided some clear guidelines as to how staff development programs can be made more effective.

Why Staff Development?

Professional growth and school improvement are the twin rationales for a strong emphasis on staff development. Outside the education sector, staff development programs have mushroomed across the country because employers are looking for gains in productivity and quality. Moreover, many realize that they are faced with a stable but aging workforce. The majority of employees are likely to stay at their current positions without moving up the career ladder. How to motivate and sustain high morale among these employees so that they will continue to be productive and maintain quality standards in performing their work has become a major issue for many managers.

School systems are faced with analogous problems. A maturing teaching force across the nation has brought relatively little new blood into the profession in recent years, increasing the need to retool existing teachers with new approaches and knowledge. This is beginning to change in many communities and will accelerate in the 1990s as many veteran teachers reach retirement. Moreover, the nationwide call for school improvement rests squarely on the shoulders of the teaching profession. Change in any organization depends on the ability of leaders (see Chapter Three) to inspire, mobilize, and prepare members of their organization to do things differently. In education, change ultimately depends on teachers for implementation. School improvement will not advance if teachers are unprepared or lacking in motivation to carry the torch forward.

Professional Growth

According to the Arizona Education Association (1986), professional growth is the process of establishing, adapting, and extending one's skills and knowledge as a teacher. Professional growth must be continuous and integrated into a collegial model of teacher relations. It implies that teachers are capable, that their decision-making powers change over time, and that organizations can promote, nurture, encourage, and enhance that growth and change. In his work on career dynamics, Schein (1978) identified three dimensions in a typical individual's career development cycle: upward mobility; functional growth (i.e., increasing areas of technical competence, sometimes referred to as *lateral career growth*); and movement toward the "inner circle" (i.e., permanent membership in an organization or profession with access to special inside information). At different stages in a career span, individuals are usually more concerned with one or another of these dimensions. Early career concerns are usually centered around upward mobility and lateral career growth, whereas later career concerns may be linked more to being admitted to the inner circle.

The recent professional and research interest on the induction of new teachers into the profession suggests that after the initial student-teaching period, most teachers take their first job on a sink-or-swim basis. As a rule, new teachers are expected to perform in the same terms as veterans. Because new teachers are low on the totem pole, however, they frequently receive the least desirable assignments, more difficult students, and, at a secondary level, maximum number of preparations.

New teachers are eager to demonstrate their competence and should be encouraged to do so. However, it should be recognized that in order to become a competent and accomplished teacher with the ability to function in a deliberate, decision-making manner requires thousands of hours of practice (Wildman and Niles, 1987). Three conditions for professional growth of the motivated teacher have been identified: autonomy, collaboration, and time. *Autonomy,* or the opportunity to experiment, direct, and experience one's own growth, is widely available to new teachers. However, *collaboration* and *time,* attendant conditions, are usually sorely lacking. Staff development efforts for new teachers, such as mentor teacher programs (discussed later in this chapter), can be especially effective if they are designed to stimulate interaction among new teachers and their experienced colleagues, thereby bringing new teachers together in supportive networks. Site and district administrators can work together to create more time for new teachers to prepare and receive feedback on their classroom teaching skills. Staff development programs designed to meet these needs will boost the lateral professional growth opportunities sought so actively by beginning teachers.

Motivation

At midcareer, many individuals (and teachers are no exception) enter a period of reevaluation (Schein, 1978). This involves a major reassessment of one's career progress relative to initial ambitions, sometimes leading to the decision to level off professional effort, change careers, or forge ahead to new and greater challenges. Choices are largely influenced by perceived opportunities for further growth and development within the existing organizational/career context. A strong, multifaceted staff development program can help to motivate and identify a constant stream of areas for lateral growth, even where upward mobility is no longer possible. Moreover, stimulating professional growth can help to avoid the disengagement or burnout syndrome frequently found among midcareer teachers as well as others in people-oriented service occupations.

Research on teaching suggests that many teachers become entrenched in a particular teaching approach and are resistant to changing or trying new techniques. However, a process of professional learning is set into motion when teachers are given the skills to identify and solve problems themselves. Districts can

either stimulate or kill a teacher's motivation to grow professionally. Evidence shows that teachers are willing to make changes in
their teaching behaviors if they believe that the changes will enhance their professional growth and increase their effectiveness
with students (Rosenholtz, 1984).

Traditional in-service approaches to training tend to stifle motivation since they are often designed around "teacher-proof"
packages and one-shot training sessions. These sessions are often
conceived and executed by outside experts or central office personnel rather than by teachers. This type of in-service approach
conveys the attitude that others know better than teachers what
skills and knowledge they need for growth. Research on the effects
of staff development on teaching illustrates that the greatest staff
development successes occur in schools where there is a norm of
collegiality and experimentation around instructional matters
(Little, 1981).

Organizational Climate

Staff development programs that are based on the professional growth model just discussed have the potential to alter
school climate as well as change the teaching practices of individual teachers. In Chapters One and Two we discussed certain attributes of the school as an organization and teaching as an activity
that have thwarted the growth of professionalism among teachers.
The organization of most schools into self-contained classrooms
severely limits communication among colleagues by inhibiting
sharing of professional experience as well as mentoring of newcomers by experienced colleagues. Certain types of staff development experiences promote collegiality by allowing teachers to
trade experiences, problems, and successes while serving to promote professionalization and helping to sustain motivation and
engagement over a long career cycle.

Changes in an organization's climate depend on how people
do their jobs and relate to each other on both individual and organizationwide bases. Changes in instructional approach, classroom management techniques, the way school goals are set, how
problems are identified and resolved, along with the methods of
decision making have all been demonstrated to affect the efficiency and quality of education as well as school climate. To implement change in either the instructional or the management

domain, people need opportunities to acquire, test, and evaluate new practices. Staff development that provides such opportunities can lead to schoolwide gains as well as improvements in the skills of individual teachers.

The Scope of Staff Development

Although teaching is acknowledged to be a complex process, one useful perspective is to analyze the roles a teacher must perform in order to stimulate student learning. Three widely recognized dimensions of the teaching process are *instruction, classroom management,* and *human relations.* Related to these dimensions is the actual or potential role of teachers as *professional leaders.* This role does not relate directly to teaching, but it has the potential to influence profoundly the instructional process.

The basic processes associated with the dimensions of teaching include *planning, implementation,* and *evaluation.* Teachers must have a repertoire of relevant skills within each dimension and they must also be able to make decisions about the application and adaptation of these skills. These generic dimensions and processes are presented in Table 7.1

With the intensive interest in new approaches to the development of instruction and classroom management, less attention has been given to developing human relations skills among teachers. With the move toward teams and ad hoc workgroups as the basis for developing individual teaching competencies, the importance for interpersonal communications and the group dynamics increases (discussed later in this chapter). Human relations as well as site management skills can be learned. Any organization moving toward a more participatory style will need to devote a substantial amount of its staff development efforts to improving human relations and site management skills for teachers.

Two critical areas of human relations are group process skills and interpersonal relations. If schools intend to build professional teams and emphasize collegial work relations, considerable training and practice is necessary to enable these approaches to function effectively. Learning how to run an effective meeting, plan and set goals, solve problems, and make decisions each involve considerable time and effort. These skills are neither inherent nor will they necessarily emerge simply through a process of trial and error. Organizations that place an emphasis on decentralization and participatory approaches to management will need to devote a

TABLE 7.1 • *Staff Development Scope Framework*

Dimensions of the Teaching Role	Basic Processes		
	Planning	Implementation	Evaluation
Instruction	Instructional planning skills	Instructional implementation skills	Instructional evaluation skills
Classroom Management	Management planning skills	Management implementation skills	Student behavior
Human Relations	Skills and concepts	Acquisition and application	Parent attitudes Staff relations
Professional Leadership	Goal setting Planning	Problem Solving Staff Development	Performance review and program evaluation

Adapted and modified from Basic Career Development Framework, in *Career Development System,* Arizona Education Association, Compensation Task Force, 1986.

fixed portion of their staff development budgets to the acquisition and refinement of human relations skills. In schools, for example, the implementation of the coaching and mentoring approaches to individual professional development requires teacher coaches and mentors to perfect their ability to give feedback. The use of quality circles for problem solving requires training in group facilitation (see Chapter Five). Skills such as these need to be nurtured as part of ongoing staff development efforts.

Because teachers are not prepared for increasing positions of professional leadership as their careers progress, there tends to be a parochial view of the professional role and responsibility. Many teachers do not see their involvement extending beyond the limits of their individual classroom. They do not have an organizationwide view, nor do they give much thought to how their work interfaces with the work of their colleagues in the school at large. The organizationwide perspective has already been discussed in detail in earlier chapters. Developing this perspective among teachers is the responsibility of the site manager and the district leadership. The case of Kenneth Hill in the Redwood City School District (Chapter Three) illustrates how district leadership can promote an organizationwide perspective through ongoing staff development.

Staff Development Policy

Policy and management are two related aspects of staff development for the teaching profession. The term *management* means the planning, coordinating, implementing, and evaluating specific staff development activities. An effective means of managing staff development, however, is unlikely to proceed without a clear and well-drawn policy. Moreover, to be effective, staff development requires, at minimum, a districtwide *policy.* The basic staff development policy issue facing any school system is how to relate staff development to the career advancement of teachers. A corollary of this issue is the relationship between career advancement and the increasing professional competence of teachers. This policy issue can be framed within the debate over career ladders for the teaching profession.

Staff Development Policy and Career Ladders

One of the common laments of the teaching profession is the absence of a professional career ladder along which the novice teacher can expect to progress over time to the level of expert. Career ladders generally involve increasing levels of responsibility and status and are frequently accompanied by extrinsic rewards. Ideally, career ladders are not exclusively based on seniority. In theory, a career ladder is linked to increasing competence in the exercise of professional activities. Within the field of education, until very recently, virtually all career ladders centered around moving out of classroom teaching into school administration or into a limited number of district-level professional positions usually linked to special programs. Within teaching itself, seniority has been the overwhelming basis for advancement and enhanced professional status. From time to time there have been calls for differential staffing based on teacher competence rather than seniority and special expertise (e.g., higher-level science and math teachers).

Establishing a career ladder involves (1) determining the basic levels linked to professional competencies, (2) identifying the means of acquiring and demonstrating competency, and (3) specifying the incentives/rewards and responsibilities linked to each level on the ladder (see Table 7.2). Professional competencies required at each level of the ladder would constitute the parameters for a staff development program linked to a district career ladder.

Recently, experiments have begun to crop up across the nation that attempt to structure career ladders for the teaching profession. California's mentor teaching program is one among these efforts. Tennessee has instituted a five-level career ladder that links assessed professional competencies and monetary incentives. The effectiveness of career ladder salary differentials depends on several factors. First, is the size of the salary differential at the upper levels significant? Studies of salary differentials as motivators suggest that these differentials need to be on the order of 20 to 30 percent to have real impact on motivation (Geis, 1987). Second, what are the chances of reaching higher levels on the ladder? Third, is the selection process generally viewed as valid by teachers and administrators? Fourth, does the ladder program actually provide teachers with the opportunity via a staff development program to increase and demonstrate their professional competence? Research suggests first that experimental career ladders in school systems are generally underfunded, and second that districts that hire at higher initial salaries are more effective in attracting and retaining quality personnel than those that hold out the prospect of a higher ceiling (Stern, 1986).

In the past, teachers' associations have objected to career ladders and merit pay schemes that differentiate among faculty on criteria other than years of service. They believe these differentiations are divisive among teachers and possibly weaken teachers' strength at the bargaining table. Recently, with the quest for upgrading professional standards and in the hope of retaining expert professionals, this position has begun to change. Merit pay is far from being a closed issue. Some of the advantages and disadvantages of merit pay in the context of teaching are presented in Box 7.1.

Managing Staff Development

The opening vignette, which describes the Petaluma School District's experiment in restructuring staff development, brings to the forefront the question of who should be responsible for managing a

TABLE 7.2 • Tennessee's Teacher Career Ladder

Ladder Level	Professional Development Criteria	Assessment Method	Responsibilities Rewards/Incentivies
Probationary Certificate	i) Graduation from approved teacher training program; ii) Qualifying score in National Teacher Examination Core Battery	i) Evaluation level by supervisory teachers/principal	1 year non-renewable certificate supervised by 2 tenured teachers at school site
Apprentice Certificate	i) State Department of Education Review; ii) State Department of Education Interview	Demonstrated competence during probationary period	3 year non-renewable certificate
Career Level I	i) Demonstrates instructional preparation; ii) Uses teaching strategies and procedures appropriate to content, objectives and learners;	2 local site evaluations, 1 State Department Review and 1 interview	5 year renewable certificate $1000 annual increment

iii) Uses evaluation to improve instruction;
iv) Manages classroom activities effectively;
v) Establishes and maintains effectively;
vi) Communicates effectively

| Career Level II | Same as Level I | 2 local site evaluations and 1 comprehensive State Board Evaluation | 5 year renewable certificate choice between 10 month certificate, $2000 incentive program, 11 month contract, $4000 incentive program |
| Career Level III | i) Training Peer Evaluation plus criteria from Levels I and II | 2 local site evaluations and 1 comprehensive State Board Evaluation | 5 year renewable certificate, peer evaluator |

Source: Carol Furtwengler, "Tennessee's Career Ladder Plan: They Said It Couldn't Be Done," *Educational Leadership* (November 1985):50–56. Reprinted with the permission of the Association for Supervision and Curriculum Development. Copyright © 1985 by the Association for Supervision and Curriculum Development. All rights reserved.

BOX 7.1 • *Merit Pay: The Yeas and Nays*

Merit pay systems attempt to link salary advancement to performance. A pure system of merit pay is the commission approach whereby a salesperson earns a percentage, sometimes increasing with the volume of his or her actual sales. Piece-rate pay in manufacturing is another form of merit pay. In most settings merit pay is mixed with a guaranteed salary base (e.g., the waitress who earns the minimum wage plus tips).

Merit pay has been experimented with widely, but rarely endured in school districts. One perspective is that merit pay is appropriate where it is clearly observable that one employee is more productive than another, and that other employees know or can be told what they must do to receive a merit increase. These conditions are difficult to achieve in the case of teaching. There are two types of merit pay—*old style,* where the supervisor/principal assesses the individual teacher's performance and decides who deserves merit, and *new style,* where teachers receive pay for student performance. Neither has been widely accepted.

Old style merit pay has frequently backfired with teachers decreasing their effort after failing to receive a merit increase. Moreover, principals report that the merit system can interfere with building a strong team effort among teachers. New style efforts have been rejected because of the number of interfering factors that affect student test scores—the problems of deciding which aspects of the curriculum should be included for testing, and how to separate the contribution of one teacher from the next on test scores in view of the cumulative nature of learning.

Proponents of merit pay argue that teachers who work harder and achieve observable results should be rewarded. Stern (1986) introduces the idea of a group or schoolwide merit pay, which could promote collaboration on curriculum, instructional technique, discipline, and keeping track of individual students from one year to the next. If a whole school is rewarded for good performance, then teachers who are already inclined to accept schoolwide responsibility might have more incentive to do so and they would also have an added argument for their colleagues to do the same.

---

staff development program. Petaluma transferred the planning and coordinating responsibilities for one component of teacher staff development from district administrators to a team of teachers, union representatives, and administrators. The team plans and coordinates the implementation of four days of district-funded in-service training.

Planning

Linking staff development activities to specific districtwide goals (e.g., the improvement of the teaching of science) to specific school goals (e.g., introducing cooperative learning techniques into the mathematics curriculum across grade levels) or to individual teacher professional development goals (e.g., mastering the inquiry approach to teaching a social studies unit or incorporating the use of manipulatives into mathematics instruction) requires a decentralized, participative planning approach to staff development activities.

First and foremost, for staff development to be relevant at individual teacher and school levels, direct input from teachers and site administrators is needed. This can be achieved through a variety of planning structures and processes. Among these are districtwide committees, as in the case of Petaluma; use of a recurrent needs-assessment procedure that captures individual teacher and school-level concerns; and school-level staff development task forces that coordinate with the school-level planning team.

The school-site administrator has a crucial role to play in planning as well as executing staff development by encouraging teachers to assess their professional growth needs and to set goals for themselves that can be translated into staff development activities. Equally important is providing the support and direction needed to develop a school-level staff development plan. Ideally, this would be coordinated with schoolwide goals and specific school improvement plans. This school-level staff development plan should be part of and simultaneously a product of a specific school improvement plan. The Beverly Hills Elementary School 1987–88 School Level Plan includes a specific staff development component (see Box 7.2). The component takes as its point of reference the district's Five Year Plan for Instructional Improvement and, through a site-level committee, elaborated five objectives, each with a specific set of staff development activities designed to achieve the objective.

Design and Execution

Well-designed staff development activities and programs are like a well-written newspaper article: The design must answer who, what, when, where, and why? The planning and policy as-

BOX 7.2 • Beverly Hills Elementary School: Staff Development Plan

Component: Staff Development (Baseline) 1987–88   **Funding Source:** _____

Current Conditions	Objectives
In the Five Year Plan for Instructional Improvement, the district identified the following staff development areas and processes as means to improve instruction:	By June 1988 the site manager(s) with the assistance of teacher leaders and support from other district support staff will have designed, implemented, and evaluated a comprehensive, coordinated staff development program which contains the following components:
Curriculum implementation and alignment of state and district curriculum standards	• Refinement of the use of existing curricular documents and programs
Instructional supervision, evaluation and support	• Use of any new district curricula, as appropriate
Teacher leadership in curriculum implementation, staff development, peer observation and feedback, and school level planning efforts	• Use of student performance data to refine programs and instructional practice
Use of student performance data to analyze and focus the school; and classroom instructional program	• Use of the PQR process and criteria as a basis for classroom, department, and schoolwide program revision
Use of Program Quality Review criteria and processes and a Five Year Plan to analyze and focus school and classroom instructional programs	• Awareness of current state and district undertakings in curriculum and staff development
	The program will be measured by staff development activities and meetings, staff self-assessments, review reports, PQR reports of classroom observations.
	In June 1988 principals and vice principals will have refined their skills in the use of instructional supervision to increase teacher effectiveness as measured by discussions between the manager and his/her district support person, joint observations and feedback sessions with the manager and district support person, and manager self-assessment.

188

Component: *Staff Development (Baseline) 1987–88*   ***Funding Source:*** _____

Activities	Timeline	Responsibility	Evaluation
1. The 87–88 school level plan will be reviewed by staff; adjustments will be made as needed	August–September	Principal	Written analysis of end-of-year principal survey to determine district effectiveness in supporting site level leadership
2. The principal (and vice principal) will support the staff in achieving curriculum implementation, instructional effectiveness, and other program objectives through:	Ongoing	Principal and Vice Principal	Written analysis of the principal's effectiveness in carrying out activities designed to promote school effectiveness through district and on-site staff development efforts
• Thoughtfully planned staff meetings and inservices addressing program objectives			Analysis of the staff development programs by: evaluation of activities and meetings, self-assessments, PQR reports of findings, and classroom observation
• Instructional supervision to provide feedback to staff on curriculum implementation and instructional effectiveness objectives			
• The teacher evaluation process in which teachers will be helped to match objectives and activities with school goals and resources			
• Assistance to staff in using student performance data to identify program objectives and tailor classroom programs to meet identified needs			
• Use of teacher leadership to provide input and assistance in planning and evaluating school objectives and activities			
• Regular monitoring and adjusting of			

Continued

189

Box 7.2 *Continued*

Activities	Timeline	Responsibility	Evaluation
activities to meet staff needs/readiness to develop staff resources and ownership for program implementation			
3. The principal (and vice principal) will ask for and use feedback and assistance from the district support person to help achieve program objectives. The district support will provide: • Observation of and feedback on instructional conferencing, workshop design/implementation, staff interactions, program planning, etc. • Assistance with developing and presenting workshops, designing assessment strategies, and determining priorities • Demonstrations of instructional conferencing, presentations and facilitation skills	Ongoing	District Support Person, Principal	
4. The staff will utilize the following to support curriculum implementation: • District Curriculum Management System for Reading, Language and Math — including continua, CRTM data, profile folders, courses of study, etc. • Social Studies Framework • Career Guidance Framework • Science Continua		Principal	

- District K-6 Report Card
- Computer Master Plan
- PQR criteria
- Model Curriculum Standards
- State K-8 Curriculum Guides
- State Curriculum Frameworks

5. The principal (and vice principal) will participate in district meetings and workshops that provide input on and assistance with:

- Instructional supervision, including:
  —Elements of effective instruction and management
  —Lesson analysis
  —Conference design and implementation
- Use of test data and materials (CRTM, CAP, Hart Bill) to:
  —Assess schoolwide needs; identify critical needs
  —Communicate school and district needs and accomplishments
- Evaluation, including:
  —Requirements of the contract
  —Ways to increase accuracy/appropriateness of objectives and activities planned
  —The Five Year Plan
  —District policies such as pupil retention and promotion, as selected for discussion

Ongoing

Superintendency
Principals

Continued

Box 7.2 *Continued*

Activities	Timeline	Responsibility	Evaluation
6. The principal (and vice principal) will participate in a principal support group and/or problem-solving sessions addressing selected topics, such as: • Use of teacher leadership • Use of district resources • Planning strategies for school improvement • Effective meeting strategies	Ongoing	Principal and Vice Principal	
7. The principal (and vice principal) will implement activities designed to accomplish yearly evaluation objective(s); the principal will ask for and use the district support person's feedback	September–June	Superintendent, Principal, Vice Principal	

Source: Beverly Hills Elementary School, Vallejo City Unified School District, 1987–1988.

pects of staff development discussed above address the "Why?" component of a staff development program or activity. (A staff development program is comprised of a number of staff development activities that fit together to address districtwide, schoolwide, and individual goals or needs.)

What Should Be the Focus of Staff Development?

Staff development needs are relative to program, department, school, and districtwide goals as well as individual professional development concerns. Thus determining the focus of a schoolwide staff development program is part and parcel of the school planning/school improvement process. The appropriate content for staff development programs should emerge from the process of (1) analyzing the school's current situation, (2) establishing goals for a specific future time horizon, (3) elaborating the human and material resource requirements needed to achieve the goals, and (4) specifying staff development activities that would augment the human resource base needed for achieving school improvement goals.

The process of conducting a needs assessment can play an important role in each of these four steps. A needs assessment, first and foremost, should give the school staff and management team an overview of the school's current situation with respect to actual resources and achievement—what can be referred to as a *baseline.* It should also serve as the basis for identifying staff development needs once specific goals relative to the baseline have been set.

There is no set format for conducting a needs assessment. Needs assessments can be focused on a schoolwide basis, examining the status of instructional, curricular, and noninstructional dimensions of the school. Needs assessments can also be very specific, such as zeroing in on one aspect of the curriculum (e.g., arts). A needs assessment can be conducted internally (e.g., by the school staff itself; see Box 7.3) or with external assistance (e.g., a consultant or team of evaluators).

Needs assessments often use one or more techniques to gather information about the school's current status and perceived needs. These techniques include surveys designed to develop an inventory of human and material resources; surveys to assess the perceptions of staff, parents, and students of their specific needs; observations of actual teaching practices; and analyses of documentation available to the school, particularly student performance on standardized measures of academic achievement.

BOX 7.3 • *Beverly Hills Elementary School: Self-Review, January 1988*

Beverly Hills Elementary School spent four days in January observing in classrooms and evaluating educational processes and how these relate to the Program Quality Criteria. The school is coming to the end of a three-year cycle and will be compliance-reviewed by the California State Department of Education.

In the 1987–88 School Level Plan, the two main areas of focus academically were Math/Problem-Solving and Literature as they relate to writing skills. The staff review teams and parents of this Self-Review kept those areas of focus in mind.

The results of this Self-Review will be used in two ways. It will help in the writing of the 1988–89 School Level Plan, and the results of the Self-Review will help in the school's efforts to clearly articulate our program to state compliance reviewers.

The Self-Review report will be laid out to help point to what we are doing well and how we are using our special program resources to help meet both School Improvement (SIP) and identified student needs. There will also be a section that addresses program planning issues for the 1988–89 School Level Planning process.

It would be very difficult to address all academic areas in one Self-Review report; therefore, our accomplishments in Language Arts, Math, and other schoolwide commendations will be listed. An attempt will be made to draw connections to the quality criteria and how our effective practices are evidence of the criteria. A special section of the report will list parent commendations for the school.

Language Arts at Beverly Hills Elementary School

In the base program, in most classrooms, there appears to be an integrated approach to language arts instruction. Students work on language arts across the curriculum. A strong thrust has been made toward a literature-based reading program with the acquisition of selections provided by the Vallejo City Unified School District. Oral and written approaches to language are stressed in every classroom, as evidenced by classroom discussions witnessed by all self-reviewers and the multitude of writing samples viewed. Here are some of the things working well in language arts at Beverly Hills:

- Students making books; they become publishers
- Written work is displayed on bulletin boards
- Group discussions
- Dental health integrated with writing
- Comparing the presentation of a story in different media (written work, movie)
- Science integrated with language arts (whale unit, bird feeders)

There is appropriate sequence of instruction in math, learning with concrete examples (having the chance to manipulate), moving on to representational level, and finally, dealing with the abstract level of numbers and math concepts. All teachers want their students to "get the concept," not just be able to do the algorithm.

Problem solving is a major area of focus in math. Beverly Hills Elementary School students are to be good problem solvers, and time is spent to teach them the strategies involved with problem solving. Here are some highlights from the classroom observations during the Self-Review:

- Students respect the manipulative materials, little abuse apparent
- All math strands addressed
- Learning builds on previous knowledge
- Geometric designs
- Patterning with "junk boxes"
- Oral group discussions
- Counting, patterning with the calendar
- Problem-solving evident across the curriculum
- Use of manipulative evident
- Well-defined math stations
- Student approaches to problem solving well thought out, therefore we can tell that good teaching is going on
- Good instructional setting

Chapter 1/SCE Program

The support for identified students in acquisition of basic math skills is a clear priority at Beverly Hills Elementary School. As in language arts, direct services to identified students are provided (classroom aides, computer proctor, basic skills teacher). These people help provide additional instruction and reinforcement of basic math skills. Materials have also been purchased to achieve identified student success in basic

Continued

Box 7.3 *Continued*

math skills. The Chapter 1/SCE computer lab also supports identified student progress in basic math skills.

Specific examples from classroom observations include:

- Teachers check for understanding constantly
- Homework charts record identified student progress
- Students work independently at their appropriate level
- Peer tutors
- Allowance for individual differences
- Student concept is stressed for success
- Good number concepts in kindergarten
- *Math Their Way* being used in many classrooms
- Students well directed in the computer lab
- Visual reminders of progress
- Charts help students achieve success
- Math centers allow identified students to accept different challenges

Schoolwide Criteria

On the nonstudent day, the entire staff spent time in a cooperative learning experience conducting a self-review of the schoolwide Program Quality Review criteria—Leadership, Staff Development, Special Needs, and Schoolwide Effectiveness.

Here are the summary statements from each Cooperative Learning group about Beverly Hills Elementary School for each schoolwide criteria:

Leadership

The leadership is broad-based at Beverly Hills Elementary School. The staff members are all responsible for all of the children. Regular feedback is given to all staff whenever an observation is made. The leadership (school site and district level) supports instruction.

Staff Development

The staff development at Beverly Hills Elementary School reflects the school-level plan and meets the needs of the school and staff. The main focus for schoolwide staff development this year has been language arts, problem solving, and the Comprehensive Health Project (CHIP). Each staff member's personal staff development goals and needs are also kept in mind. There is administrative support for staff development from the principal and through the district's Professional Development Center. The program is flexible, presenting new methods and strategies, while also refining older practices. Staff development is ongoing at Beverly Hills Elementary School with assessment and planning for the future.

Special Needs

Students with special needs at Beverly Hills Elementary School have equal access to the total curriculum. Beverly Hills is proud of its mainstreaming program, allowing students with IEPs to participate in the regular program. Here, students with special needs are accepted by their peers in the school. Here is what is going well in Special Needs:

- Mainstreaming—accepted/supported by teachers, accepted by students
- Communication between special education teachers and classroom teachers
- Special Needs Committee
- Reading teacher
- Speech and language program
- Resource Specialist/Basic Skills teacher communicates through notes, verbal interactions, and negotiates times for students to work in program

Schoolwide Effectiveness

The academic program at Beverly Hills Elementary School is developed by all staff and parents, as evidenced by:

- The school level plan
- SSC/SAC involvement
- Return of PTA

Some examples of the schoolwide programs are:

- Citizen-of-the-Week
- B.E.A.R.S. time
- "Bear Tracks" newsletter
- Continua
- Honor Roll

Students receive a broad-based curriculum, as evidenced by mainstreaming, cross-age tutors, problem solving across the curriculum, and the CHIP activities.

Continued

Box 7.3 *Continued*

Instruction is coordinated with the goals and objectives of the curriculum. Examples of this coordination are:

- Student work, including homework
- Self-Review
- CAP, CRTM, Hart Bill Testing
- Direct instruction
- Continua
- Teacher evaluating process
- Staff inservice
- Profile folders

The above goals and objectives of the curriculum are clearly defined in the above examples. In addition, they are evident in:

- Lesson plans and classwork
- The selection of instructional materials
- Assessment practices (tests)
- Book Room
- CHIP curriculum ("Health Skills For Life")

Source: Beverly Hills Elementary School, Vallejo City Unified School District, 1987–1988.

The outcome of a needs assessment should be (1) an inventory of actual resources and practices that characterize the school currently, (2) an indicator of the school's current performance, and (3) a list of perceived needs by significant members of the school community. With this information in hand, goal setting and specific program planning (including the type and content of staff development activities) directed toward achieving goals can be elaborated.

Who Should Be Involved?

Teachers as well as administrators should be involved in the design of a districtwide or schoolwide staff development program. When considering the design and execution of specific staff development activities, such as workshops, courses, or in-service training sessions, research indicates that design should be done in consultation with actual or potential participants. However, design does not have to be conducted exclusively or even primarily by the participants—in this instance, teachers. Similar findings are true for the actual execution of staff development activities. Although there are ample justifications for drawing on the in-house expertise of teachers within a school or district, this is not a condition *sine qua non* for effectiveness. Later in this chapter, we will examine two staff development activities, coaching and mentoring, that do utilize in-house expertise.

There are aspects of staff development that may be more appropriately executed by nondistrict or school personnel. One example is broadening and deepening teachers' knowledge base. University coursework or specially designed seminars for teachers, such as the National Endowment for the Humanities summer seminars or the Bay Area Writing Project based at the University of California, Berkeley, bring teachers into contact with subject matter specialists and can be highly successful vehicles for additional knowledge acquisition.

The Bay Area Writing Project selects teachers, elementary through college level, to participate in a five-week intensive course that focuses on the teaching of writing. The participants are exposed to a variety of writing activities and are asked to write extensively during the course of the workshop. The members also participate in response groups, which are sounding boards for early and later-stage work. The group listens to each of its members read his or her work aloud and gives objective, supportive feedback to help the writer advance his or her skill. Participants learn that writing is an iterative process. They learn how to give feedback and appreciate their own progress in writing through successive attempts at improving a given assignment. After completing the course, some participants are selected as trainers. They receive additional training during the school year following the summer workshop. The focus of this training is to enable them to assist with the establishment of ongoing in-service workshops in their respective school districts.

The actual presence and participation of the principal at in-service staff development programs communicates the importance of the activity as well as the principal's commitment to further professional growth. In contrasting two comparable staff development programs undertaken by similar school districts, Little (1981) identified several steps that preceded a program that was evaluated as effective in altering classroom teaching practice. The antecedents of success include extensive communication between the trainers (who were off-site personnel) and the site administrators; communication between the site administrators and the staff regarding the nature of the program, its rationale, and the time and resources required for implementation; and the opportunity for participating teachers to discuss the program and adapt its goals to their own needs at the onset of the training.

When Should It Take Place?

The question of when staff development should take place depends on the specific goals of the staff development activity at hand and the resources available. If the learning/training process is thought of as three successive phases—the acquisition of skills or knowledge phase, the application phase, and the adaption/extension phase—it is easier to see that the staff development activities frequently may need to combine in-service and extra-service settings. The acquisition of skills in any of the four dimensions of Table 7.1 (instruction, classroom management, human relations, and professional leadership) can be carried out under a variety of circumstances. The application and adaptation phases need to be in the context of the actual or simulated situations where they are utilized. Very few staff development activities are actually designed to span the application and adaptation phases of the learning and mastery process.

Where Should It Be Done?

Siting of staff development activities is contingent on the actual scope and sequence of the events contemplated. On-campus and off-campus locations have advantages and disadvantages that should be evaluated in terms of the space requirements of the activity being planned.

Methods of Staff Development

The appropriate methodology for staff development varies with the objectives of each activity. Two approaches to ongoing in-service staff development that are being experimented with widely are peer coaching and mentoring. These two approaches serve as models for a wide variety of efforts that combine skills acquisition and simultaneously foster collegiality and professionalism.

Coaching

Coaching, a term borrowed from the world of athletics, is based on a simple four-step model. This model includes the essential steps needed to acquire a complex teaching skill and use it in a variety of classroom situations: (1) a presentation of the theory or concepts underpinning a specific skill; (2) a demonstration of the skill; (3) repeated opportunities to practice the skill under both simulated and actual classroom conditions; and (4) repeated feedback on the practice efforts. Research indicates that the combination of these four elements is necessary in order to promote the incorporation of the skill into the teacher's daily teaching repertoire.

The initial learning period for understanding a complex idea or theory behind a practice is estimated to be between 15 and 20 hours. To actually acquire proficiency and use, the skill requires another 15 to 30 hours with directive and supportive feedback (Showers and Joyce, 1987). In essence, coaching is preoccupied with the process of transferring what is learned through staff development programs to the classroom situation. Until recently, the coaching approach has been used almost exclusively with student teachers. Most staff development programs focus on the first step—presenting theory and concepts—and sometimes the second step—demonstration of an actual practice. However, once teachers are back in the classroom, faced with the pressures and need to perform effectively, these ideas are rarely utilized.

Why is feedback so crucial? First, the new learner is often so focused on the mechanics of performing the task that there is little or no sense of whether the job is being done right or wrong. Second, the learner lacks familiarity with what mastery feels like. Third, it is very important for new learners to experience success and a sense of progress in their efforts toward mastery. Thus, an observer, well-versed in the skill being learned, acts as both coach and cheerleader, giving the learner feedback regarding both accuracy and progress.

Three distinct types of coaching have recently emerged with regard to staff development in schools (Garmston, 1987). *Technical coaching* is focused on the acquisition and transfer of new teaching skills (just described). *Collegial coaching* emphasizes the fine tuning of skills through supportive interaction among experienced teachers observing each other teach. Finally, *challenge coaching* has evolved to resolve persistent problems teachers have discovered, such as how to explain a specific topic in the curriculum to students or how to manage a difficult classroom situation. Through challenge coaching, teachers work together, observing each other in action and looking for and experimenting with possible solutions to teaching challenges.

Implementing coaching-based staff development programs

requires understanding, commitment, and ingenuity. Many site managers and teachers object to the idea of coaching, insisting that their colleagues will fear the presence of another teacher in the classroom. Although some teachers are indeed fearful, this fear can be overcome. When school climates are hostile to coaching, the process can be introduced on a voluntary basis, emphasizing collegiality and explicitly separated from evaluation. Moreover, by making the objectives of different coaching models clear and by demonstrating the coaching process, teachers are more likely to see the advantages of participation.

To introduce coaching, the site administrator must be committed to the process and the staff. Critics of coaching suggest that it is a nonaccountable procedure whereby teachers decide on the areas in which they would like feedback and avoid areas where they really need to improve. Moreover, coaching is viewed as a teacher-driven process and therefore tangential to wider school goals and priorities. We can respond to these objections by noting that coaching is a developmental process, not an evaluative procedure. It does not necessarily supersede performance appraisal (see Chapter Eight). Accountability is not the focus; professional growth and development are. If an administrator and staff jointly agree, coaching can be used to strengthen weaknesses or improve strengths. Moreover, coaching is a technique that can be used to help implement schoolwide instruction goals where these have been identified and agreed upon jointly by the management/professional team.

Because coaching requires observation and feedback on actual classroom teaching, a certain amount of ingenuity is required at the site level to make coaching work. In the Orion School (see the case study at the end of Chapter Eight), which had no administrator to step in to release one classroom teacher to observe another, the staff came up with a videotaping solution. Other solutions to the need for release time have also been devised. If a strong management/professional team exists, ingenuity is usually forthcoming. Coaching is labor intensive, but the research indicates that it produces results. The effects on teacher performance are much greater than from other staff development approaches (Showers, Joyce, and Bennett, 1987).

Mentoring

The mentor, an experienced professional, opens the pathway to the new professional who is in the process of becoming established. Mentoring has been a widely recognized process in many professional settings, such as law, medicine, and especially higher education. However, it is still predominantly an informal arrangement—a mutually established bond between the mentor and the protegé.

Mentoring as an approach to staff development has multiple applications in education. It is an especially appealing support for novice teachers entering the profession. Mentoring also holds the potential for on-the-job training of more experienced teachers, and promises benefits for the mentors themselves. These benefits accrue in terms of professional recognition, expanded responsibility, and a sense of satisfaction from helping new colleagues establish themselves in the profession.

To implement a mentor teacher program requires planning and specific training for the mentors because the role and skills of a mentor are distinct from those of a teacher. The mentor is more than a buddy. He or she is expected to share professional knowledge about teaching and learning that is precise and concrete. This sharing generally takes place informally and in the context of a personal relationship. When mentors assume paid positions and as well as formal responsibilities, careful orchestrating of the process is necessary (Levine, 1989).

Mentoring relationships in a variety of organizations have been studied in depth (Kram, 1985). Certain conditions need to exist for the mentoring relationship to be fruitful. First, there needs to be a certain degree of personal empathy between the mentor and his or her protegé. Without this empathy the quality of the mentoring experience is likely to be lacking. Additionally, the relationship requires time to develop so that the protegé can benefit from continued reflection on his or her teaching practice over an extended period of time—at least one year. Studies of mentor-protegé relationships suggest that the relationship grows slowly, reaches a period of fairly intense interaction and often dependence of the protegé on the mentor, and then turns to a new phase when the protegé wishes to move on toward greater professional independence. Allowing this process to evolve naturally in the context of formal mentoring programs is one of several issues that must be confronted.

The potential uses of mentoring for staff development are great, but there are built-in barriers in the school as presently organized (see Chapter Two). Moreover, one must question the degree to which the strong personal attachments of the traditional mentor-protegé relationship can be mandated. However, formal mentor programs have been established in schools as well as other work settings. One of the most notable examples is California's mentor teacher program enacted by the state legislature in 1985. Funds and guidelines for selecting and rewarding mentor teachers at school-site levels for their recognized professional excellence are provided. Mentors receive a monetary stipend, plus classroom release time to work with other teachers. This work with colleagues is not restricted to mentoring new teachers. More broadly defined, mentor teachers can also work with experienced colleagues. Preliminary evaluation of the initial years suggest that the mentor teacher program is working, but remains limited by traditional organizational obstacles in schools, preventing teacher-teacher interaction. Moreover, teachers' associations have been somewhat reluctant to embrace the program enthusiastically because selection of mentor teachers is based on merit as judged by the site administrator.

Mentors, themselves, report that they are faced with the dilemma of how to establish contact with colleagues in environments where teachers have not generally worked together. In the first stage of implementation, mentors reported spending nearly half of their time engaged in improving curriculum materials, in contrast to less than one-third of their time working on the improvement of instructional methods. Of their total release time, they were spending slightly more than one-third engaged in work with other teachers—and during that time they were three times as likely to be working with experienced as with novice teachers. This is, of course, influenced by the small proportion of new teachers in the educational system at this moment. However, the situation will be changing rapidly in the 1990s with the retirement of many veteran teachers (Bird, 1985).

In order to work well, mentoring programs must first take steps to train mentors. Research strongly suggests that successful mentors take a personal interest in proteges' careers, that they share power and expertise, and that they encourage their proteges' ideas and help them to gain self-confidence. Moreover, the relationship between mentor and protege must evolve over time toward one of greater collegiality as the novice gains in experience, confidence, and skill.

Evaluation

No discussion of managing the staff development process is complete without considering evaluation. How does one know that a particular staff development activity is effective in achieving its objectives? Does the districtwide staff development program designed to promote professional growth and delineate career advancement accomplish its goals? In both respects, the evaluation of staff development must be viewed from the perspective of the management cycle (see Figure 7.1). Staff development activities should be evaluated by both participants and planners/designers as to whether or not specific goals and objectives are being met. When teachers and administrators are involved in goal setting for their individual careers and schools, and these goals have been integrated into the planning and design of staff development, there are criteria upon which to base an evaluation.

One of the major evaluation issues surrounding staff development is whether or not staff development should be tied to individual teacher performance review. Proponents of linking staff development activities to formal teacher evaluations argue that without this linkage there is no incentive for teachers to incorporate new skills and ideas on the job. Opponents argue that if staff development activities involve some professional risk taking—such as the peer coaching method for acquiring new classroom instruction and management skills—and are too closely tied to individual performance review, teachers will by and large resist experimentation. In the case of the Orion School (see the case study at the end of Chapter Eight), the faculty has chosen to delink their version of peer coaching from the contracted biannual evaluation procedure. Although there is no simple solution to this dilemma, there are options that can mitigate the inevitable conflict between evaluation for purposes of accountability and willingness to experiment for the purpose of potential growth.

FIGURE 7.1 • *The Management Cycle*

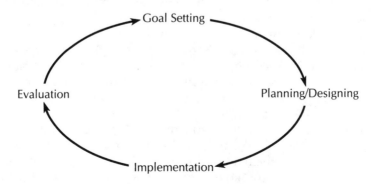

Among the options that can mediate this tension are the following:

1. Move away from the one-shot workshop approach to inservice staff development without the chance to stimulate, practice, and receive feedback in the application and adaptation to real teaching situations.
2. Integrate specific staff development activities into a larger scheme of career development so that these activities are part of moving from one stage of career advancement to the next. An example might be training for participation in peer coaching for classroom management and instructional skills among experienced teachers as a development activity prior to a teacher moving to the stage of mentor teacher along a career ladder.
3. Include a team, department, or school-level focus in evaluation that reaches beyond the performance of individual teachers and lodges individual effort within a larger organizational context.

Summary

Staff development encompasses a wide gambit of professional and organizational concerns—especially for the participatory school. There is an important interface between the needs of individual teachers and the school as an organization that must be constantly addressed and readdressed. This requires collaboration between teachers and site managers as well as among teachers themselves.

In this chapter we have emphasized managing the staff development process, keeping both individual career advancement and organizationwide objectives in mind. In addition, the importance of staff development to the participatory management of schools cannot be underestimated. Developing human relations and self-management skills among teachers is one of the keys to creating a participatory school. This requires the commitment of both the teaching staff and the site managers. Strong leadership regarding staff development demonstrates to teachers that the manager cares about professionalism and quality teaching. Staff development reaches in several directions simultaneously: to motivate, to stimulate, to enhance teaching skills and knowledge, and to build collegiality and self-management capacity. Without a school staff

development thrust, it is difficult for teachers to grow professionally or for schools to thrive as organizations.

Case Study _____

Participative Renewal in a
Suburban School

*(Authors' Note: This case illustrates how one school linked school-
site planning with staff development. Readers may want to consider why this proved to be a successful strategy for Beverly Hills
and why the staff accepted the approach. Looking at staff development from another perspective, what resistance might one expect to encounter from an approach that begins with the
identification of school problems and needs and determines staff
development needs as a function of these organizational requirements? Why is it important to conceptualize a staff development
program from an organizational rather than an individual professional perspective? Can you think of examples whereby these
two levels of staff development needs might conflict? What might
be management strategies for reconciling divergences if and
when they crop up? What role, if any, does a staff development
exercise like the preservice retreat at Beverly Hills play in elaborating a relevant and acceptable staff development program?)*

Background

Beverly Hills Elementary School is set amidst a lower- and
middle-income housing tract that was constructed on the out-
skirts of Vallejo, California, in 1948. Once a typical middle-class
neighborhood, Beverly Hills is now populated by few of the original, now aging residents and a growing transient population of
low-income renters. The school has a high proportion of ADFC re-
cipients among its 450 ethnically diverse students. About two-
fifths of the school's children are black, a third are Caucasian, and
the remainder are largely recent Filipino immigrants. In the
evenings, when the school is closed, the neighborhood is often a
site of drug transactions.

The Problems

In 1985, when Barbara Armstrong was asked to consider the
job of principal, she encountered a fragmented staff who commu-

nicated "we don't feel supported here." There were extensive disciplinary problems and a laundry list of minor irritants, ranging from the length of the lunch period to teacher gripes about lunch duty. The former principal, on the verge of retirement, was not happy in his position, and the teachers felt neglected. Instead of working as a team, teachers were guarding their turf and ignoring the playground problems. For example, there was a sense that few cared what "other teachers' kids were doing."

Participative Renewal

It was this situation that Armstrong inherited in September of 1985. All in all, Beverly Hills Elementary was an unlikely candidate for a model school program. She began her work by identifying the problems. "I first interviewed each teacher; I talked to each one and said, 'What do you see as the main problems here?' I found a number of simple problems that were easy to fix. We lengthened the lunch period from 30 to 40 minutes and put in lunch monitors so that teachers wouldn't have to supervise during their lunch period and could meet and talk."

The strong support of the school district was also helpful. "When I started, the superintendent said, 'What would you like?' I said I would like an enlarged and painted office for the staff."

Little by little, Armstrong began a series of small changes that altered the school climate. Her daily presence in classrooms and on the playground demonstrated her support of the staff. "One of the aides said to me the other day, 'Gee, I was out on the yard at recess and it's nice to have a principal that's out in the playground too.' " She adds, "The kids know my name and they like to hug me. I guess that they find me accessible."

Discipline was a deep-seated problem that required careful work over a period of time. When Armstrong arrived, she had a long list of rules that teachers did not feel were being upheld—nor did they get support from the previous principal. "Teachers would discipline a child on the playground and the child would 'mouth off' and no one would support them. The teachers felt powerless. They really weren't working as a team."

Building a Team

Site improvement planning was placed in the hands of the Support Team, which consisted of three teachers, an instructional assistant, and the principal. Armstrong had to show the teachers that she would back them up, and she had to create a team spirit where there was little before. Rules were discussed and revised.

Teachers were encouraged to support each other. Teamwork was encouraged in the Site Improvement Plan; for example, teachers chose to release each other to observe one another and to create new computer-education lessons. And teachers started to share their ideas and methods of classroom instruction. After three years, the results began to be evident. At a staff planning meeting one teacher remarked how different things had been in the course of three years. Moreover, there was a sense that all the kids are everybody's kids.

The Change Process

One of the first and most decisive ingredients in developing a participatory climate occurred a week before school started. Armstrong, who had just been appointed, organized an overnight staff retreat. Focused on the need to improve the school's service to its Chapter I children, this first group encounter began a process of breaking down walls that existed between teachers as well as between teachers and administrators. It was an opportunity for open-ended discussion of the behavior policy, classroom management, and long-range school plans. It was also an opportunity for recreation and interaction in an entirely different mode. This first preservice retreat is now an annual event.

Staff Development

Staff development is a prime area of focus. It is the school's policy to use teacher leadership to provide input and assistance in planning and implementing in-service training. For example, teachers identified several areas for emphasis, including literature and writing skills and problem solving in mathematics. Retreats and shortened days provide an opportunity for the staff to work on these skill areas. In addition, a state-funded program in health education has identified Beverly Hills to be one of five statewide pilot sites.

Armstrong's approach to staff development has received enthusiastic support from the teachers. Since staff development involves teacher participation in the planning of educational programs, this is accomplished through a number of committees. Participation in the committees is voluntary. For example, in 1986, the Learning Environment Committee, a committee composed of teachers, was given responsibility for implementing a schoolwide "affective education program."

Each year a one- or two-day preservice retreat is held to discuss areas identified by the teachers as their own priorities for further training. In past years these topics have included classroom management, problem-solving methods, research on mainstreaming Chapter I children, and long-range planning of student skill development. At the retreat, a good bit of time is devoted to group process team-building activities. Brainstorming solutions to the school plan and activities was one effective technique. "It prompted group interaction and was also stimulating. It reinforced my feelings that we sure are a good team," remarked one teacher.

Integrating Staff Development

Integrating staff development and school planning provided an opportunity for teachers to reflect on prior years' activities and to map out critical areas for future attention. One teacher commented, "There was a feeling of sharing. Departmentalizing into committees was very successful in terms of dividing responsibilities and sharing of ideas. I really felt the enthusiasm and commitment to implementing the Comprehensive Health Program." Another remarked, "Committees certainly got a lot accomplished as far as setting objectives for the school year and planning how to meet these objectives as well as setting time frames for the school year." And still another added, "I thought that going over the school level plan and then brainstorming as a group to develop ideas from each group . . . helped each group focus on schoolwide concerns and suggestions."

Results

Although it is still early to measure the entire results of the change in management style, early indications are that California Achievement Program (CAP) scores have risen in the written language skills, which the school identified as an area of emphasis in its curriculum and staff development.

Several exemplary approaches to learning have been implemented, including the use of cross-age tutors, a computer lab, writing across the curriculum, literature-based reading instruction, and cooperative learning.

Perhaps one of the most telling pieces of evidence comes from a 1987 Program Quality Review conducted by a team of external examiners. "The staff serves as excellent models of leadership and cooperation. Especially strong leadership from the principal and the willingness of each of you to take on leadership responsibilities makes it possible for you to capitalize on this unique combination of strengths to move the school toward the best program for your students. The staff sees themselves as equal leaders, unselfish and willing to give time and expertise to each other. Keep up the good work!"

Beverly Hills School is a good place to go to school. It is seen as a place you come to learn. Teachers expect students to be on task and succeed. Students are eager to participate in class and their answers are respected.

We saw and heard numerous instances where both students and teachers were treated with respect. Students laughed freely and received a large dose of hugs and other appropriate personal support. They respected school and classroom procedures.

Both students and teachers obviously like each other and work together to solve problems. Students freely shared materials, talked during cooperative lessons, and made special efforts to help each other as they worked.

References

Arizona Education Association Teacher Compensation Task Force. *Career Development System.* Arizona: AEA, February 1986.

Bird, T. *Prospects and Demands of California Mentor Teacher Program.* San Francisco: Far West Laboratory for Educational Research and Development, 1985.

Bird, T., and Alspaugh, D. *Applying Research in Teacher Education: 1985 Survey of District Coordinators for the California Mentor Teacher Program.* San Francisco: Far West Laboratory for Educational Research and Development, January 1986.

Fagan, M. M., and Walter, G. "Mentoring Among Teachers." *Journal of Educational Research* 76 (November/December 1982):113–118.

Furtwengler, C. "Tennessee's Career Ladder Plan: They Said It Couldn't Be Done." *Educational Leadership* (November 1985):50–56.

Garmston, R. J. "How Administrators Support Peer Coaching." *Educational Leadership* (February 1987):7, 18–26.

Geis, A. A. "Making Merit Pay Work." *Personnel* (January 1987):52–60.

Gray, W., and Gray, M. "Synthesis of Research on Mentoring Beginning Teachers." *Educational Leadership* (November 1,1985):37–43.

Kram, K. E. "Mentoring in the Workplace." In E. Schein (Ed.), *Career Development in Organizations.* San Francisco: Jossey-Bass, 1985.

Levine, S. L. *Promoting Adult Growth in Schools.* Boston: Allyn and Bacon, 1989.

Little, J. W. *School Success and Staff Development: The Role of Staff Development in Urban Desegregated Schools.* Washington, DC: National Institute for Education, 1981.

Rosenholtz, S. *Political Myths About Reforming the Teaching Profession.* Denver: Education Commission of the States, July 1984.

Schein, E. *Career Dynamics: Matching Individual and Organizational Needs.* Reading, MA: Addison-Wesley, 1978.

Showers, B., and Joyce, B. "Low-Cost Arrangements for Peer Coaching." *Journal of Staff Development* 8 (Spring 1987):22–24.

Showers, B. J.; Joyce, B.; and Bennett, B. "Synthesis of Research on Staff Development: A Framework for Future Study and State-of-the-Art Analysis." *Educational Leadership* (November 1987):77–87.

Stern, D. "Compensation for Teachers." *Review of Research in Education* 13 (1986):285–316.

Wildman, T. M., and Niles, J. A. "Essentials of Professional Growth." *Educational Leadership* (February 1987):4–10.

CHAPTER EIGHT

Evaluation: Teachers, Programs, and Schools

Introduction

Several science teachers in the Kentfield Unified School District began to experiment with a cooperatively based science curriculum after attending an intensive summer workshop. After nearly one and one-half years, the teachers—supported by two school principals—proposed that the district consider revamping its science curriculum along the lines of the experimental program. Much discussion ensued, involving other science teachers throughout the district as well as the district-level science resource specialist. What was the evidence to justify generalizing the cooperative approach to all classrooms? What would such a change involve in terms of time and cost? The district resource specialist suggested that an evaluation of the cooperative science curriculum already used by three teachers be evaluated before making any districtwide decisions. The issue then rapidly became: How could the program be evaluated?

All educators recognize that evaluation is endemic to the educational process. Increasingly, management specialists acknowledge that evaluation is one of four key aspects of the management process (see Figure 7.1 in Chapter Seven). Teachers are concerned with the evaluation of students, and principals have traditionally been concerned with the evaluation of their teaching staff. In recent years administrators and teachers are concerned with the evaluation of pilot projects, special programs, and their school's performance as an organization.

This chapter takes up two processes: evaluating the school and its programs as well as reviewing the teacher performance of individual teachers. We believe it is important to link these two processes conceptually. The performance of individual teachers will naturally influence a school's effectiveness as an organization. Likewise, the impact of program and/or organizationwide performance has an affect on teachers.

We begin our consideration of evaluation via an examination of the various functions of evaluation relative to individual, program, and school-level performance. Following these general considerations, we turn to the topic of school and program evaluation, addressing the questions: What should be evaluated? Who should be involved in program evaluation? and What are some standard evaluation techniques and processes? We then discuss the topic of individual teacher performance evaluation. Our concerns include the following: (1) What constitutes effective teacher performance? (2) What criteria should be used to evaluate teacher performance? (3) What are the salient approaches to individual performance appraisal? and (4) What is the nature of the performance appraisal process?

Functions of Evaluation

Table 8.1 presents the three major reasons for evaluating individual, program, and schoolwide performance: information, feedback, and accountability. It is not uncommon for parents and prospective students to want information on teachers' effectiveness. Meanwhile, teachers themselves need feedback on their professional performance in order to assess their developmental needs. And the school-level and district management evaluate teacher performance from an accountability perspective that can be related to personnel decisions regarding career advancement and professional placement (Beer, 1981; Cook, 1988).

Performance evaluation of specific school programs provides information for interested audiences: students, parents, the implementors themselves, as well as school- and district-level management. It also provides crucial feedback for future planning and for making adjustments in ongoing programs. Finally, program evalu-

TABLE 8.1 • *Functions of Evaluation*

Level	Purpose		
	Information	*Feedback*	*Accountability*
Teacher	Students, parents	Professional development	Personnel decisions
Programs	Student, implementors, parents, school management, district management	Implementation plans and changes	Funding decisions
School	Parents, school staff, district management	School improvement plans	Resource allocation decisions

ation is important in the determination of future funding decisions. Programs that are effective should receive priority over those that are less effective in the use of discretionary resources.

The functions of evaluation vis-à-vis the school as a whole are in most ways similar to that of program evaluation. For example, the audience for information is the same. Schoolwide evaluation has an important feedback role in terms of future planning and resource allocation. Determining the priorities for a school improvement plan should depend on the results of a schoolwide quality review. In terms of accountability, year-to-year and long-term resource allocation decisions need to be based on priorities that have been determined by a careful evaluation of the school's existing strengths and weaknesses.

School and Program Evaluation

Over the past three decades, the topic of evaluation has grown dramatically in scope and importance within the educational system. In the space of one decade, spanning the late 1960s to the late 1970s, the funds spent on educational evaluation climbed from a few hundred thousand dollars to hundreds of millions of dollars (Evans, 1984). The growth in schoolwide and program-specific evaluations has roots in the increased involvement of federal and state authorities in education, both as financiers and instigators of educational reform efforts (e.g., see Timar and Kirp, 1988).

Traditionally, some states have a mandated accreditation process that all schools must undergo on a regular basis. Accreditation evaluations are conducted by a team of external evaluators selected by the state or a regional accrediting agency. The role of the site management and staff is basically to present their entire school program to the accrediting team, focusing primarily on curriculum, academic standards, and personnel qualifications.

Evaluation of specific federal, state, and privately funded educational programs has also become a routine activity in which the school site can be either directly or indirectly involved. Most large-scale programs have their own district- and/or site-level coordinators who assume responsibility for orchestrating evaluations. In general, however, program evaluations are conducted by external specialists with expertise in the technical aspects of evaluation. Nonetheless, administrators, program directors, and teachers are often called upon to participate in a program evaluation.

Increasingly, school personnel may be given the responsibility of organizing, designing, and interpreting the results of an evaluation—often without the assistance of evaluation specialists. These evaluations are usually pieces of "action research," emanating from specific questions like "How is the implementation of a new curriculum proceeding? Is the intervention program designed to keep high-risk students from dropping out of high school achieving its objectives? and How well is the school performing in both academic and nonacademic dimensions in relation to other schools in the district?"

The field of evaluation makes the basic distinction between formative and summative evaluations. *Formative evaluations* examine programs, projects, or individual performance while in the process of execution. Formative evaluations tend to focus on management and technical aspects of a program rather than actual outcomes. Information collected on an ongoing program can be used to detect flaws in the program, to provide key supporters and constituents with interim information about its status, or occasionally to give an early reading on implementation success or failure.

Summative evaluations, by contrast, are conducted at the end of a program and generally focus on outcomes. Summative evaluations answer specific questions concerning expected results. For instance, "Did the program designed to prevent secondary school students from dropping out actually reduce the drop-out rate or keep it from accelerating?" Although summative evaluations are results-oriented, they need not neglect a review of how the management of the implementation process affects the program's outcomes. Both formative and summative evaluations are important. They have different objectives, but a common set of evaluation procedures applies to both.

Although educational evaluation has become a highly specialized and technical field, the nontechnical roles of evaluation are equally important. These roles include public relations, accountability, and building cohesion and vision within the school. The public relations function of evaluation serves to inform constituencies of the school and/or district (see Chapter Nine) about current activities and performance. The results of either an external or internal evaluation can be very valuable or damaging vis-à-vis the district board of education, parents, or the wider community.

Closely related to the public relations aspect of evaluation is the accountability role of evaluation. Agencies funding special programs inevitably want to know how their money has been spent and what impact it is having. In order to maintain a continuous flow of external funds, school sites must be prepared and willing to engage in ongoing monitoring and evaluation of special programs. High marks on accountability increase the organization's chances of receiving additional funds from the same and new agencies.

An evaluation can be seen as an opportunity for reflection, rather than as an added obligatory responsibility with which the school must comply. It can be used as a positive motivator to build a broader vision of the school among the staff. It can also be seen as a chance to engage staff members in dialogue regarding the organization's or program's performance vis-à-vis its goals, and to stimulate specific planning for future improvements.

School-Based Evaluations

Recently educators have begun to pay much more attention to the effectiveness of the school as an organizational unit. School-based evaluations have been introduced as a recurrent process in some states. For example, California has instituted a triannual Program Quality Review process: All schools must be reviewed by a team of external evaluators in accordance with a set of criteria developed by the district. This review involves a self-assessment by the school-site personnel (principals and teachers) in preparation for the external evaluation (see Figures 8.1, 8.2, and 8.3).

The schoolwide evaluation perspective is extremely important because it focuses the attention of the staff on the performance of the organization and it relates individual teaching efforts to the performance of the school as a whole. School-based evaluation requires a team effort on the part of the site staff who must prepare for the evaluation both through the provision of background materials and teaching performance. Moreover, school-based evaluations are generally multidimensional. Drawing from the research on effective schools that has accumulated over the past decade, school-based evaluations look at a variety of aspects of the school's performance, including school climate, staff development, leadership, planning and goal setting, as well as the quality of teaching at the various different grade levels.

What Should Be Evaluated?

Frequently evaluations are necessary either to secure additional funding for a program in progress or to decide whether or

FIGURE 8.1 • *Letter from Principal to District:*
Program Quality Review

VALLEJO CITY UNIFIED SCHOOL DISTRICT

April 24, 1987

Special Projects
Instructional Division
Members of the Board

Beverly Hills is excited and committed to Program Quality Review and how it ensures quality education for Vallejo children. We are looking forward to our next PQR in the 1988-89 school year. We wanted to make sure our school level plan would be aligned with the district's efforts in Program Quality Review.

Our "Current Conditions" section is aligned and each component has a structure which perhaps needs some explanation. Current Conditions at Beverly Hills School begins with references from the QUALITY CRITERIA. We believe that is what "should be" going on at a school site. Beverly Hills School has already been "matched up" to the Quality Criteria, and so references from our first Program Quality Review are cited.

The Self-Review is an extremely important dynamic to Program Quality Review, and Beverly Hills School will conduct a Self-Review every year in our striving to keep improvement on-going at the school site. References from the 1987 Beverly Hills School Self-Review are cited.

For the past two years, Beverly Hills School has surveyed the parents and staff members, using a productive input-gathering instrument. Comments were made by some individuals. References are made to the PARENT/STAFF SURVEY results.

Finally, OTHER SOURCES OF DESIGN DATA, which helped us design the objectives and activities stated in the School Level Plan are cited.

Please take the time to review our current conditions. We are working hard to provide excellence for Beverly Hills School students, and this working document, the School Level Plan, reflects this excellence.

Sincerely,

Barbara J. Armstrong, Principal

Source: Vallejo City Unified School District.

FIGURE 8.2 • *Description of the School: Beverly Hills Elementary School*

Name of School: Beverly Hills Elementary School
Address: 1450 Coronel Avenue, Vallejo, California 94591
Phone (707) 644-5557
Number of Students This Year: 356
Approximate Number Next Year: 335
AFDC Count: 29.5%
Racial/Ethnic Composition of Student Body: 64% Minorities

Narrative Description

Beverly Hills School is a Kindergarten through 6th grade elementary school located in the city of Vallejo at the junction of Interstate 780, near Benecia and Interstate 80, near Carquinez Bridge. The attendance area includes students from within the city limits and from an unincorporated semi-rural area. In recent years the Beverly Hills student population has increased due to the construction of new homes in the Glen Cove area.

The Beverly Hills area is served by the city bus system. As there are no parks and recreational facilities in the area, the school is frequently used as a gathering place for neighborhood youth and organized groups.

The K–6 enrollment at Beverly Hills is approximately 345 students. This includes students from two special day classes for communicatively handicapped children. A federal childcare program and a state preschool program are also located on the campus.

The student population is 36.8% white, 36.5% Black, 16.8% Filipino, 8.1% Hispanic, .6% Asian, .3% American Indian, and 1.7% Pacific Islander. The transiency rate for the 1986–87 school year was 40%.

Using a variety of effective teaching approaches, Beverly Hills teachers' instructional programs are aligned with state and VCUSD curriculum products. Student needs are assessed using CRTM and CAP test scores each year.

Each Beverly Hills student's basic education is enhanced by School Improvement funds. The identified students (those who score below the 50th percentile) have their learning experiences reinforced and receive extra practice with State Compensatory Education and Chapter 1 monies. These funds provide a multitude of services and materials, including a computer lab. The school is a pilot school and part of the California Comprehensive Health Project, the goal being increased student and staff awareness of health and wellness issues.

There are a variety of staff development opportunities at the school. These include on-site workshops on Monday afternoons, release time at the district professional development center, and Saturday and afterschool workshops provided by the VCUSD staff development program. In addition, teachers continue to increase their skills and knowledge by attending local Bay Area colleges and conferences.

To involve as many staff members as possible in school decisions, there are two structures—the support team and committees. The support team consists of the principal, the Instructional Associate, and three teachers. The support team works with the staff on inservices, school level planning, and school-wide decision making. The committees function on an ad hoc basis. The 1986–87 school year saw three committees focused on reading, math, and the learning environment.

Source: Beverly Hills Elementary School, Vallejo City Unified School District.

FIGURE 8.3 • *School Program Quality Review: Summary of The Report of Findings*

California State Department of Education Instructional Support Services Division

Date: February 24, 25, and 26, 1986

District Vallejo City Unified	School Beverly Hills Elementary	Lead Reviewer (signature)
(Signature)	(Signature)	(Signature)

Curricular Criterion	*Directions:* Briefly identify major findings for each curricular area. Curricular areas that are not pursued in depth may be addressed separately or under the umbrella of the Schoolwide Effectiveness Criterion.
Math	The math curriculum is clearly defined in the district continuum. There is a commitment toward the establishment of a strong math base throughout the grades. Whole class, small group, and individual instruction is evidenced in the school. Textbook usage as well as supplementary material is utilized.
	Different types of manipulatives and a variety of teacher strategies were apparent in the classroom. The computer software has been selectively chosen to support the classroom math program. The different strands of the curriculum were represented by examples of student work in geometry, algebra, problem solving, and graphing.
	Suggestions: To ensure that problem solving is a major part of the math program as set forth in the quality criteria, you might plan a specific time each day which would be devoted to estimation, probability prediction and logic.
Written Language	Area of strength: It is obvious that the staff has commitment to a strong, quality schoolwide written language program for all students. Students write daily and writing is well integrated into other curricular areas. Student success is assured through the conscientious use of brainstorming, word mapping, and other prewriting strategies. Students and teachers love writing. Student books and

Continued

FIGURE 8.3 *Continued*

compositions are valued as important literature, used as choral reading material, presented in public speaking situations, and published for others to enjoy.

There is clear progression in the sophistication of writing skills from grade to grade.

Opportunity for improvement: We saw students revising and editing their own and each other's work in some classrooms. To ensure that all students consistently experience all stages in the writing process, it is suggested that the staff spend some time agreeing on what the editing process is. The Program Quality Review criterion for written language also explains these elements.

You were very successful in using your staff development days and each other's expertise to implement the pre-writing/writing and responding stages. You could use this process to refine revising and editing. The Bay Area Writing Project would be an effective model for these strategies and procedures.

Your approach to reading is a forward-thinking, continuum-based approach in which you look at a continuum of skills for instruction and then create a reading program to teach those skills. You have supported this reading approach through your SI/SCE with a special reading teacher, the kindergarten teachers helping students in the afternoon, and cross age tutoring. Your computer software has been carefully correlated to your reading objective.

As your self-review showed, a Razzle Dazzle reading day and home-reading program would further enhance the enthusiasm for and love of reading at Beverly Hills.

Your literature program, which consists of individual and group literature selections followed by discussions and/or skill lessons, is exposing your students to quality literature on a regular basis.

As you help students love reading and learn to use it to gain knowledge and understanding, continue your focus on the grade level CRTM and consider developing interim assessments to insure skill acquisition at each grade level. Perhaps topics might include a schoolwide silent reading time, teachers reading to students daily, and alternatives to written book reports. You might also consider establishing a reading committee to help coordinate these efforts.

Fine Arts

We found art integrated throughout the school program in the writing, science, and social studies projects as well as in crafts and displays of children's work.

Music and performing arts are found in classrooms (singing, movement, exploration, listening to music). Upper-grade students participate on a voluntary basis in instrumental music.

Schoolwide Effectiveness

The staff at Beverly Hills has high standards and expectations for their students. They believe students can behave and learn. A schoolwide discipline program, consistent homework, accountability for assignments, and a "you can do it and I'm here to help you" attitude all contribute to these high expectations.

The district has supported your effectiveness through continuums aligned to your assessments. The long-range plans you did this year help ensure that students learn a progressive sequence of skills in each subject area. Your instructional support team, instructional associate, computer proctor, and the teacher computer group all positively support the teachers efforts.

Students are interested in learning and teachers use whole class instruction as well as small group and individual strategies to help students master skills and concepts.

Your preservice retreat days and weekly planning/staff development days allowed you to get schoolwide goals and work together to implement them.

You have a unique combination of strengths at Beverly Hills. Barbara is a well-respected, strong, supportive leader, the instructional support team and key planners keep communication going and problem solving possible; Dave and Tom (staff assistants) are obviously service and student oriented; Rex keeps the grounds safe and clean and teaches students responsibility; the classroom aides, computer proctor, and clerical staff also support both the kids and teachers, all of you as classroom teachers, who implement the fine instructional program for students, and, of course, Daly (instructional associate), who bakes brownies and is the glue that holds it all together.

Special Needs

Area of strength: During the Quality Review at Beverly Hills School, it became very apparent that the special needs of students were being met positively in a number of ways, largely due to the cooperative efforts of the teachers, aides, the bilingual program, the Special Needs Committee, and the principal. The SI/SCE categorical funds have made many aspects of the program possible, an extra day for the psychologist, a reading teacher as well as aide time. All students and each child's program has been carefully coordinated between Support Staff, resource teacher, and classroom teacher.

The curriculum is well defined and challenging for all students with special needs. A definite focus on goals and expectations is apparent. A model program of interclass mainstreaming has been especially successful with opportunities for all special need students to be included into

Continued

FIGURE 8.3   *Continued*

	the regular classroom activities. Cross-age tutoring has afforded additional opportunities to the student.
Oral Language	Your oral language program is demonstrated by brainstorming, choral reading, sharing of reports, and public speaking, and has been nicely integrated with your written language program. Opportunities for students to share their written words are an established priority within the classrooms.
	Effective communication skills are also being encouraged by the use of the Standard English Program.
	Your ideas to purchase videotape equipment and to use assemblies to enhance your oral language program are good.
Science	As we found in our self-review, all students K–6 are involved in the instructional science program on a regular basis. The curriculum is well defined and generally science lessons are teacher directed and/or textbook oriented. Students have some opportunities to investigate and use the scientific method. The Savi-Selph program and materials that you plan to purchase will further enhance your program.
Planning, Implementing, and Evaluating the School Program	We have heard from all of you about the strong feeling of working as a team this year. The preservice retreat was the starting point and that ongoing collaborative problem solving has continued.
	There has been a clear definition of roles and responsibilities, which has encouraged good working relationships and communication. The needs of students have been addressed with the establishment of goals and objectives.
	The planned program is known and evaluated during planning times to ensure that modifications reflect changing needs. All support activities, resources, and personnel are directly linked to the program for students.
Staff Development	Area of strength: There is evidence of a large number of staff development activities covering topics identified by the school as areas of need. You use your support team and Instructional Associate effectively to help implement your staff development goals.
	The Monday afternoon planning time provided by the district enhances your staff development efforts. Staff members willingly share knowledge and strategies with each other.
	The preschool retreat planning session was said by all to have contributed to your abilities to work together and to

implement common goals and programs. This commitment makes everyone a winner—the district, the principal, the teachers, and especially the students.

Continued use of peer observations is encouraged as it has certainly helped you implement the staff development techniques you have learned.

Special Note: Many of you mentioned that you were not fully aware of all the materials available in the Resource Room. Perhaps Daly could arrange an informal field trip to share information about available materials.

Source: California State Department of Education, Instructional Support Division.

not a particular project should be continued. It is very important to ask "Who wants to know?" at the same time we begin asking, "What do we want to know?" Evaluation is a political as well as a technical process. The questions asked in a program or schoolwide evaluation should be designed to respond to the concerns of key decision makers as well as various constituent groups, be they teachers, parents, district personnel, or external funders.

Formative evaluations can usually be designed around two key questions: What has gone well up to this point? and What is currently or likely to become problematic? It is very important that evaluations give emphasis to both strengths and weaknesses. This gives the school or program staff recognition for their achievements as well as ideas and directions for improvement in the future. Because formative evaluations are developmental in emphasis (i.e., their objective is making a diagnosis that will improve the future health of the program), they should reflect carefully on the human process dimensions of a program. Many programs fail to reach their potential because they are weak in a management rather than a technical area.

Summative evaluations, in contrast, examine the relationship between program goals and actual outcomes: Did the program achieve its results and if not, why not? Were there spinoffs and unanticipated benefits that resulted from the program? Were some of the specific goals of a program modified in the process of execution and if so, why? A summative evaluation may bring out positive results that were unanticipated at the onset, as well as initial objectives that were not accomplished. This situation can be treated as an opportunity or a catastrophe. Obviously, it is best to take the "What have we learned?" approach rather than simply looking at "What have we failed to accomplish?"

The Choice of Evaluators

The choice of evaluators depends both on technical and political criteria. Evaluations may be undertaken by an individual or team external to the program itself, or conducted completely in-house by those who design, implement, and participate in the program. Between these two extremes there is a mix of options, which should be determined by the particular circumstances surrounding the evaluation. Are the program implementors the primary consumers of the evaluation, or is the evaluation being directed toward funders who might want a degree of detachment and external legitimacy? Is it important to engage the program participants as a means of increasing their commitment to this or future programs? Direct involvement of program implementors may not be necessary or even desirable under certain circumstances, but input from program personnel can be very helpful at the planning stage of an evaluation. Moreover, the school staff involved in the program should be well-informed on the objectives and procedures of the evaluation as well as having access to the results. Rapport between program staff, clients, and the evaluation team is essential for a successful evaluation. Every effort should be made to include these individuals prior to, during, and following an evaluation.

Technique: Design, Sampling, and Data Collection

Although evaluation can be a highly technical process, it is important not to lose sight of its basic objectives: to provide usable information, give feedback to participants, and underscore the importance of accountability for present and future decision making. Many educators are more familiar with evaluation techniques and their attendant caveats than other professionals because of the pervasiveness of standardized student testing. Basically evaluation techniques are concerned with producing a reliable and valid assessment. A reliable evaluation is replicable; that is, if the evaluation was conducted again on the same or a similar program, the results would be consistent with earlier findings. A valid evaluation accurately reflects important processes and outcomes of the program or school.

Design

The design of an evaluation will affect both reliability and validity. In the social sciences there are two basic evaluation designs: experimental and nonexperimental. *Experimental designs* compare a control group with an experimental group. Using the example of the cooperative science curriculum at the opening of this chapter, an experimental evaluation design might compare the learning of students exposed to the cooperatively organized science curriculum (the experimental group) with students of the same grade levels who were not exposed to the curriculum (the control group).

Experimental designs are highly desirable, but generally more expensive and time consuming than nonexperimental designs. *Nonexperimental designs* do not compare the results from two or more groups that have undergone different circumstances; instead, they focus only on the group program or project in question. Thus a nonexperimental evaluation design of the cooperative science curriculum would study results only of the students who actually used the curriculum. Results from nonexperimental designs are usually based on comparing information from before and after exposure (pretests and posttests). The limitation of this procedure comes from the possibility that factors other than the cooperative curriculum itself are responsible for changes in student learning (e.g., special abilities of the teachers' involved or special characteristics of the students). To deal with the impact of intervening factors that might influence the results in nonexperimental designs, sampling techniques and certain types of data-analytic techniques may be used to "control" for external influence.

Sampling

Tests and examinations that are commonly used in education to measure results generally do not take a sampling approach. Educators generally believe that all students need to be examined rather than just a percentage that might represent a cross-section of the group. This is, of course, because educators are interested in individual learning accomplishments as much, if not more, than the performance of the group as a whole. However, when a program or schoolwide evaluation is undertaken, testing of all the clients, implementors, and others affected by the program may not be necessary. Evaluations frequently select only a sample of the entire group involved. This sample may be selected at random or it may be chosen with the idea of being sure to include representatives from specific groups of people (nonrandom selection). There are advantages to both of these methods.

Another approach is to use a stratified random sample. Returning to the example of the cooperative science curriculum, to evaluate its effectiveness in producing desired learning results, one probably wants to know its impact on all three grade levels (fourth through sixth). One may also be interested in knowing whether girls respond equally well to boys in this approach. An evaluation focusing on these issues might want to "stratify" the students by grade level and sex for each of the participating schools (see Table 8.2) then randomly select 10 percent from each group of girls and boys at each grade level.

A nonrandom approach might be also be used. For example, to evaluate how the cooperative curriculum affected low achievers among the pilot classes, one might handpick a group of low achievers in some grade-level classes that did not use the cooperative curriculum. This, then, is a nonrandom, experimental design—comparing an experimental group (the students using the cooperative curriculum) with a control group (the students using another science curriculum.)

The importance of sampling is that the actual number of cases studied can be reduced and yet valid results can be achieved from the evaluation. Ultimately, this means saving time and resources.

Data Collection

The basis for making an evaluation is the collection of data regarding processes and outcomes from the program or school being evaluated. Sometimes relevant evaluation information is already available through existing school and program records. In other instances, information needs to be collected firsthand (referred to as *primary data*). Written questionnaires and tests, interviews, direct observations and documents generate primary data.

The choice among data-collection techniques depends on what questions are being asked in the evaluation and which method is most appropriate for getting relevant and reliable information. Additionally, constraints such as difficulty in locating the information, reluctance of certain people to provide information, difficulty in classifying the data in a meaningful and generalizable form, and the expense of collecting the data also influence one's choices among the various data-collection techniques. Table 8.3 summarizes the methods of collection, degrees of resource intensity, as well as the advantages and disadvantages of different data-collection techniques.

Written *questionnaires and tests* are usually self-administered by the respondents, and therefore are relatively inexpensive to use. They offer the security of anonymity so that respondents may feel more comfortable being candid about sensitive issues or expressing personal opinions. *Interviews,* by contrast, require a one-on-one situation between data collector and respondent, making them a high-cost approach to gaining information. However, interviews do provide the possibility of unanticipated information and probing topics in much greater depth than is generally possible via a questionnaire or test. One disadvantage is that the interviewer may influence the quality of responses through manner or personality.

Observations focus on actual behavior rather than reported behavior obtained from interviews or questionnaires and tests. Unfocused observations can be diffuse and fail to yield useful information, therefore, observers need training in observation techniques. The problem of obtaining a representative cross-section of behaviors arises with observations. This is especially true for observations that focus on teaching behaviors in the classroom. Another major disadvantage is that without careful focus the observer may be inundated with too much information—much of it extraneous. Nonetheless, observations can yield a data base and provide a dynamic picture of behavior. *Documents,* such as reports, school records, and teacher records, can also be useful data sources. Obtaining this information requires someone to research the available material and read for pertinent data. Using documents is low in cost and, if the materials are confidential, access is relatively easy. One disadvantage of using existing documents is that information has already been preselected and certain relative facts and details may be missing.

Because each technique tends to focus on different aspects of reality, it is often desirable to use several information sources. Returning to the cooperative science curriculum example, to evaluate its effectiveness in terms of student learning, one can see the advantages of testing students both with a written format and through observing them while they are engaged in "scientific problem solving." To understand why the curriculum may be working in one classroom and not another, it might be informative to both interview and observe teachers in action. And to evaluate

TABLE 8.2 • A Stratified Random Sample for Evaluating a Cooperative Science Curriculum

Sex	Grade 4		Grade 5		Grade 6	
	Population	Sample	Population	Sample	Population	Sample
Girl	75	8	74	8	77	8
Boy	75	8	76	8	74	7
Totals	150	16	150	16	151	15

TABLE 8.3 • Data-Collection Techniques

Technique	Method of Collection	Resource Intensity	Advantages	Caveats
Written questionnaires and tests[a]	Self-administered	Low	Anonymity	Low response rates; limited information
Interview	Interviewer	High	Spontaneity; unanticipated information	Impact of interviewer responses
Observations[b]	Trained observer	Very high	Ability to observe processes	Extraneous action and information
Documents	Reader	Low	Accessibility	Information preselected; incomplete

[a] Written questionnaires and tests may be composed of "open" and "closed"/forced choice.
[b] Observations may be unstructured (i.e., an observer records actions, events, etc., as noticed) or structured (i.e., the observer looks for and records specific actions or events).

how the students who learned with the cooperative curriculum compare to students who did not, one might want to compare the performance of the "experimental" group to other students with similar characteristics at the same grade levels on standardized science achievement tests.

Conclusion

Evaluating schools and specific school programs is a multidimensional undertaking. It involves technical, resource, and political considerations. Both external and internal evaluations require the understanding, voice, and commitment of school personnel. Administrators and teachers need not be evaluation experts to understand and share their ideas and concerns regarding any specific evaluation. Ideally, evaluations are done in collaboration with those involved in the programs or schools being evaluated.

Evaluating the Performance of Teachers

On Thursday at 2:50 P.M., Wilda Gardella, a resource teacher and part-time administrator at Orion Elementary School, arranges a cheese log and crackers on the table. The VCR unit is already in place. The teaching staff arrives promptly at 3:00. Joe, a teacher for a combination third/fourth-grade class, explains to the group that the video about to be viewed is a segment of a lesson on values awareness he has developed. He says that one of the objectives is to help children become aware of their own value position as well as be able to listen respectfully to the value statements of others. The group watches the 15-minute segment attentively. Immediately following the viewing, teachers are busily writing their comments on an evaluation form. Then the discussion begins; one colleague starts with, "I really liked the way you were able to draw all the children into the discussion. How do you do that?"

Information, feedback on performance, and accountability are three key functions associated with evaluation of individual employee performance (see Table 8.1). Traditionally, individual performance appraisal has been used by employers as an instrument for making personnel decisions (i.e., promotion, transfer, and release decisions). If the employee receives a positive appraisal he or she will get a raise or promotion; if not, the employee may be transferred or lose his or her job. From this perspective, many employees view the process as threatening and potentially punitive. Consequently, both employees and managers are known to experience substantial degrees of anxiety in conjunction with performance appraisal when used primarily for this purpose.

For these reasons, school principals are often reluctant to identify weaknesses in teacher performance for fear of reducing morale. Moreover, school principals have demonstrated an hesitancy to report poor performance among their staff. Dealing with a weak performer may cause additional administrative work, bring about intervention from an unwanted outside authority, or affect the organization's perception of the principal as an effective manager (Bridges, 1986). Clearly, there is a tradeoff between the development/improvement functions of performance appraisal and the accountability functions. In the following sections of this chapter we will examine the characteristics of an effective teacher performance appraisal system, present criteria for developing performance appraisal instruments, and discuss several effective approaches that have been developed to assess the performance of teachers.

Effective Performance

An effective performance appraisal system is marked by several features. First, it is compatible with the specific goals and objectives of the organization in which it operates, and it changes as the goals change. Second, top-level leadership and institutional resources are provided for its implementation. Third, evaluators receive the specialized training they need to perform their task. Finally, both managers and employees share an understanding of goals and processes of the evaluation (Wise, Darling-Hammond, McLaughlin, and Bernstein, 1984).

Because schools grow and change in response to internal and external conditions, the performance appraisal process should not be written in stone. *Organizational compatibility* means that the criteria upon which teachers are to be evaluated are consistent with school or districtwide goals. A comprehensive study of teacher evaluation in 32 school districts across the United States by RAND revealed that articulating the performance appraisal system with districtwide goals was characteristic of districts with especially effective systems. Although the goals and appraisal systems varied from district to district, where there was a close fit between the larger district policies and the appraisal system, the system received high marks from both employees and administrators (Wise et al., 1984).

One of the most salient choices that needs to be made is determining the dominant function of the performance appraisal system. Is its goal to weed out incompetent teachers? Or is the dominant goal to help new teachers develop their competency in the classroom? Is the system to be used as the basis for the organization's reward system? These are policy decisions that must precede the actual design or redesign of a performance appraisal system.

The support of *top-level leadership* along with the commitment of an organization's *resources* to the performance appraisal process is another element of success. Because performance appraisal is a process that takes time to set up and implement, top-level management in the educational system must be willing to participate in and commit administrative resources to the system (see the example of the Toledo Unified School District in Wise et al., 1984). Studies have shown that in school systems that emphasize the importance of performance appraisal, principals may spend between 10 to 20 percent of their time on the process. Superintendents may spend less time, but they will nevertheless need to commit part of their own time, as well as that of managers and professionals in the system, to this activity.

The third aspect of successful performance appraisal systems is that the evaluators—whether they are school principals, teachers, or district-level personnel—receive *specialized training* in the concepts and techniques of performance appraisal. This means that administrative time and resources must be allocated for such training. Research has demonstrated that a minimum of 12 hours is needed to train experienced administrators or teachers in teacher evaluation procedures. Less time (8 hours) may be needed to train administrators evaluating nonteaching personnel—either professionals or support staff. Evaluators must be thoroughly familiar with the goals of the evaluation process and how the evaluation instruments relate to those goals. They must also be trained to observe teaching behavior in the classroom and record it reliably. Finally, they must have strong interpersonal skills needed to establish constructive dialogue regarding the results of an evaluation with teachers.

The final characteristic of an effective performance evaluation system is that both managers and employees *share an understanding of the goals* and workings of the evaluation. This is achieved through allocating adequate time to the performance appraisal process. Effective performance appraisal processes generally include a preevaluation interview between the employee and manager to discuss the purpose, characteristics, and actual process of the evaluation. This is a time to clarify doubts and misunderstandings and to allay apprehensions regarding the evaluation. In many school districts, management/employee agreement and understanding goes beyond the level of the employee/manager conference. The performance appraisal system is actually adopted as part of an employee's (teacher's or classified employee's) union contract. This mutual acceptance of the performance appraisal system relates directly to the specific technical criteria for building an effective performance appraisal instrument.

Criteria for Appraising Performance

Deciding what criteria should be used to evaluate the performance of a classroom teacher is a controversial matter. One view of the profession is that teaching is an art and therefore permeated with subjectivity, innuendo, and subtle complexities. These qualities do not readily lend themselves to formal, objective evaluation. As an art, teachers practice their profession through the expression of personality and the use of creativity and intuition. The best teachers may, in fact, be those who are the least conventional and approach both subject matter and classroom management in a highly individual manner.

Another commonly held perspective is that effective teaching is indeed a systematic process that can be analyzed in terms of specific skills. These skills are learnable and transferable from one teacher to another. Skills such as providing students with feedback, establishing behavioral objectives, and giving clear instructions are observable in effective teachers, and can be developed in new as well as experienced teachers who do not display these behaviors regularly (Hunter, 1976).

Many teachers object to current techniques of appraising their performance (Turner, 1987) because they believe that neither the technique nor the process accurately assesses or reflects their teaching competence. In effect, these teachers are saying that the performance appraisal techniques and procedures are not valid. If the evaluation of teachers' performance is going to be useful for teachers themselves, as well as administrators, it must be considered to be a legitimate process by all involved. Building an understanding of both the goals and procedures of an evaluation process is an important task at a district and school-site level. Developing a degree of consensus among teachers with regard to the criteria, instruments, and procedures used to appraise performance is an essential aspect of performance appraisals. Actively engaging teachers in discussion about the practice as well as their philosophy of teaching helps to facilitate a common understanding among a school staff in this respect.

Technical Considerations

The concept of performance appraisal validity also has an important technical component. Technically, validity means that the criteria used to evaluate performance are accurate and relevant measures of what constitute acceptable, exceptional, and unacceptable levels of competence. In a highly complex profession such as teaching, establishing these criteria involves considerable research and experimentation as knowledge about the teaching process expands.

The reliability of an evaluation system is equally important to its technical and political validity. A reliable performance appraisal instrument has several aspects. First, it yields a similar rating of a teacher's performance by two different evaluators, referred to as *interrater reliability.* Another type of reliability refers to the reliability of the items in the instrument measuring the same dimension of the job being evaluated. For example, most teacher evaluation instruments have more than one item to measure a teacher's instructional skills. The Lake Washington School District classroom observation schedule identifies seven separate activities that indicate a teacher's performance with respect to instructional skills (see Figure 8.4). If these are indeed reliable measures, they each should be more closely related to one another than they are to other items on the evaluation checklist measuring different dimensions, such as classroom management and lesson planning. (Technically this is referred to as the *differential ability index* (DAI); see Bernardin and Beatty, 1984.)

Finally, being free from outside contamination requires that the picture of the employee's performance be independent of factors and circumstances beyond his or her control. For instance, a teacher working with a class of students who have noted discipline problems should not be penalized in his or her evaluation with regard to student discipline. Notice that criterion 3 (Figure 8.4) of the model teacher evaluation form, "Handling Student Discipline," is conceived in such a manner that teacher actions to establish discipline and deal with problems are elaborated as indicators (rather than using student behavior as the primary indicator) of the teacher's performance in this dimension.

FIGURE 8.4 • *Lake Washington School District No. 414 Evaluation of Certified Teachers: Evaluative Checklist*

Pre-observation Conference Date _____
Teacher Objective _____

	Satisfactory	Needs Improvement	Unsatisfactory	Comments

Criterion 1: Instructional Skill

1.1   Plans instruction
1.1.1 Identifies learning needs
1.1.2 Teaches curriculum
1.1.3 Develops plans
1.2   Implements planned objectives
1.2.1 Gives clear instructions
1.2.2 Assists student to develop work habits and study skills

Criterion 2: Classroom Management

2.1   Develops classroom procedures
2.2   Organizes the physical setting
2.3   Prepares materials
2.4   Exercises care for physical safety and mental health of student
2.5   Maintains record appropriate to level/subject
2.6   Maintains records as required by law, district and building
2.7   Organizes individual small group, or large group learning experiences

Criterion 3: Handling Student Discipline

3.1   Follows up disciplinary procedures
3.2   Encourages self-discipline
3.3   Recognizes conditions, develops and implements strategies
3.4   Makes known to student clear parameters for pupil conduct
3.5   Deals consistently and fairly with students
3.6   Enlists assistance

Criterion 4: Interest in Teaching Pupils

4.1   Develops rapport with students
4.2   Recognizes unique characteristics of each student
4.3   Guides learning

Criterion 5: Effort Toward Improvement When Needed

5.1   Continually assesses self
5.2   Acknowledges recommendations

Criterion 6: Knowledge of Subject Matter

6.1 Keeps abreast of new developments and ideas

6.2 Relates subject matter to general body of knowledge

Criterion 7: Professional Preparation and Scholarship

7.1 Possesses and maintains academic background

Signature of Evaluator	Date	Signature of person being evaluated	Date

(Both signatures are required. Signing acknowledges participation in, but not necessarily concurrence with, evaluation conference.)

Source: A. Wise, L. Darling-Hammond, M. W. McLaughlin, and H. T. Bernstein, "Case Studies for Teacher Evaluation: A Study of Effective Practices," a RAND Corporation Note (N-2133-NIE). Reprinted with permission.

Appraising the Performance of Teachers: Four Approaches

There are many performance appraisal instruments and inventories available. However, most evaluations rely on one or two techniques for collecting information on a teacher's performance. Direct observation of classroom teaching is the most widely used method. In addition, documentation and attestation, tests, and simulation are also other useful means of gathering relevant data on teacher performance.

Observation

The vast majority of teacher performance reviews that take place across the United States each year are done in the form of a one-time visit to observe the teacher in action, in his or her classroom. The observation approach is widely accepted in part because of its immediate appeal as being valid. After all, during an observation one can see teachers engaged in the most time-consuming aspect of their profession—teaching students.

Most districts develop a specific instrument or checklist of items to guide the observer in rating the teacher's performance. In the Lake Washington School District (see Figure 8.4), teachers being evaluated are observed three times during the school year by the site administrator. These observations are guided by the checklist. However, each observation is preceded and followed by a conference between the teacher and administrator.

The advantages of using behavioral observations to assess performance are obvious. Observations are specific and lend themselves readily to data for feedback. Moreover, they focus on a very important aspect of the job: actual classroom teaching. Nonetheless, observation as a basis for generating information upon which to evaluate the performance of teachers has some drawbacks. One disadvantage is that a few observations, lasting anywhere from 20 to 50 minutes, cannot possibly reflect a teacher's competence. An observer may not be able to see the most relevant behavior in a few sessions. For example, no student discipline problems may arise or the session may not provide adequate insight into the teacher's knowledge of subject matter—especially at the elementary school level where teachers are responsible for all areas of the curriculum. Another limitation is that direct classroom observation may not reveal anything but a number of important aspects of teaching beyond classroom instruction, for instance, lesson planning, curriculum development and adaptation, relating to students and parents, or helping colleagues. Finally, observation tends to focus on the "stand-up-and-teach" model of instruction, which is a teacher-centered (see the study at the end of this chapter) rather than a student/learner-centered model.

In combination with other documentation on teacher performance, observations can provide both valid and reliable information (if the observer has been trained and the instrument is well-designed). As mentioned earlier, most teacher evaluations are carried out by administrators. With the trend toward peer coaching (see Chapter Seven), some schools are moving toward models of peer evaluation. The Orion School (see the case study at the end of this chapter) is one of the growing number of examples of this trend. At present, teacher associations are beginning to move away from their previous reluctance to involve teachers in the process of evaluating other teachers. The starting point has generally involved mentor/consultant teachers in supporting and evaluating new teachers (see Chapter Seven).

Documentation and Attestation

Less frequently used to assess the performance of teachers, but nonetheless an important source of information, is documentation or testimony provided by the teacher, colleagues, administrators, mentors, and students. Documentation and attestation are usually linked to observation, such as videotaping a teacher's performance. Where videotaping is not possible, mentors or colleagues who have observed another in action can provide testimony regarding competence.

Documentation reaches beyond the act of teaching. Teaching involves planning, assembling special materials, and developing and adapting the curriculum. These aspects of the job are often best demonstrated as a collection of written documents that a teacher has compiled over time. Lesson plans and curriculum can be readily presented to an evaluator—although these have not been systematically used as evidence of performance. Documentation portfolios are likely to include such artifacts as lesson plans, examples of student work with teacher comments, videotapes of teaching, observer's notes, and commentaries by mentor teachers.

Testing

Recently, in the sweep of a national concern with educational quality and the preparedness of teachers, written tests such as the California Basic Educational Skills Test (CBEST) have been used to screen potential teachers on mastery of basic skills and specific subject matter knowledge prior to entry into the profession. Although tests are being used and advocated as an entry bar, they should not be the only criterion of competence. Periodic tests (every 5 to 10 years) may also be useful for evaluating tenured teachers' competence over the subject matter, which may have changed considerably since the time of their initial university education. Some would argue that this may be one relevant criterion upon which to base merit increases (see Chapter Four).

Simulation

Teaching has hardly experimented with simulation as a method of evaluating a teacher's performance, as in medicine, business, and other fields, but this may be a wave of the future. With the current interest in establishing a National Board of Professional Teaching Standards, as advocated by Shulman and Sykes (1986) and others (see the discussion of external review in the next section of this chapter), simulation could play an important role in the evaluation process. An example of a simulated teaching assessment might involve teaching a mock class before a group of observers/assessors.

The Performance Appraisal Process

The preceding discussion of performance appraisal techniques focused on different methods of obtaining information for evaluating performance. Some techniques are based on output measures of performance, others are based on the judgment of significant others regarding performance, and still others are based on self-evaluations. At this point, we will consider the performance appraisal process itself. Some of the reasons why performance appraisal is anxiety provoking to so many people (managers as well as employees) are rooted in ineptly conducted appraisals rather than the particular technique that was used. In the final analysis, whatever appraisal method is chosen, how it is put into motion will largely affect the efficacy of the process as well as its acceptance by both management and employees.

Performance appraisal requires sensitivity and well-developed interpersonal skills on the part of the rater vis-à-vis the employee being appraised. These skills can be learned, and an organization can either support or undermine the process with the resources it devotes to the development and recurrent implementation of the appraisal system.

Several of the choices that must be made regarding a performance appraisal system have already been examined—what should be appraised and how the appraisal data should be generated. Other equally important considerations are Who should be responsible for conducting the appraisal? When should appraisal occur? and What are the optimal conditions for assessing performance?

Evaluators

There are several key candidates for the role of teacher evaluator. Traditionally, evaluation has been the purview of the school principal or deputy principals. In this chapter, and in Chapter Seven, considerable attention has focused on the possibilities for involving teachers in generating information and giving feedback on classroom teaching performance to their peers. Mentor teachers are sometimes involved in the evaluation of first-year and non-tenured faculty. Some districts have gone so far as to use peer evaluations as the basis for recommending rehire and tenure (see Box 8.1).

Another approach is to involve the teacher in his or her own evaluation process, usually in conjunction with an administrator, mentor, or group of colleagues. There are numerous varieties of this approach. The strict *self-assessment model* relies on the teacher to self-report his or her accomplishments during the evaluation period and also to identify areas of difficulty and needs for professional growth. The self-assessment model assumes a high degree of trust between the teacher and site-level manager, as well as a strong sense of professionalism and knowledge of what constitutes professional competence as a teacher.

A self-assessment combined with an administrative or collegial assessment is called the *cooperative assessment method.* Management by objectives (MBO) relies on a cooperative assessment approach, which is closely linked to the larger processes of organizational management. McConkie (1979) describes MBO performance appraisal as a process of bringing together organizational goals with individual employee work objectives, as mutually agreed upon by employees and managers. These objectives are specific, measurable, time bounded and stated in a written action plan. Progress towards goal attainment is measured in appraisal sessions which center on mutually determined criteria. Regardless of the degree of the formality or informality, the cooperative assessment method consists of three steps: (1) the teacher and administrators mutually set performance goals; (2) there is freedom for the teacher to pursue these goals during a specified period following the goal-setting exercise; and (3) performance with regard to achieving the goals is reviewed jointly by the teacher and administrator at the end of the preestablished time period.

MBO performance appraisals depend largely on the effectiveness of the goal-setting process. When goals are clear, measurable, and specific, the employee and supervisor have little difficulty with the third step of the appraisal process (i.e., reviewing performance vis-à-vis goals). If the goals are ambiguous or difficult to measure, problems may arise. Another area at issue is the degree of consistency between individual employees' goals and broader organizational goals. Bernardin and Beatty (1984) report that although individual employee objectives can be made consistent with the organization's goals, they are not a substitute for them. All teachers in a school system may have obtained their goals

BOX 8.1 • *Cincinnati Public Schools Peer Assistance Program*

History

The Peer Appraisal evolved from an agreement between the Cincinnati Federation of Teachers and the Cincinnati Public Schools in the 1985 collective bargaining contract. Functioning initially as a pilot program, a Peer Review Panel composed of four teachers appointed by the union and four administrators appointed by the superintendent developed guidelines for the program. During the second year of the pilot program these guidelines were revised and the Peer Review Panel was expanded to include ten members—five teachers and five administrators. After two pilot years, the program was extended districtwide.

Purpose

The Peer Assistance and Appraisal Program has two components. The first is an Intern review component, which seeks to assist teachers in their first year in the Cincinnati Public Schools by helping them to refine teaching skills and providing orientation to the Cincinnati district, including its goals, curriculum, and structure. Each intern is assigned a consulting teacher who observes classroom teaching, meets regularly with the intern, and provides assessment information to the Peer Review Panel on a regularly specified basis. The evaluations of the consulting teacher are ultimately used to determine renewal or nonrenewal of the intern teacher's contract and/or to recognize outstanding performance.

The second element is referred to as the Intervention component. It seeks to assist experienced teachers who exhibit serious teaching deficiencies. Teachers requiring intervention are assigned a consulting teacher who works with them to improve their instructional skills to a satisfactory level of performance. A clear system for referring teachers with an appeals process is part of the intervention component. The intervention procedures include a diagnosis by the consulting intervention process and a time table for improvement. If improvement occurs in accord with the designated time table, the teacher is removed from the intervention program by the Peer Review Panel upon recommendation of the consulting teacher, recommended for further assistance through the intervention process, or designated for dismissal.

Source: Adapted from Cincinnati Public Schools Peer Assistance and Appraisal Program Guidelines, November 1988.

under an MBO system, but the school system itself may not have reached its goals. For example, many teachers may have set and reached goals concerning such aspects of the job as planning, managing, and organizing instruction; providing a favorable psychological environment for learning; or increasing reading levels by two months. Generally, self-assessment and cooperative assessment techniques do not permit inter-employee performance comparisons, nor do they yield any type of quantifiable measure of performance, but they have been used with success in some states (e.g., Texas) since the mid-1980s.

The idea of *external assessment* (i.e., by qualified experts outside the school and local district) is an approach to evaluation that has been often used for programs and schools, but yet to be applied to evaluating individual teachers. The growing attention to teacher professionalism has provoked discussion of the possibilities of creating an external assessment board, such as the National Board of Professional Teaching Standards. Such a board, according to Shulman and Sykes (1986), would be engaged in certification of excellence rather than licensure of minimal competence. It would rely on expertise and professional support rather than function as a legal regulator, based on the assumption that such a body is most likely to achieve its purposes of creating professional standards of excellence when it supports voluntary assessment and certification.

Client Evaluators

At the postsecondary level, students are routinely asked to evaluate instructors. Their evaluations may weigh considerably in faculty retention and promotion decisions. However, very few precollegiate districts involve students in any aspect of the teacher evaluation process. We believe that students at the secondary level and possibly upper-primary level should be encouraged to provide feedback that is well structured and in line with specific criteria that are understandable by the students. This would constitute an added information source for performance evaluation (discussed more fully in Chapter Nine).

Frequency of Evaluation

The frequency of the performance appraisal is yet another key aspect of its success. The labor-management contract usually specifies the frequency with which formal evaluations on non-tenured and tenured teachers must take place. Requirements vary from district to district, mandating evaluation as often as once annually for tenured teachers to as infrequently as every three to four years. First-year teachers and experienced teachers new to the district are often evaluated more frequently than tenured staff. Although formal appraisals may not be possible more often than once a year, a well-managed school will create informal opportunities for feedback on a consistent and regular basis (see Chapter Seven). Goal-driven appraisal systems like MBO tend to engage in performance appraisals that coincide with the work flow and cycle of projects and programs in the organization rather than occurring at regular six-month or annual intervals. Other approaches can be segmented. In the educational system, teacher performance tends to be evaluated less frequently than the performance of professionals in other service-oriented occupations. This may be an indication that more emphasis needs to be given to the role of performance evaluation in school-site management and improvement.

Conditions of Evaluation

The conditions under which the performance appraisal occurs are particularly important to control. If a behavior observation technique is going to be used—as is common with classroom teachers—it is important to schedule the observation(s) in advance with the teacher, for a limited time period, and at a time when the observation is likely to be free from as much outside contamination as possible. The same holds true for a performance appraisal interview between a principal or peer evaluator and the teacher. The interview should be scheduled for a time without other pressing matters and should be carried out without interruptions. It is essential that employees be aware of how they are being appraised prior to the appraisal. This usually is carried out via a preappraisal interview to discuss the objectives of the appraisal, review the dimensions being appraised, and familiarize the employee with the appraisal process.

The most sensitive and important part of the appraisal process comes when the evaluator and the teacher sit down, face to face, to discuss the results of the appraisal. This is the performance appraisal interview that many administrators dread as much, if not more than, the evaluatees. Evaluators can be trained to conduct more effective performance appraisal interviews. The purpose of the interview should always be clarified by the evaluator before discussing the substance. There are several formats for the interview: sandwich, spinach, and dessert. In the *sandwich format,* the evaluator inserts areas for improvement between slices of praise. The *spinach format* discusses all the weaknesses at the beginning of the interview so that the teacher does not sit on pins and needles waiting for the bomb to drop, and has the further advantage of ending the interview concentrating on strengths. Finally, the *dessert format* begins the interview by emphasizing the employee's strengths, and ends with a discussion of areas in need of improvement followed by an improvement plan. These suggested formats work for many evaluators, however, each principal should develop a style with which he or she is comfortable. Chances are that if the evaluator is comfortable, the employee will also feel at ease.

Experienced evaluators know how to phrase criticism constructively. The evaluator should give a concrete suggestion on how to improve each area of weakness, so that the teacher can take action in the following appraisal period. Some school systems insist on a thorough ongoing improvement plan devised and agreed upon by both employee and evaluator (and the school administrator if different from the evaluator). The principal should try to balance the amount of talking done by both parties during the interview. The 50–50 principle is a good guideline. If the evaluator is doing more than half the talking then he or she should pull back and attempt to draw the employee into the process.

In the Orion School (see the case study at the end of this chapter), the appraisal session has become the responsibility of a group of teachers rather than a single evaluator. This is extremely useful in terms of providing the teacher with multiple perspectives on his or her performance, as well as increasing the reliability of feedback. Because the Redwood City School District, where Orion is located, takes the position that effective evaluators are generally made, not born, it has chosen to devote considerable time and resources to develop its cooperative assessment model.

Summary

Teacher evaluation is a complex process. In general, schools devote too little time and attention to defining, structuring, and supporting effective evaluation procedures. Multiple sources of information regarding the performance of teachers is of the utmost importance, given the complexity of the teaching enterprise. Buy-in and support by teachers within the district for the evaluation procedure is also extremely important. Training of evaluators, whether they are administrators, mentor teachers, or colleagues, and adequate time to carry out an evaluation are also important requisites for success. Perhaps most critical, however, is a mutual understanding by teachers and administrators that evaluation is a process for the purpose of providing feedback for professional growth.

The tension between the developmental and appraisal aspects of an evaluation process can never be completely eliminated. Some districts are choosing to disassociate with peer-review programs of individual teacher performance from the formal evaluation process required in most district contracts (see the case study at the end of this chapter). Others districts, such as in Cincinnati, are linking peer assistance to the performance review process of special categories of teachers (i.e., interns and nonperforming tenured teachers). Both programs emphasize the feedback developmental function of evaluation, although only the Cincinnati model incorporates the accountability function as well.

The other key aspects of this chapter focus on program and schoolwide evaluation as an important task of the school management team. Involving site personnel in programmatic evaluations is an effective way to build organization circle awareness. Even when evaluations are being conducted by an external body, site-level personnel can be actively involved in preparing for the evaluation. In this respect, the organizationwide evaluations have a strong formative/developmental aspect that pushes the school in the direction of self-evaluation. Engaging in an effective evaluation process is dependent on creating an organizational attitude that is receptive to feedback/evaluation. This type of attitude tends to emerge in situations where working relationships are based on trust and mutual respect, and where there is leadership pushing for growth and excellence at all levels—individual, program, and organization.

Case Study _____

Orion School: A Cooperative Teacher Assessment Model

(Authors' note: This case illustrates one of many possible arrangements for introducing more collegiality into the performance appraisal process. Keeping the case in mind, devise a

peer coaching plan for your school or one with which you are fa-
miliar. What are some of the immediate logistical problems you
might encounter? What would be possible objections or sources
of resistance to this approach? How might you overcome these?
Do you think that it is necessary to separate peer coaching from
the formal performance appraisal process as described at Orion
School? Teachers' unions often insist on this. Why? How, if at all,
does the collegial model of performance appraisal used in higher
education, as well as other professions, apply to the K–12 school
system?)

Background

Orion School is a K–6 alternative school established in 1984
in the Redwood City School District. The school has 140 students
(1987–88), five full-time teachers, and one resource teacher who
serves as a half-time administrator. Parents elect to send their children to Orion School because it offers an open-structured, hands-
on, student-centered learning environment. The students come
from a cross-section of the Redwood City community. About 30
percent of the children are minorities, which is slightly below the
district average. However, Hispanic students are underrepre-
sented.

Orion's Cooperative Assessment Model

Five years ago, the teachers at Orion "dreamed-up" a peer-
coaching approach to assessment, with the assistance of a district
consultant. Because the school size is so small, arranging release
time for teachers to observe each other in action was discarded by
the staff as an unworkable option. Soon, however, the group hit
upon an alternative: videotaping demonstration lessons that could
be viewed by the teacher actually teaching the lesson as well as by
all other colleagues.

During the first year, while developing cooperative assessment, the teachers operated with borrowed equipment. They began by trying to work with Madaline Hunter's model to format an
assessment model (i.e., criteria) and help prepare demonstration
lessons. The Hunter model, however, was not appropriate for the
school's student-centered instructional approach. As a spinoff
from an unrelated staff development workshop, the teachers
serendipitously began to experiment with other approaches that
more closely approximated the type of teaching strengths they

were trying to develop as a school faculty as well as individual classroom teachers. Because they were not within the "stand-up-and-teach" approach, the staff eventually came up with a choice of five lesson types that could be used for the videotape sessions: concept development, information acquisition, values clarification, problem solving, and skill-building lessons.

The Process

Videotaped assessments take place two times each year for each teacher. Each assessment follows a clearly defined procedure that has been developed and agreed upon by the teachers themselves. It is a five-step process. First, the teacher being assessed chooses and develops a lesson to be filmed. The lesson should be directed at values clarification, problem solving, or skill building. Teachers estimate that this takes an average of two hours. Then the teacher meets with a colleague he or she selects for a planning session prior to the actual videotaping. During this session the two teachers discuss the classification of the demonstration lesson as well as its objectives and techniques. Frequently the demonstration teacher will walk through the lesson with the colleague, who will ask questions about different aspects of the lesson. This planning session helps the demonstration teacher to think the lesson through more carefully before it is actually taught and videotaped. Generally, planning sessions last from 30 to 45 minutes.

The third step in the cooperative assessment process is actually teaching the lesson, which is videotaped. The video work is done by a person from the district office with special skills in this area. The availability of only one person with adequate technical skills to do the video recording currently limits the extent to which the procedure can be used. Increasingly, the taped sessions have focused on the teacher and a subgroup of students rather than the entire class, due to the technical problems associated with getting good quality video for an entire class (e.g., noise, confusion, and interruptions). The taping session typically runs about one hour in length.

Following the video session, the teacher personally views the demonstration lesson. This prescreening gives the teacher an opportunity to edit out and target in on parts of the tape with greatest relevance for the group assessment. It also offers the teacher the option of a retake if he or she is not satisfied with the initial results. Retakes however, are rare. The prescreening usually takes the teacher about one hour.

Finally, the entire faculty of six teachers meets for a cooperative group assessment session. The group views the video together. Using criteria for the particular category of lesson, they give the teacher feedback on his or her performance. These sessions concentrate on strengths as well as areas for improvement. The sessions and the video recordings are not part of the annual performance review required under union contract with the district for all teachers. The processes are completely independent.

Results

The resource teacher, Wilda Gardella, believes that the cooperative assessment model has several very important advantages over the one-to-one observation model of peer coaching. First, the teacher receives feedback from several colleagues rather than just one. Second, the lesson serves as a model and learning experience for the colleagues engaged in giving feedback. When new teachers have joined the staff of Orion, demonstration lessons have been taped with the primary objective of modeling teaching. Gardella says, "I truly believe [that] collegiality develops in the conferences among the teachers." Observations of one staff session revealed a high degree of supportiveness by colleagues and acceptance of suggestions by the teacher.

Gardella thinks that the video approach may not be as time efficient as the one-to-one peer-classroom observation approach, but believes that the benefits outweigh the added time. The greatest problem in working with the video approach relates to the technology of using the video itself: Equipment is limited, and there is only one person in the district with adequate filming skills. The school is developing a video for the school board, in which the cooperative assessment approach is demonstrated. Gardella says that the board, which has been very supportive of their effort, has seen relatively little of what they are doing and the teachers want to provide them with a sample of what is happening.

References

Beer, M. "Performance Appraisal: Dilemmas and Possibilities." *Organizational Dynamics* (Winter 1981):142–155.

Bernardin, H. J., and Beatty, R. W. *Performance Appraisal: Assessing Human Behavior at Work.* Boston: Kent, 1984.

Bridges, E. *The Incompetent Teacher.* Philadelphia: Falmer, 1986.

Cincinnati Federation of Teachers. "Cincinnati Public Schools Peer Assistance and Appraisal Programs Guidelines." Memorandum, 1988.

Cook, D. "A Design for Program Evaluation." *Thrust* (February/March 1988):41–43.

Darling-Hammond, L.; Wise, A. E.; and Pease, S. R. "Teacher Evaluation in Organizational Context: A Review of the Literature." *Review of Educational Research* 53 (Fall 1983):285–328.

Evans, J. W. "Is Educational Evaluation Dying?" *Evaluation Comment* 7 (December 1984).

Hunter, M. "Competency: Problem and Theory." *Theory to Practice* 15 (April 1976):62–71.

McConkie, M. C. "A Classification of the Goal-Setting and Appraisal Process in MBO." *Academy of Management Review* 4 (1979):29–40.

Shulman, L., and Sykes, G. *A National Board for Teaching? In Search of a Bold Standard.* Paper prepared for the Task Force on Teaching as a Profession, Carnegie Forum on Education and the Economy, May 1986.

Timar, T., and Kirp, D. L. "State Efforts to Reform Schools: Treading Between a Regulatory Swamp and an English Garden." *Educational Evaluation and Policy Analysis* 10 (Summer 1988).

Turner, R. R. "What Teachers Think about Their Evaluations." *Learning* 86 (February 1987):40–43.

Wise, A.; Darling-Hammond, L.; McLaughlin, M. W.; and Bernstein, H. T. "Case Studies for Teacher Evaluation: A Study of Effective Practices." A RAND Note, 1984.

CHAPTER NINE

Managing School-Community Relationships

Introduction

Although students, parents, and school board members are tied together through their direct involvement with schools, the wider community is also part of the school's constituency. There are varying degrees and numerous ways in which the school is connected to the community—through school boards, PTAs, and site councils. It is not unfair to say that some schools exist in their communities without being closely connected to them. In urban areas, court-ordered desegregation has created a pattern of nonneighborhood-based clients in many schools. Children are bused out of their own neighborhoods to attend schools across the city. Consequently the neighborhood does not necessarily identify closely with the schools located within its boundaries. Some communities resent or resist schools—especially secondary schools. Businesses fear the potential consequences of thousands of unsupervised adolescents moving in and out on a daily basis. Residents see secondary schools as disruptive in terms of noise, traffic congestion, and the potential for illegal activities, especially drugs. Given the extent to which schools rely on members of the community, some of whom are not parents, to support them through their voice in public policy, schools cannot afford to alienate the community or to remain aloof and detached.

Connecting the community and the schools is often a tough task. Dennis Chaconas, principal of Oakland Technical High School, illustrates the commitment and strong community relations orientation that are necessary to build this important tie. Built in 1915 after the great San Francisco earthquake, Oakland Technical High School was hailed as an architectural classic and flourished for decades, first as a vocational-technically oriented high school and later as an academic institution. The school's image became a problem after 1961, when district boundaries were redrawn to make room for a newly constructed high school that began to syphon off a growing segment of Tech's student clientele. The school became increasingly racially and socioeconomically unbalanced and the campus rocked with protests during the Civil Rights era. In 1976, the school was moved from its original campus because of earthquake regulations. Sited on a temporary substandard campus, the enrollment declined from 1,800 to 900 and was nearly 100 percent minority.

When the original campus, refurbished to meet earthquake standards, was about to open in September 1983, the school's ingrained reputation in the community preceded its move. In an interview, Principal Chaconas said that the community had not been accustomed to having a school there. "When we came in, we had a community meeting with business and homeowners to tell them about how we were coming back and how we wanted a community partnership. We asked them what would make them feel better, and some of them said, 'We don't want the school to reopen.' I responded, 'Well, I know that's not going to happen, because we just spent $10 million to fix the school, but okay, I'll patrol everyday at lunch. I'll work with you guys, and if you have a problem, you call me. I have a walkie-talkie and I'll be there in two minutes.' So I'm doing it."

Chaconas has kept his promise. Daily at 12:15, he gets into his Jeep and drives around the campus perimeter, looking for trouble spots in the neighborhoods. He stops into local businesses regularly to make sure things are okay and he follows up on complaints. Chaconas sees the neighborhood as a little city within the larger community. One of his largest concerns is enforcing the city ordinance that prevents nonstudents from loitering in the vicinity of a school. If he sees a 21-year-old talking to one of the 13-year-old students, he calls the parents saying, "Look, maybe this is none of my business, but are you aware of this?" Almost every time the parents say, "No, I am not, thanks for calling." In response, the community now takes the initiative to call the school when they believe students may be acting disruptively.

Because of his good-neighbor policy, the school can count on the community. Businesses willingly donate materials and services to help augment both regular and extracurricular programs. They have also become increasingly involved in building stronger links with the students who may become their future employees. A Labor Education Week was jointly sponsored by the local trade unions and the school. The editor of the local newspaper speaks regularly to the high school journalism class.

As an educator, Chaconas is primarily concerned with the students. "I think we need more [financial] resources, but I don't think we're using the resources we have in creative and flexible ways. . . . I try to look at education as a business and think of each kid as a client, and I want him to graduate and go on and tell everyone what a great school Tech is." This principal feels strongly that the public hasn't really come to grips with what it wants from education. He argues that test scores are only one aspect. What about driver's education, sports, and job training? Oakland Tech is a turn-around school. When asked why the school has succeeded, the principal says, "I think this can work anywhere, if people go after it, but unless you create an environment and try to meet the kids' needs, they won't be willing to come in. Then you'll be out of business."

Professionalizing the work environment of teachers and creating a collaborative school management team involving teachers and site administrators increases a school's responsiveness to student needs. This chapter concentrates on managing the relationships between key constituencies of the schools: parents and the wider community. Closely related to the issue of client responsiveness is the issue of making schools more organizationally responsive to the needs of the students by examining the relationship between professionals and clients as well as how schools can restructure themselves to better meet client needs.

Community Involvement and Client Responsiveness

Recent studies of especially effective organizations in the private sector suggest that client involvement and client responsiveness are related. One of the most salient characteristics of successful companies is that they are preeminently occupied with being "close to the customer" (see Peters and Waterman, 1982). In fact, the former editor-in-chief of *Business Week*, Lew Young, said:

> *Probably the most important management fundamental that is being ignored today is staying close to the customer to satisfy his needs and anticipate his wants. In too many companies, the customer has become a bloody nuisance whose unpredictable behavior damages carefully made strategic plans, whose activities mess up computer operations, and who stubbornly insists that purchased products should work. (Peters and Waterman, 1982, p. 156)*

Schools do not have customers per se; instead, like most service-oriented organizations, they have clients. A *client* is defined by *Webster's New Collegiate* dictionary as "a person under the protection of another; a person who engages the professional advice or services of another, and a person served by or utilizing the services of a social agency." In the case of public schools, student clients are defined both by the concept of being persons under the protection of another and as persons served by a social agency. Public schools, with few exceptions, do not select their clients, as do private companies and some social service agencies. They are mandated to accept all the children of a specified age group residing within a defined geographic location.

Also, unlike other social service agencies, such as hospitals and welfare bureaus, schools have more broadly drawn goals and social functions: (1) transmitting knowledge and skills in both the broad sociocultural and the narrow job-oriented sense; (2) socializing the next generation in terms of values, attitudes, and behaviors that prepare them to function in and accept the existing social relations of the society into which they are born (Bowles and Gintis, 1976; Carnoy and Levin, 1976); and (3) providing safe, supervised custodial care for children in the absence of their parents. Not only are these roles for schools extremely wide reaching, but they are conflict ridden, competing with each other for limited time and scarce resources. For example, providing a broad sociocultural knowledge base through the school curriculum competes with job-specific training, and intensifying the efforts to increase student learning is increasingly in competition with funds for extending the custodial care service provided by schools, such as before- and after-school programs.

Another complication schools face when dealing with the challenge of trying to be "close to their customers" is the great diversity of their clientele. Unlike private businesses and service agencies, public schools have not tailored their services to a specific or limited segment of the entire market for schooling. They are faced with a highly diverse clientele and a legal mandate to provide equal opportunity for all. This has involved compensating for segments of that clientele which have not had equal access to educational services in the past. To do so, in large part, schools have responded not by organizational restructuring, but by developing special programs, such as compensatory education, Title I, special education, and bilingual education. However, the basic relationships between teachers and students as well as among teachers themselves remain unaltered. Moreover, the traditional "one teacher, one classroom" model of learning primarily through the "listen and learn" or "read and learn" modes of instruction prevail (Goodlad, 1984). This limitation will be discussed later in this chapter when we examine the question of restructuring the school for client responsiveness.

Models of Constituent Relationships

Schools have several important constituencies. Strictly speaking, a *constituent* is someone who authorizes another to act on his or her behalf. Parents and the wider community are key constituent groups for schools. Parents authorize schools to educate their children (the schools' clients), and school boards authorize schools to implement school policy. The wider community is also a constituency of the schools in that it is a group involved in or served by an organization. Although none of these constituencies partake directly of the school's educational services, each has a strong vested interest in how and what services are provided to the student clientele. Concern with constituencies is very important for schools from a resource and operational perspective. Moreover, there are distinctive relationships between organizations and their constituencies. Below we examine three such models: the professional/client model, the advocacy model, and the partnership model.

Professional/Client Model

The professional/client model is based on the assumption that education is a specialized service to be delivered by professionals (teachers) to clients (students). The professional/client model assumes that the professional has knowledge and expertise, and that the client wants or needs that knowledge and expertise. Moreover, the professional's training, knowledge, and experience place him or her in the position to diagnose client problems and needs and to prescribe appropriate action in response to those diagnoses. The client is fundamentally a passive recipient of the professional services. Moreover, diagnoses, judgments, and prescriptions are based on pertinent information gathered by the professional. The relationship between the professional and client is designated as impersonal and one that should be permeated by a certain degree of "scientific" objectivity.

The professional/client model delineates a specific configuration of participatory behaviors for clients. The motive for participation is the desire to acquire the professional's knowledge or expertise. In the case of schools, students are in attendance to learn what teachers are able to teach them. Parents send their children to school based on the premise that teachers possess knowledge and expertise that their children can learn. What is to be learned is generally not open to discussion with the clients.

Communication between professionals and clients—especially teachers and students—tends to be unidirectional. This holds for the relationship between the school and other constituent groups, particularly parents. Teachers (the professionals) are usually the initiators of communications, and parents (the clients) are respondents. Communication is organized around evaluative concerns or conveying information (e.g., what will be covered and expected during the school via an open house or back-to-school night; learning problems a student might be having; report cards; etc.).

There is very little room for the initiation of action on the part of the client in the professional/client model. The client is expected to act in response to directives of the professional, but usually not the reverse. In terms of the distribution of power, the professional—especially in the public school setting—tries to retain most of the power. In a marketplace setting, clients may seek another professional if they are dissatisfied with the services delivered. However, in the realm of education, there are few genuine alternatives. In summary, the professional/client model commonly found in public schools does not always stimulate active or sustained parent participation.

Advocacy Model

The advocacy model implies a far more activist stance on the part of constituents than does the professional/client model. It concentrates on political participation rather than participation in the educational process itself. The primary emphasis of the parent participation movement of the 1960s and early 1970s was focused on the issue of involvement in decision making at the school site and the school district levels. The motive underpinning the demand for involvement in decision making came from the parental perspective that decisions were being made against the interests of their children, whether these were decisions regarding curriculum, use of funds, hiring of teachers, or school discipline policy.

Communication between the school and its constituents

changes dramatically in the advocacy model. Parents may band together and communicate with the school as an organized group rather than through individual client/teacher contacts. Moreover, clients are likely to be the instigators of communication. These communications are frequently formulated as critiques or demands. Occasionally, advocacy groups form to defend a specific school against actions or policies of the district administration. Recent instances have been associated with advocacy groups protesting the closing of neighborhood schools in districts with declining enrollments. The political mobilization that characterizes the advocacy model is often generated by emotionally charged issues such as sex education or busing.

Participation through advocacy is difficult to sustain, however. It functions primarily as an opposition force rather than in support of positive educational processes or reforms, and it operates in a political arena rather than as part of the school organization. Also, constituents involved in forms of participation that involve advocacy usually represent a small proportion of the total school constituency. By forming a political base, advocacy groups attempt to shift the balance of power away from the school. This may be effective temporarily, but the long-term adversarial approaches to power sharing are difficult to perpetuate in the face of well-institutionalized educational bureaucracies. From the perspective of school management, advocacy groups can be troublesome. The partnership model presents an alternative to both the advocacy and professional/client models.

Partnership Model

The partnership model of participation occurs when home, school, and community members collaborate to produce educational achievement with shared initiative and responsibilities (Seeley, 1982). This is in contrast to the professional/client model (where the primary relationships are derived from the delivery of educational services by professional staff to students, parents, and the community) and the politicized advocacy model.

The partnership model relies heavily on self-interest as the compelling motive of parents and other community groups to participate in school-related activities. Partnerships expand participation to include almost everyone—students, parents, teachers, administrators, citizens, businesses, and local organizations of all kinds. All interested individuals are viewed as useful and able to help improve educational quality.

Partnerships emphasize involvement where the point of interest is greatest, rather than concentrating specifically on decision making or particular areas of educational policy. Although parental demands to participate in decision making are understandable when parents feel that decisions are being made against their childrens' best interest, if this is not the case, parents and community groups tend to focus their participatory energy on other domains of action, such as providing additional educational and financial resources, homework support, and direct support of their childrens' classroom teacher.

The distribution of power within the partnership model is closely aligned with the division of labor that evolves among the various members of the partnership. District or school-specific educational foundations—a relatively new approach to fund raising—are organized and administered by community members. The involvement of school personnel is of an advisory nature. For example, the foundation for Kensington-Hilltop Elementary School in California's Richmond Unified School District is controlled by a foundation board and operates in close conjunction with the principal of the school (see the case study at the end of Chapter Six). Together, the board and the principal play complementary roles: The principal indicates the priority school needs and the board works in the community to raise money. In this partnership the board and the principal are the two main partners; each has a distinct role and responsibility.

Benefits of Community Involvement

The school effectiveness movement has focused primarily on successful factors within the school (instructional leadership, orderliness, etc.). Relatively less attention has been given to the external factors that exert a powerful influence over individual student achievement and the general organizational effectiveness of schools. Community involvement in the schools brings benefits in four important areas: student achievement, incremental resources to supplement and complement the existing program, opportunities for staff renewal and organizational innovation, and political support. The nature of these benefits is examined below.

Student Achievement

Ample evidence demonstrates that when parents of students are constructively involved, individual student and organizational performance are augmented. The National Committee for Citizens in Education has reviewed 35 studies related to parent participation and concluded that parent involvement—in almost any form, from classroom tutoring to recess supervision—improves student achievement (Henderson, 1981).

Evaluations of preschool programs where intensive forms of parent involvement have been tried also show that participation can have positive effects on children. Head Start programs typically find that the children of highly involved parents retain their learning gains better than children of parents who do not have high levels of participation. One study found that there were significant IQ gains for children whose parents were involved. These gains are attributed primarily to changes in the parents' perceptions of themselves as teachers of their own children (Seeley, 1982). In a study of second- and third-grade classrooms that were part of the Early Childhood Education program funded by Title I, Herman and Yeh (1983) found that parent participation is positively related to both student achievement and parent satisfaction with the school.

Added Resources

The closest and most obvious constituency within the community is parents. However, other important constituencies include the business community, institutions of higher education, private voluntary organizations, and external foundations.

Each of these constituencies has important resources to offer the school. Parents and voluntary agencies may mobilize volunteers to help with special events such as field trips, or with ongoing school programs such as tutoring or a homework hotline. The business community is also a rich resource. Not only will businesses make in-kind and financial contributions to schools in their community but they can supplement the school's academic program through field-placement opportunities for students who are participating in special academic programs.

School-university partnerships are another form of school-community collaboration. Partnerships have taken various forms: special after-school and summer school programs for minority students as well as enrichment programs for gifted students; professional development programs for teachers and principals (see Box 9.1); and school-specific programs in areas such as curriculum and instruction, evaluation, and classroom management.

Foundations have traditionally played a role in providing financial resources to education. In the past, foundations tended to concentrate their efforts on educationally related research and programs connected with university-school partnerships. More recently, some foundations have begun to make grants directly to individual schools as well as school districts for innovative and special programs. In some states, educational foundations serving specific school districts or in some instances a single school have been established to raise tax-exempt resources from the community for direct allocation to schools (see Chapter Six). Resources of this kind provide schools with discretionary funds for programs that the district is unable to support from its general budget.

Staff Renewal and Innovation

School-community partnerships can be an important source for innovation and renewal. The availability of outside resources (e.g., educational foundations and university-sponsored programs) creates an outside impetus and incentive for innovation sometimes difficult to mobilize within the school itself. Moreover, these partnerships frequently provide renewal opportunities for school staff, such as a sabbatical in a computer software company for a mathematics teacher or peer training for an English teacher (see Chapter Eight).

Professional development can result from the collaboration between professional and constituent groups. At the Claire Lilienthal Alternative Elementary School in the San Francisco Unified School District, parents were anxious for computers to be introduced in the curriculum. However, the teaching staff had no computer experience. As a result of parental interest and the strong parent-school partnership at Lilienthal, the third-grade teacher decided to devote her half-year sabbatical to learning about computers. Upon return from the sabbatical, with a grant for release time, she trained her colleagues and led students in the use of computers. This type of professional-client involvement produced positive results for all concerned: teachers, students, and parents (see the case study at the end of this chapter).

Participation via partnerships can also extend to nonparent constituents. As part of an effort to make its school more responsive to the varied interests and needs of an inner-city predomi-

---

BOX 9.1 • *School-University Partnerships*

Overview of Project

There are a great many new teachers in SUPER schools this year—some new to teaching and some experienced teachers at new schools. Additionally, there are some new member schools in SUPER. To all of you: Welcome to the School-University Partnership for Educational Renewal (or SUPER Project as we are more commonly known).

To acquaint you with SUPER and encourage you to pursue your particular areas of interest and to take advantage of opportunities to collaborate with your colleagues, here are brief answers to some of the most commonly asked questions about SUPER, and some people to contact for more information.

What Is SUPER?

SUPER is a working partnership between the UC Berkeley Graduate School of Education and K–12 Clusters of schools in the Albany, Richmond, and Oakland Unified School Districts. SUPER also welcomes individual educators from other school districts who wish to participate in its activities.

What Is SUPER's Goal?

SUPER's goal is to work toward educational reform in five general areas: preservice and inservice professional education, school-site planning, practice-sensitive research, policy analysis and professional discourse, dissemination.

How Does SUPER Operate?

SUPER is administered collaboratively by UC-based participants and school-site based participants. The central coordinating group includes: Prof. Bernard R. Gifford, principal investigator of SUPER; Nina Hersch Gabelko, director; Carrie Brown, administrative assistant; Maureen Gravett, El Cerrito High School: Fran Paxson, Kensington Elementary School; Robin Davis, Albany Middle School; Ed Allen, Emerson Elementary School (Oakland); Charlene Kalagian, Stege Elementary School (Richmond). Additionally, each participating school has a School-Site Liaison who keeps the faculty informed about SUPER activities, and keeps SUPER Central informed about events at the school. As schools new to SUPER have not yet selected Liaisons, we will publish the completed list of SUPER representatives in the October issue of *SUPER News*.

If your school does not have a Liaison, and you would like more information about the job, please contact Maureen Gravett.

What Kinds of Activities Can I Participate In?

SUPER offers workshop series for teachers, counselors and administrators based on areas of interest articulated and developed by the participants. The first SUPER Saturday set of workshops this school year will be held October 7 at Albany Middle School. A flyer with workshop descriptions should have been placed in your school mailbox. See future issues of *SUPER News* for other SUPER Saturday dates.

SUPER offers monthly School-Change Seminars. The first seminar is being held October 12, from 5:30 to 7:30 p.m. As always, a light supper is offered from 5:30 to 6:00, the presentation runs from 6:00 to 7:00 p.m., with open discussion from 7:00 to 7:30 p.m. This month's topic is: The Looking Glass Self: Media Images of Minority Students. The featured speakers, who all work in media, are Lynn Kidder, Jesus Mena, Jr., and Johnny Barnes Selvin.

The topic of the November 9 SUPER Seminar is: An Update on Education from the Capitol. The featured Speaker is Assembly Member Tom Campbell.

Seminar dates for the year are:

October 12
November 9
January 11
February 8
March 8
April 12
May 10

How Can I Take a Leadership Role in SUPER?

Individuals participate in SUPER in a variety of ways. Some find that SUPER meets their professional needs by affording them opportunities to take part in workshops, attend seminars, and meet colleagues with similar interests. Others wish to develop their own capacity. They can do so in the following roles:

- *Partnership Fellow:* An individual who coordinates the SUPER activities for a Cluster of participating schools.
- *School-Site Liaison:* An individual who represents his or her school within SUPER at the school site.

Continued

BOX 9.1   *Continued*

- *Design Team Leader:* The chair of a team of educators who are interested in investigating a common area or problem. In previous years, there have been Design Teams in E.S.L. instruction, gifted and talented education, social studies education, and computer use in the classroom.
- Others take a leadership role in SUPER by offering hands-on workshops in a wide range of areas at SUPER Saturdays, by presenting points of view at SUPER Seminars, and by participating in SUPER-sponsored research projects.

For more information about any of these areas, please call the SUPER office.

What if I Want More Information?

Super Contacts
Prof. Bernard R. Gifford, P.I.

Nina Hersch Gabelko, Director

For general information:
Carrie Brown

For information about Liaisons, Partnership Fellows, SUPER Saturdays, special activities:
Maureen Gravett

SUPER Peer-Support Program:
Fran Paxson

SUPER Saturday Workshops:
Robin Davis and Charlene Kalagian

Newsletters, Publications, Seminars, Summer Institutes:
Carrie Brown

Source: SUPER News 6, no. 1 (October 1989). University of California, Berkeley. Reprinted with permission.

---

nantly minority client, Oakland Technical High School has initiated a health services major for students. It is based on a partnership with local health service agencies (public and private) who provide internships, speakers, and some instructional assistance for students enrolled in the program.

Partnerships between schools and the community work in two ways. The principal of Oakland Technical High School (see this chapter's opening vignette) makes participation on boards of various local business associations (realtors, retail merchants, etc.) part of his job description. This helps to bring members of the business community who do not have students enrolled in the school into a closer contact with the school. He also makes personal visits every month to businesses in the neighborhood surrounding the school in order to enhance community relations and troubleshoot any complaints. Furthermore, the school has initiated a semiannual open house during school hours for members of the local realtors' association to come and see for themselves what the school has to offer the children of prospective owners.

Political Support

A latent benefit of school-community collaboration is the political support that schools gain from increased interaction with the community. Schools are ultimately dependent on constituencies outside their organization for support in terms of public funding, so it is critical to strengthen the school's community base. Because a smaller proportion of the adult-population has school-aged children than in earlier decades, efforts must be made to involve community constituencies other than parents in the educational process. This involvement helps to build crucial political support for public education, not least of which is greater financial support from the local level.

Thus the evidence suggests that there are substantial benefits to be gained if schools involve the community in collaborative actions. Crucial to fostering involvement, and thereby heightening responsiveness, is a management system for school-community relations. The key aspects of such a system are discussed next.

Managing Involvement

Involvement does not just happen. It results from a well-orchestrated and constantly managed effort to build collaboration between the school and the community. Conditions for building involvement include tapping the desire for collaboration, time, focus, and a management system.

Desire for Involvement

There is strong evidence that indicates that both parents and teachers want parents to be involved in their children's education.

The National Education Association's survey of teachers found that over 90 percent of all teachers favor more home-school interaction than currently exists (NEA, 1981). Since 1969, Gallup has conducted an annual poll on attitudes toward education. Results show that teachers feel that many school problems can be solved only by involving parents in the educational process itself (Gallup, 1978).

Studies of parent attitudes toward involvement with their children's education indicate that parents are willing to participate in school-related matters. The Southwest Educational Development Laboratory studies show that, in general, parents are more interested in helping with the education of their *own children* than in decision making about school management (Seeley, 1982). For example, most parents would rather volunteer in their child's classroom than sit on a districtwide committee. In some instances, roles have been mandated by state and federal programs (e.g., School Improvement Councils and school-site compensatory education committees), giving parents a voice and access to programs and policy on a schoolwide basis.

Time

Time is commonly cited as the greatest obstacle to parent participation in school. Changes in the structure of the family, especially the substantial number of working mothers and the single-parent families, are repeatedly referred to as a primary obstacle to greater involvement in their children's education. In a synthesis of research on parent participation in their children's education, Moles (1982) found that working mothers and parents with low educational levels help with schoolwork and other forms of participation with student learning as much as mothers who are homemakers. Other studies also indicate that working mothers help their children with schoolwork and are equally active in school-related events as are homemaker mothers (Medrich and Roizen, 1982; Tangri and Leitch, 1982). Although working and single parents may be less able to help during school hours, their collaboration can be engaged at other times and in ways that do not always require their presence at the school site.

Focus

In spite of the desire to participate and the willingness to allocate time for home-school collaboration, studies also indicate that parents are unsure of their role as participants in schools (Williams, 1981). Although there are strong indications that parents would like to participate and that teachers desire more parental involvement, surveys, interviews with teachers, parents, and administrators indicate ambiguity regarding the general role of parents in collaborating with schools and their specific role in such activities as the completing of homework assignments (Seeley, 1982). Even though teachers clearly indicate that they desire more parental help with homework and tutoring under teacher guidance, they are not enthusiastic about parental involvement in matters of curriculum development, instruction, or school governance (Williams, 1981). There are many possible areas for parent and community collaboration with schools. It is crucial, however, to identify and agree on an emphasis and to communicate it clearly to everyone on the school staff as well as members of the community.

In general, parent and community collaboration with the school is the result of individual teacher efforts. There is very little in the way of structure within schools to support involvement and few if any rewards at the site level for encouraging it. In a study of 3,968 Maryland elementary schools in 16 districts, teachers expressed the feeling that if they are going to get any cooperation from parents beyond those who would participate anyway, they would have to rely on their own energies and efforts to organize such a system (Becker and Epstein, 1982).

Management System

There are two key elements of a management system for school-community involvement: leadership at the school site for the partnership and a well-established management structure for promoting and overseeing participation. With these conditions, a change in attitudes and perceptions about the respective roles and responsibilities of parents and other community members will gradually begin to take place.

Leadership

To grow and flourish, a participatory partnership must have leadership at the school-site level from the principal. Leadership involves establishing a policy of participation and supporting that policy with a management structure. Publicizing the policy to staff, parents, and the community, recognizing and rewarding partnership activities, and allocating school resources to increasing participation are actions that help to build the partnership.

Although principals can simply mandate a policy, one of the most effective ways to establish both policy and practice of greater client participation is to begin with a needs assessment. A needs assessment is designed to determine what parents and community members might realistically contribute to the educational process, and what the staff would like them to contribute. The assessment provides the basis for establishing a policy that can be supported by the parents, staff, and school administration. It also aggregates essential information to help set priorities, develop an action plan for parent participation, and establish a workable structure for managing the partnership. At Claire Lilienthal Elementary School (see the case study at the end of this chapter), a parent volunteer began by compiling a list of activities and ideas with which teachers and the principal wanted help. This list eventually became the basis for establishing the priority areas for parent collaboration. Each year the list is updated and modified by the parent volunteer coordinator who has a key role to play in managing the parent participation process.

Structure

Participation occurs within a framework. Earlier, the professional/client, advocacy, and partnership models of participation were compared and contrasted in terms of motives for participation, communication patterns, areas of involvement, and the distribution of power. In addition, each of the models has a typical management structure with which it is generally associated. The professional/client model usually delegates the management of participation to the discretion of the individual professional. As discussed earlier, this means that participation will vary from teacher to teacher and be largely an ad hoc activity. Parents and community members have limited initiative and limited responsibility for sustaining actions. In contrast, the advocacy model shifts management entirely onto the shoulders of participating parents and community members, with little if any input from teachers and administrators. The partnership model assumes joint responsibility for management, with school staff (professional and administrative) and parent-community members each having well-defined, but differentiated roles.

The first management task in establishing a partnership is to assess the needs of the school from the perspective of parents, teachers, students, and the administration. The second task is to undertake a program to train parents and staff in preparing for the partnership. This may be similar to the types of training used in problem solving, decision making, and goal setting already discussed in Chapter Five. As the partnership begins to grow, parents are often invited to participate in certain staff development trainings. For example, the principal of Claire Lilienthal Alternative School has developed a variety of joint parent-staff training opportunities to enhance the participatory partnership at that school.

Coordination is the critical management function that must be institutionalized if the partnership is going to grow and thrive. Careful selection and assignment of parent and community volunteers to match the partnership action plan is also extremely important. For example, one principal, who was dedicated to establishing a strong partnership, matched teacher and parent personalities on classroom-related activities and required the two to work together in order to ensure the growth of positive attitudes about the partnership approach. To assure that parents develop a sense that their involvement is worthwhile, their interests, skills, and availability must be taken into careful consideration.

In general, most school principals do not have the time to undertake primary responsibility for coordinating the partnership. This task needs to be delegated. In some schools (e.g., Claire Lilienthal Alternative School), a parent volunteer coordinator works with the school to identify needs, communicate with the volunteers what has to be done, and ascertain that volunteer activities are carried through. In addition to a volunteer coordinator, which is a nonpaid parent-held position at Claire Lilienthal, the principal has also designated a part-time paraprofessional position called the *parent liaison worker.* This individual has a distinct role from the parent volunteer coordinator. Responsibilities include interfacing between teachers and parents about student-related matters; contacting parents when a student has recurrent academic, social, or discipline problem; writing notes to parents; and assisting teachers with some record keeping.

The salient aspect at Claire Lilienthal is that there is a simple, yet well-defined system for managing the large volume of volunteer support and community participation at the school. This management system can be staffed by volunteers or paid personnel. Clarity regarding the roles, responsibilities, and lines of communication is essential. The Lilienthal system actually relieves teachers from the burden of organizing and overseeing parent and outside community involvement. Moreover, it gives parents a wide range of options for involvement. They may choose among activities directly associated with their child's classroom (e.g., field trips and classroom assistance) or schoolwide committees.

Building a Responsive School

Returning to our opening vignette, we see how the principal at Oakland Technical High School provided the leadership and management to involve the community in his school. Community involvement and client responsiveness are closely related. In concert with the effort to create a better quality of work life for teachers and administrators, community involvement contributes to the effort that must be exerted to create learning environments that are more attuned to the diverse needs of the heterogeneous student population. An effort of this nature, which is frequently referred to as *restructuring* schools, entails some basic changes in the traditional ways teachers are expected to work and students are expected to learn.

A more participatory-managed school will not necessarily make teaching easier for all teachers, nor will it necessarily remedy many of the limitations of standard teaching practices as they are institutionalized in many schools across the nation. What a participatory school does, however, is open options and encourage teachers, administrators, parents, and students to think beyond the limits of the organizational and educational paradigms within which they are functioning.

Making schools more responsive to the needs of students (more student-centered) is the ultimate challenge to contemporary public education. Indicators of nonresponsiveness are legion: The increasing high school drop-out rate; the declining test score trends; the shift of upper-income families in some communities from public to private schools, particularly in urban areas; and the growth of student discipline problems are all signs that there is a growing gulf between what schools offer students and what students and parents want and get from schools.

Creating responsive and responsible education is both an educational and an administrative undertaking. In this concluding section, the barriers to responsive education are examined and the characteristics of a responsive school are identified.

Barriers to Responsive Education

Among the barriers to responsive education are societal and organizational factors. Societal factors are by and large beyond the control of individuals and relatively small organizations such as schools. Nevertheless, some schools have been more successful than others in minimizing the impact of these factors. Organizational factors are more within the control of the school and school district. The competent school management team is aware of the limiting conditions in the environment and must work within as well as around these limitations to build school responsiveness.

Societal Barriers

As social service organizations, schools are impacted by two related problems. One is the multiple, broad, and, at times, conflicting functions of schools from a societal perspective. Historically, schooling began to expand rapidly after the Industrial Revolution to meet the increasingly complex problem of socializing the next generation in vocational, cultural, and sociopolitical domains (see Dreeben, 1968; Bowles and Gintis, 1976). In the latter part of the twentieth century many analysts found that schools have increasingly become "holding institutions" for youths who cannot be absorbed into the labor market (Bowles and Gintis, 1976). More recently, with the increasing participation of women in the workforce, the educational system has assumed the role of caretaker.

Meanwhile, social and political activists expect schools to play a role in redressing deep-rooted inequalities among various ethnic and socioeconomic groups. Not only are these roles extremely wide reaching but they compete with each other for limited time and scarce resources. For example, busing students to achieve racial balance within each school in a district may compete with funds for advanced placements programs in the secondary schools. Or extending before- and after-school care to children of working parents may compete with resources to hire more classroom aides. These extremely diffuse functions have left schools adrift with respect to their goals and purpose. Because the function of schools extends beyond teaching academics, schools are responding to demands for services they are neither designed, staffed, nor funded to provide.

Coupled with an array of different social functions, public schools have a legally mandated clientele. This clientele is extremely diverse—culturally, ethnically, linguistically, socially, and economically. Unlike private businesses and some other social service agencies, public schools in general have not tailored themselves to specific segments of this vast, heterogeneous student population. Rather than restructuring organizationally to meet the wide range of interests and needs, special programs within existing organizational structures have evolved to try to address some more specific client groups (e.g., compensatory education, bilingual education, and special education). The basic organizational relationships—between students and teachers, teachers and teachers, and students and students—remain unaltered.

Organizational Barriers

There are salient organizational aspects of schools that inhibit the emergence of a more responsive learning environment. These barriers arise primarily from the increasing bureaucratization of schools as well as the growth in school size. One hundred years ago, the school "belonged" to the community. Communities were relatively small and were served by single schools or, in urban areas, small groups of schools. As the urban population grew, schools began to form districts. With the advent of school district administration, communities and schools began separating— physically, organizationally, and functionally. The role of district administration came to be regulatory as well as financial. Standardization of curriculum, personnel policies, school hours, specifications for school facilities, and so on were gradually incorporated in the central, district administrative functions. The school, as we know it today, has become an organizational structure that teachers, administrators, students, and parents do not generally question.

Related to the formation of school districts and district-level administration is the general growth in the average size of the school and district. Not only have schools become highly regulated organizations from without, but from within they are large and complex. Although the growth in average school size has been justified in terms of lower unit cost and increase in curriculum offerings associated with a larger student body, recent research does not unequivocally support these justifications. Moreover, a larger-sized organization is generally associated with a more impersonal environment, less flexibility, and more decision making in conjunction with given regulations rather than analysis and responsiveness to the specifics of a given situation. Each of these characteristics tend to make schools less, rather than more, responsive to the needs of their students.

Responsive Schools: Student-Centered Environments

Responsive schools give student needs top priority in designing the learning environment. They provide different learning options, curricular focus, and a sense of community.

Learning Options

The vast array of research on how children learn amply demonstrates that there is no one best method of learning for all students. Responsive students, schools, and school districts recognize this and try to provide as many learning options as possible. These options occur at the classroom level, through skilled teaching that varies the learning and instructional modalities constantly throughout the class and school day. One example is the *quarter system,* in which the teacher divides the class or lesson time into four equal segments and plans a different type of activity for each segment. Within the school, options can be made available through specialized programs that offer an individualized instructional approach; cooperative learning programs, practicals, and laboratories; and field settings for upper elementary and secondary school students.

Another dimension of the optional characteristic is that responsive schools give their students varying degrees of choice over what they learn. This option has been commonly practiced at the upper secondary level, but it has been less vigorously pursued at the elementary and lower secondary levels. Providing students with choices and opportunities to explore a variety of academic and nonacademic topics encourages children to be active rather than passive in deciding what they want to learn. In one small, alternative school, there is a weekly two-hour block designated as "sign ups." During this period, regular classroom teachers offer something special, such as pottery, photography, or biology. Students sign up for their first and second choices. Sometimes the sign up is a series of classes over a period of weeks, other times it is a one-time activity. In a larger, traditional elementary school, electives have been institutionalized more formally. Students select two electives for a nine-week period. These classes meet up to four times weekly and have specialist instructors in areas such as dance, drama, foreign languages, and science.

Curricular Focus

Educators are increasingly recognizing that almost any subject or field can be used as a pathway to learning basic skills in the language arts and physical sciences if the subject or area focus is interesting to the student. Reading and writing skills can be developed via the study of history, art, cooking, or chemistry. Likewise, scientific methods and mathematics can be learned via carpentry, photography, and social studies. The key is to focus the learning environment on subjects and activities that are vitally interesting to students and to move outward from this focus.

Most elementary and secondary schools have a *comprehensive* curriculum, which does not provide a strong focus. Although such a curriculum may work well in the lower grades, after six to eight years, the approach no longer captures and holds the interest of the majority of students. Examples of alternatives to the comprehensive curriculum are magnet schools and schools-within-schools.

Magnet schools are growing in popularity at both the elementary and secondary levels. Their focus ranges from arts, science, health, ecology, communications, and language arts. Magnet schools provide a strong sense of educational and personal identity, giving students the opportunity to develop a depth of knowledge and practical skills in a particular area far beyond traditional school offerings. Magnet schools are not for all students, but they can be solutions for students who find a burning interest frustrated by the traditional comprehensive curriculum.

Schools-within-schools are similar to the magnet approach. The health academy of Oakland Technical High School (mentioned earlier) is a school-within-a-school. Students who are interested in a career in the health profession enroll in the program that offers health education. They also take some of their classes in the regular high school program.

Sense of Community

In her studies of secondary schools that evidence a high degree of organizational well-being, Lightfoot (1983) found that each of these five highly differentiated schools had a sense of community. That sense of community included students, teachers, the administration, and parents. There is no single factor that can create a sense of community; however, certain features are associated with close-knit educational communities. One characteristic includes an identification with the school as an organization. This identity most frequently arises when members share common goals, have time to interact with each other in both formal and nonformal situations, and perceive that their specific concerns are being taken into account. In the responsive school, students have vehicles for articulating their needs and concerns (e.g., teachers who listen, student government, etc.). Schools that are responsive to students are likely to have higher degrees of collaboration among the staff and a sense of partnership between the school and the parents.

Perhaps one of the greatest organizational weaknesses of schools today is the absence of *informal* time. There are few opportunities for teachers and students to interact informally due to the pressure for "time on task," and equally limited time for teachers to interact among themselves (discussed in Chapters Two, Six, and Seven). Informal time is very important because it allows people to express feelings more freely and to communicate in nontask-related contexts. Given that the sense of community is a feeling—a perception shared by members of an organization— there must be time to exchange feelings and noninstructional communications for the sense of community to evolve.

Another contributor to the sense of community is the size of an organization. Although some very small organizations may not offer a sense of community, large organizations face relatively more difficulties in creating the sense of community, which comes from direct face-to-face interaction with people over an extended time period. The size of many schools is a serious obstacle to developing an organizationwide sense of community. Large elementary schools have to rely on the classroom itself as the students' primary community. Secondary schools face greater obstacles because students change classrooms, peer groups, and teachers as much as seven times each day. Under these conditions, a sense of continuity is frequently lost. Some secondary schools that are plagued with high drop-out rates have designed programs for high-risk students. These programs are organized around a single teacher and student, the premise being that high-risk students need to receive personal attention and establish a sense of belonging if they are to identify with others in the school community.

Summary

Strong community involvement in schools brings important benefits: additional resources, political support, opportunities for innovation and professional development, and increased student achievement. The degree of involvement will depend, however, on the model a school chooses. Consistent, high-level participation of parents and other community members is not likely to be achieved without planning. The principal, together with the school management team, must provide leadership and delegate explicit responsibilities for managing participation.

A high level of school-community involvement is one of several avenues toward creating a more client-responsive school environment. The better the school knows the community and the better the community knows the school, the greater the possibilities for tailoring schools to meet client needs. Restructuring schools to provide more learning options, a stronger curricular focus, and a greater sense of community requires the active participation of parents, teachers, administrators, and students. Involvement and responsiveness are part and parcel of the same educational process—a process that requires participation and careful management.

The emphasis of this chapter has been on extending the concept of participation as a school management strategy to the various community constituencies: parents, the business community, universities, voluntary agencies, and nonprofit foundations. Community involvement brings benefits to the school as an organization in terms of added resources as well as staff renewal and innovation, and it helps to build broad-based political support. In addition, direct parent involvement in their children's education produces benefits in terms of improved academic achievement.

Participation can take many forms. Three basic models of participation are the professional/client model, the advocacy model, and the partnership model. In terms of maximizing collaboration and benefits, the partnership model has great potential. Its success, however, depends on establishing the necessary conditions for a partnership to flourish, including a clear focus, a management system with strong leadership, and a well-defined management structure.

Case Study

Claire Lilienthal Alternative Elementary School

(Authors' Note: Claire Lilienthal Alternative Elementary School presents a picture of parent involvement par excellence. Readers may want to consider how this model might be translated and adapted to a larger secondary school where no explicit decision to send their children to the school has been made by the par-

ents. Likewise, is it ethical and practical to insist that parents be involved in their children's schools? Considering another aspect of parent involvement, how might an administrator work with teachers who are resistant to having parents actively involved in the classroom? And from the administrator's perspective, what might be some of the possible pitfalls associated with parental involvement?)

Background

> *Of all the elements of Lilienthal's success, the support of our parents is perhaps most pivotal. Prospective Lilienthal parents should understand that, without exception, they will be expected to participate in their child's education. . . . Parents are expected to provide a variety of skills and services otherwise unavailable from the school district and to complement and enrich those that are. There are many ways parents can participate and support the school. No parent is without talents or resources.*

> —*Excerpt from the Claire Lilienthal Alternative Elementary School brochure for parents of prospective students*

In 1981, Kathy King, a teacher-in-charge and long-time union activist in the San Francisco Unified School District, was presented with an enviable opportunity of putting together a public alternative elementary school in the northwest section of the city. King went about hiring a staff that she felt could work together well as a team. Moreover, she wanted teachers who were committed to putting in the extra time and effort she felt it would take to make this experiment work.

An advocate of management-by-consensus and shared decision making, King described the first years at Lilienthal as dealing with nuts and bolts: Getting equipment, furniture, and materials took much of the early year's time and effort. Because Lilienthal is an alternative school, any child in the San Francisco Unified School District is eligible to apply through the district's Optional Enrollment Request process. The school, however, participates in the at-random, districtwide, open-enrollment process in order to maintain a racial and ethnic mix that reflects the demographics of the city itself. Also, there is a conscious effort to keep each class balanced in terms of the proportion of boys and girls.

Aside from the logistical problems of starting a school from scratch, the staff soon recognized that they were getting more than their fair share of children with behavioral and learning problems. This is not unusual for an alternative school. Parents of children who have experienced some difficulties in adapting to traditional public schools often seek placement in an alternative setting in the hopes of finding a better fit between their child's needs and an educational environment. Faced with this situation, the principal, staff, and parents began to ask the question, What is going to be the core emphasis of this school?

The Core Emphasis of the School

In order to get through the most difficult years and fill the gap left by the school district, Kathy King turned to the parents for support. In her words, "The parents were there to support the school." Carefully and systematically, King and the faculty began to build a basis of parent support and involvement in the school life. Having spent the first years of her career working with the Campfire Inc. organization, King was comfortable with volunteerism and was experienced in mobilizing voluntary support. She began with the PTA in spring 1982, which had about 30 percent of the parents as members.

A survey was conducted in order to determine what the parents wanted for the school. (Surveys are used once or twice annually at Lilienthal and channeled to parents as part of the students' homework assignments.) Out of this survey, one of the first major parent projects emerged: a creative play structure for the school yard. Together, the parents, teachers, and children visited other play structures throughout the city to gather ideas. A design was submitted to the district and city by a parent volunteer architect. Parents took charge of fund raising for the materials. After two years of planning and fund raising, the parents broke ground for the structure and completed it within 18 weekends of volunteer work.

The play structure elicited new dimensions for the school's curriculum. The momentum gained from this successful effort led to the development of a sensory-motor program for the children using the play structure. Designed with the assistance of a specialist in the field, parent volunteers were trained in program activities and staffed the program throughout the school year. Enthusiasm for the sensory-motor program spawned a creative dance program. Together, the parents and the principal raised funds to pay for the services of a children's creative dance teacher through the San Francisco Performing Arts Workshop.

To support the classroom, teachers organize additional activities such as field trips, a school library program, and outdoor education programs culminating with an annual class camping trip. King established a program of room parents, two per classroom, and she admits that there was some resistance initially from the teachers. She had to demonstrate gradually that parents, especially those trained to give specific support in the classroom, were not a judgmental threat. The experience of teaching in a self-contained classroom for years not only can lead to isolation but limits experience in working with other adults.

Carefully orchestrating direct parental help, King instructed parents on exactly what they were to do when helping in the classroom or a field trip, and tried to match parent and teacher personalities. She also encouraged parents to organize appreciation luncheons and surprise birthday parties for teachers. "Lots of stroking for teachers by parents has helped the teachers to realize that their efforts really are appreciated and valued by parents," King stated.

The acceptance of parental involvement is manifest formally as well as informally. When something needs to be done, the teachers often say, "Ask the parents to help us." "I don't think they realize how much they have changed," said Kathy, in reference to the teachers' attitudes toward parent involvement. The vitality of parental participation is also reinforced by the parent liaison worker, a position that evolved with the school. In 1982, the school decided to create the position through grants and then through part of its School Improvement Funds. The liaison worker is an highly experienced paraprofessional from the school district, whose main priorities are to act as an intermediary between the classroom teacher and parents, to facilitate parent-teacher communication when academic or student behavior problems arise, and to make referrals when outside intervention might be necessary. In addition, the liaison worker helps with organizing school activities, coordinates the library program, monitors budgets, acts as an intermediary for the PTA, and coordinates special projects on an ad hoc basis.

In order to ensure participation by all parents, the school has made specific efforts. A parent volunteer coordinator (a parent volunteer position) keeps parent participation organized in the various school committees (e.g., library, fund raising, sensory-motor program, computer program, the tutorial program) and other parent participation activities; keeps track of parental participation; and handles the annual volunteer sign-up checklist that has developed over the past five years and is, according to one parent who held the position of parent volunteer coordinator for three years, continually evolving.

Lilienthal's responsiveness to parental input has also been a source of professional development for the teaching staff. Parents encouraged the school to introduce computers into the curriculum. The teachers themselves had no prior experience with computers and felt the normal computer shyness of newcomers to the field—especially when they were so busy with an already full curriculum. As a result of the parental interest, one teacher decided to devote her sabbatical to learning about computers. Upon return from the sabbatical, with a grant for release time, she trained her colleagues and led students in the use of computers. Now, most of the teachers are computer literate. One colleague who still remains a bit computer shy has established an exchange: art time for computer time between the two teachers' classes.

Reactions and Results

Claire Lilienthal is one of those fortunate schools that can boast of traditional and nontraditional successes. On the California Test of Basic Skills, the students have consistently scored well, statewide since the school's inception in 1981. The principal attributes this to the solid cooperation between parents and teachers.

The school is highly stable amidst an environment of urban flux. Of the 180 students enrolled, only 9 students moved away from the school between the past and present academic year. It is common for siblings to follow older brothers and sisters to Lilienthal. Six of the original eight founding staff members remain at the school after seven years of operation. Describing herself as a maverick in all respects, Kathy King reports that the district has provided increasing support for the nontraditional ways of the school and encourages continued growth of parent involvement. She does admit that many colleagues are curious or puzzled about why a principal would want to spend so much time with parents. King emphasizes that she enjoys the stimulation and interaction with the parents, teachers, and students, which is a well of enthusiasm for the daily challenges the school faces.

References

Becker, H. J., and Epstein, J. L. "Influences on Teachers' Use of Parent Involvement at Home." Report No. 324. Baltimore: Johns Hopkins University Center for the Social Organization of Schools, 1982.

Bowles, S., and Gintis, H. *Schooling in Capitalist America.* New York: Basic Books, 1976.

Carnoy, M., and Levin, H. M. *The Limits of Educational Reform.* New York: David McKay, 1976.

Dauzberger, J. P., and Usdan, M. D. "Building Partnerships: The Atlanta Experience." *Phi Delta Kappan* (February 1984):393–396.

Dreeben, R. *On What is Learned in School.* Reading, MA: Addison-Wesley, 1968.

Gallup, G. H. "The 10th Annual Gallup Poll of the Public's Attitudes Toward the Public School." *Phi Delta Kappan* 60 (1978):33–45.

Goodlad, J. *A Place Called School.* New York: McGraw-Hill, 1984.

Gray, S. T. "How to Create a Successful School/Community Partnership." *Phi Delta Kappan* (February 1984):405–409.

Henderson, A. *Parent Participation—Student Achievement: The Evidence Grows.* Columbia, MD: National Committee for Citizens in Education, 1981.

Herman, J. L., and Yeh, J. P. "Some Effects of Parent Involvement in Schools." *Urban Review* 15(1) (1983):11–16.

Lightfoot, S. L. *The Good High School.* New York: Basic Books, 1983.

Medrich, E. A., and Roizen, J. *The Serious Business of Growing Up: A Study of Children's Lives Outside of School.* Berkeley: University of California Press, 1982.

Moles, O. "Synthesis of Recent Research on Parent Participation in Children's Education." *Educational Leadership* (November 1982):44–47.

National Educational Association. "Nationwide Teacher Opinion Poll." Washington DC: National Education Association Research, memo, 1981.

Peters, T. J., and Waterman, R. H. *In Search of Excellence.* New York: Harper and Row, 1982.

Saxe, R. W. *School-Community Interaction.* Berkeley, CA: McCutchan, 1975.

Seeley, P. *Home-School-Community Partnership as an Educational Reform Strategy.* Michigan: C. S. Mott Foundation, 1982, p. 81.

Tangri, S. S., and Leitch, M. L. "Barriers to Home-School Collaboration: Two Case Studies in Junior High Schools." Final Report submitted to the National Institute of Education, Washington DC: The Urban Institute, May 1982.

Van Hoose, J., and Straham, D. *Young Adolescent Development and School Practices: Promoting Harmony.* Columbus, OH: National Middle School Association, 1988.

Williams, D. L. *Final Interim Report: Southwest Parent Education Resource Center.* Austin, TX: Southwest Educational Development Laboratory, 1981.

CHAPTER TEN

Labor-Management Relations: Collective Bargaining and Beyond

Introduction

From the moment principal Mary Gardiner awoke Monday morning and turned on her radio, she knew that her careful plans for a perfect school year at Charles Eliot Junior High School had been dashed. The school was surrounded by a mob of picketing teachers and milling students. She had gone to bed Sunday night hoping that the school board and the teacher's union would settle their differences. It was going to be a difficult day. As she dressed for work, she wondered how many teachers would show up, whether she would have any substitutes, and how long the strike would last.

As Gardiner drove to school, she listened to an interview with a union leader and a parent. The teacher was reciting a litany of complaints that had developed over the past years. Complaints about discipline, excessive yard duty, lack of facilities, overcrowded classrooms and insufficient channels to air grievances all surfaced. There was also the matter of low starting salaries. The mother of a first-grader, exasperated by the prospect of being absent from work, interjected, "Why can't teachers get the money they need? Doesn't the administration care about the teachers?"

Gardiner arrived at the school and was met by circling lines of placard-carrying teachers and a few police officers. Crowds of students milled about. Upon entering her office, she learned that 15 of her 18 teachers had phoned in sick. The district had been able to find only three substitutes.

As the day wore on, she was able to herd the increasingly restless children into the auditorium and a few classrooms for babysitting. One group of students being led to the cafeteria broke loose and stormed the front gate. Leaving exhausted at the end of the day, the day's events played in her mind. She couldn't help thinking about how unnecessary it all was. As she entered the traffic for the drive home, Gardiner reflected on a fragment of conversation she had had with one of the picketing teachers—"It will take 10 or 15 years for these wounds to heal."

In the preceding chapters we have presented the elements of a participatory approach to educational administration in the critical areas of leadership, decision making, and personnel management. Many of these activities occur within the boundaries of the school. However, as is well known, schools exist in a social milieu or environment. Perhaps nowhere is the existence of the external points of interface more apparent than in the realm of contract bargaining and administration. The collective bargaining process transcends the school and the district as it is influenced by the broad legal and political environment. This chapter addresses the nature, the process, and the consequences, particularly with respect to participation, of collective bargaining in education.

Several critical elements of this multifaceted topic are highlighted. A bibliography is provided for administrators who wish to examine some of these areas in more detail. We begin with a discussion of the nature and function of collective bargaining. The second section reviews the history of collective bargaining, especially as it pertains to teachers. The next section presents a model of the collective bargaining process, the steps and patterns of contract negotiation. This section also includes a discussion of important elements in contract administration and grievance resolution. The fourth section examines how collective bargaining has affected schooling, and includes a critical discussion of the problem with conventional approaches to collective bargaining. This leads us to examine the current forces that are impelling a movement beyond traditional collective bargaining and some of the forms that the new approaches have taken. We conclude this section with five principles for creating a collegial, participatory, and productive environment for labor negotiations and contract outcomes.

The Functional Imperatives: What and Why of Collective Bargaining

In reviewing the recent history of public education in the United States, one can identify few changes that have so influenced the nature of educational administration as collective bargaining. In 1988, an estimated 90 percent of all teachers were unionized, either part of the 1.9 million members of the National Education Association (NEA) or of the 700,000 strong American Federation of Teachers (AFT). The introduction of collective bargaining has sharply restructured the role of the educational administrator from a unilateral decision maker to one who must act in a multilateral decision-making environment. The policy space of the school or district is sharply restricted by the union contract, which is itself a product of a political process that takes place between teachers' representatives and the school board, under the ever-present eye of public opinion. One result has been to heighten the tension on the tightrope that stretches between the poles of cooperation and competition on which relations between teachers and administrators balance. In part this is due to the fact that a contractual relationship has replaced the former informal relationship. When the informal relationship was good, cooperation flourished. However, in a significant number of instances teachers felt the need for the legal protection of a contract and for improvements in the conditions of work. This need has produced increased competition between labor and management, which has occurred in the context of collective bargaining in the dual processes of contract bargaining and contract administration. It is worth noting that collective bargaining has produced substantial gains for teachers in compensation as well as in noncompensation areas such as hours and conditions of work.

What Is Collective Bargaining?

Collective bargaining refers to the organizing of employees for the purpose of negotiation and administration of a contractual or legally enforceable agreement between the employee and the employer. A central characteristic of collective bargaining is the concept of "meet and confer." If employees have voted for collective bargaining, the employer must agree to meet at a reasonable time and confer in good faith with respect to wages, hours, and other terms and conditions of employment. Collective bargaining is the product of struggle by industrial workers for fair wages and working conditions and the need by government to ensure a rudimentary level of industrial peace and security.

The history of the labor movement in the 1800s and early 1900s was marked by repression and violence. Theoretically, unions were lawful organizations but in practice the courts and corporate entities acted to deny unions the liberty of engaging in collective activity. The legal and political environment was hostile to workers, many of whom felt abused and exploited as a result of low wages, poor working conditions, and unfair management. Frustrated in their attempts to create peaceful change, some union activists resorted to violence. Ironically, the Depression of the 1930s created the conditions for the widespread acceptance of improved bases for labor-management relations. The long record of industrial violence and strife in the nation's industries finally convinced Congress in 1935 that legislation was needed that would secure a degree of industrial cooperation to the benefit of both employees and employers.

The National Labor Relations Act (NLRA) of 1935 (also known as the Wagner Act after its sponsor, Senator Robert Wagner of New York) established the "right of employees to self-organization, to form, join, or assist labor organizations, to bargain collectively through representatives of their choosing, and to engage in concerted activities, for the purpose of collective bargaining or other mutual aid or protection" (Section 7, National Labor Relations Act of 1935). The NLRA provided the basis for union growth in the industrial sector; it did not apply to public employees.

It was not until 1963 with the issuance of Executive Order 10988 that President John Kennedy, responding to the growing role and strength of public employees and the imperatives of a national movement for the protection of civilian rights, established a federal policy to grant recognition to unions in the public sector. Kennedy's executive order provided a legal precedent, and within the public sector the favorable political climate of the 1960s and 1970s served as a spur to the development of collective bargaining in education. It is important to note that Executive Order 10988 pertained only to federal employees; the responsibility for regulating labor-management relations at the state and local levels where teachers are employed lies with a host of state legislatures, courts, and administrative agencies. Until the 1960s, most state legislation was decidedly hostile to teacher unions. For example, as late as 1930, the state of Washington enforced, and the courts upheld, a "yellow-dog" contract for teachers, which required job applicants to sign a statement that they were not members of a union and promised not to join a union (Cresswell, Murphey, and Kerchner, 1980).

At this point it is useful to trace some of the early roots of teacher unionism, for the two dominant teacher organizations had their roots long before the advent of public sector collective bargaining.

A Brief History of Teacher Organizations and Collective Bargaining

Unionization of teachers in the United States has a long and colorful history. The National Education Association was formed in

1857. In 1887, New York teachers formed a Mutual Benefit Association, and in Chicago, led by the militant organizer Margaret Haley, the Chicago Federation of Teachers, formed in 1897, was a leader in securing teacher pensions and prodding political reform. In 1903, Philadelphia teachers organized themselves into the Philadelphia Teachers' Association, enlisting practically every teacher in its drive for better salaries. In Atlanta, teachers formed the Atlanta Public School Teachers' Association in an effort to pressure the city council to provide more funds for education. Later, the Teachers' League, led by socialist Henry Linville, John Dewey, and suffragist Charlotte Perkins Gilman, formed an association that sought far more than economic issues. Its purpose was to give teachers a vote in determining school policies, to acquire representation on the New York Board of Education, to help settle school problems, to eliminate politics from promotion decisions, and to encourage free public discussion of educational issues. In 1916, the Teachers' League changed its name to the Teachers' Union and affiliated with the American Federation of Labor (AFL), joining with the CFT and other locals to form the American Federation of Teachers (Urban, 1982).

During the early part of this century, teachers' wages and working conditions were still surprisingly oppressive (Apple, 1986). Figure 10.1 shows an example of a 1923 teacher's contract.

During the pre-World War I period and again in the 1930s, teachers made further sacrifices by taking cuts in pay as school boards responded to declining revenues by cutting teachers' salaries, increasing class size, and reducing the length of the school year. For example, between 1931 and 1934, the average teacher's salary in Illinois declined by $385 per year while the per capita cost of education dropped from $119 to $94 (Cresswell, Murphey, and Kerchner, 1980, p. 75). Then, in the 1940s and 1950s, teachers failed to participate in the wage growth experienced by private sector employees. As a consequence, the decade of the 1950s was marked by a growth in strikes by teachers and a growth of teacher unionism led by the AFT. Meanwhile, the NEA, which had been an organization composed of teachers and administrators but led by administrators (from 1857 through 1945 only three classroom teachers had served as presidents of the NEA, the rest being administrators or college presidents), began in the 1950s to move aggressively in support of the welfare of classroom teachers. Nevertheless, despite the long history of teachers' unions, until the end of the 1950s teachers still had not attained the right to collective bargaining except in a few districts.

Two factors radically affected this course of events. The first

FIGURE 10.1 • *Teacher's Contract, 1923*

This is an agreement between Miss _____, teacher, and the Board of Education of the _____ School, whereby Miss _____ agrees to teach for a period of eight months, beginning Sept. 1, 1923. The Board of Education agrees to pay Miss _____ the sum of ($75) per month. Miss _____ agrees:

1. Not to get married. This contract becomes null and void immediately if the teacher marries.
2. Not to keep company with men.
3. To be home between the hours of 8:00 P.M. and 6:00 P.M. unless in attendance at a school function.
4. Not to loiter downtown in ice cream stores.
5. Not to leave town at any time without the permission of the chairman of the Board of Trustees.
6. Not to smoke cigarettes. This contract becomes null and void immediately if the teacher is found smoking.
7. Not to drink beer, wine or whiskey. This contract becomes null and void immediately if the teacher is found drinking beer, wine or whiskey.
8. Not to ride in a carriage or automobile with any man except her brother or father.
9. Not to dress in bright colors.
10. Not to dye her hair.
11. To wear at least two petticoats.
12. Not to wear dresses more than two inches above the ankles.
13. To keep the schoolroom clean.
    a. To sweep the classroom floor at least once daily.
    b. To scrub the classroom floor at least once weekly with hot water and soap.
    c. To clean the blackboard at least once daily.
    d. To start the fire at 7:00 so the room will be warm at 8:00 A.M. when the children arrive.
14. Not to use face powder, mascara, or paint the lips.

Source: Michael W. Apple, *Teachers and Texts* (New York: Routledge, 1986). Reprinted with permission.

was the passage of state legislation establishing the right of teachers to organize and bargain collectively in Wisconsin in 1959. This was closely followed by a successful teachers' strike in New York City in November 1960, which led to an overwhelming vote by city teachers in favor of collective bargaining in June 1961. These two events marked a change in the pace and movement of teacher unionization and set the course for the following decades.

Following the direction of Wisconsin, many states then passed legislation that established the right of public employees to bargain collectively. By 1975, some 41 states had legislation that required school districts and other public employers either to "meet and confer" or bargain collectively with employee unions (Cresswell, Murphey, and Kerchner, 1980). By 1988, the number of states that had passed similar legislation increased to 45.

Why Teachers Unionize

The universal reason why people organize is to enhance the individual through a collective presence. As Aristotle noted, man is a political animal, congregating with those who are similar to develop and promote policies of common interest. Teachers formed unions to advance their economic and professional policies and to increase their political power. For example, the early history of the NEA is marked by a campaign to reform the governance and to professionalize the administration of public education (Tyack, 1974). In forming a union, there was hope that by cementing a unity of interest, teachers could effect greater political influence. Since its inception, the AFT has emphasized an interest in securing better pay for teachers as well as in the professionalization of working conditions. A major issue has been to secure due process in hiring and firing decisions. Figure 10.2 lists some of the main economic and professional reasons for teacher unionization.

The economic motives center around demands for higher wages and improved benefits. As noted, this issue has been stimulated by the notoriously low salaries paid to teachers. Today, teachers are among the lowest paid professionals. Related factors are the desire to obtain fringe benefits, such as health and dental care or life insurance. An added economic motive is that of job security. Although this issue may overlap with noneconomic or professional aspects (i.e., protection of academic freedom), it is an important economic item as well.

The issue of professionalization is a complex one. Some individuals still see teacher professionalism and collective bargaining as antithetical. They argue that a true professional will always place duty before self. An early AFT pamphlet sought to address this issue in the following terms:

Teaching Is a Profession, Not a Trade

For generations public school teachers salved their pride with this pitiful substitute for adequate remumeration and

FIGURE 10.2 • *Reasons for Teacher Unionization*

Economic Motives

To improve salaries

To secure health and other fringe benefits (e.g., credit union, life insurance, professional liability insurance)

To secure job security

Professional Motives

To lobby for improved educational quality

To lobby for additional funding

To gain influence over school policy

To protect academic freedom

To gain influence over teacher professional development

To secure gains in school safety

To secure limits in class size

To achieve due process in hiring and firing through a formal grievance procedure

a position of influence in the community. They have refused to face the obvious fact that whereas doctors, lawyers, architects and other professional men can control their hours, the conditions under which they work, and the amount of their fees, teachers, as individuals, have almost no control over these matters vital to their welfare. The results are that the vast majority of teachers receive a smaller annual wage than unskilled laborers and exert far less influence in their calling and in the community than skilled workers. (Freeland G. Stecker, cited in Urban, 1982, pp. 139–140)

A good deal of the force behind the growth of the NEA and AFT is in their professional lobbying activities. Among the noneconomic issues that motivate teachers to seek professional association are those that contribute to improved educational quality. Ranking high in this area are lobbying for additional resources and policies that provide for better working conditions. During the past two decades, the fiscal crisis faced by many districts has contributed to increasing class size and deteriorating school facilities. These are examples of factors that undermine the learning process to which teachers are committed. Collective bargaining has proven to be an avenue by which teachers have been able to secure some redress. Through the process of collective bargaining these motives are articulated and translated into negotiable demands and, where successful, ultimately into provisions. At this point we will now explain the process.

The Collective Bargaining Process

The process of collective bargaining occurs in two conceptual phases: contract negotiation and contract administration (see Figure 10.3). The nucleus of the labor-management relationship is the contract. It is a legally enforceable agreement between two or more parties, usually the union and the school board. The contract is the point of reference in all discussions, informal consultation, or formal arbitration. Contract negotiation and contract administration include a range of activities and may be divided into several phases.

Step 1: Prenegotiation Planning

In prenegotiation planning, both sides review the previous contract, grievances, organizational factors, as well as recent settlements by similar districts. The union representatives consult with the membership and review member demands, whereas the administrative bargaining team analyzes cost and revenue projections. A good deal of time must be spent in preparing information prior to the commencement of negotiation. On the basis of this information each team then prepares a contract bargaining strategy.

The strategy is built around a guiding philosophy. Clear, deci-

FIGURE 10.3 • *The Collective Bargaining Process*

Contract Negotiation ◄─────────────────────► *Contract Administration*

1. Prenegotiation planning	5. Contract communication and education
2. Proposed presentation and negotiation	6. Contract implementation
3. Impasse resolution	7. Contract dispute and grievance resolution
4. Contract agreement and ratification	8. Contract evaluation

sive goals and objectives guide each team during labor-management bargaining sessions. The strategy specifies the most
significant policies guiding or limiting action. For example, if the
main issue is reduction in class size, then other demands will be
subordinated to that issue. An effective bargaining strategy develops around a key concept that provides cohesion, balance, and
focus (i.e., a selective posture). In addition, the strategy includes a
plan for the unknowable (Quinn, 1988). Some of the issues to be
decided at this stage are: What should be bargained? How should
strikes and impasses be handled? What should be the nature of
labor-management relationships?

Step 2: Proposed Presentation
and Negotiation

Collective bargaining is necessarily adversarial. Sources of
conflict stem from limited resources, the concept of managerial
rights or prerogatives, perceptions of opposing roles, and differences in values. Once inside this dynamic, roles tend to become
reified and positions tend to harden into "we" and "they." Bargaining in this context involves each side seeking advantage by forcing
the other side to make concessions or by trading and exchanging
items. Occasionally, it will involve finding new acceptable forms of
agreement. There are a number of tactical approaches to the bargaining process (Cresswell, Murphey, and Kerchner, 1980).

The actual content of bargaining is wide, varied, and the subject of considerable legal dispute. The NLRA specifies mandatory
items, permissive items, and items that are illegal for consideration during bargaining. With regard to schools, the state law will
determine precisely what must or may be bargained. Generally
speaking, the substance of bargaining must include wages, hours
of employment, and conditions of employment. For management
to refuse to bargain in good faith over any of these items would be
illegal and subject to legal remedies. In practice, what constitutes
"conditions of employment" is a matter open to dispute. California's Education Employment Relations Act defines and limits the
meaning of the term as follows: "Terms and conditions of employment mean health and welfare benefits . . . leave and transfer policies, safety conditions of employment, class size, procedures to be
used for evaluation of employees, organizational security . . . , and
procedures for processing grievances" (Section 3543.2).

However, in contrast, the Michigan statute fails to make any further clarification, leaving the meaning of the term to be filled in by decisions of the state labor relations board and the courts. Table 10.1 provides an outline of the contract provisions that are likely to be included or negotiated in most collective bargaining agreements. Clearly, each of the thousands of contracts will differ in a variety of areas but some or all of the usual provisions can be found in the contract of any district. Nevertheless, special circumstances or state legal constraints may lead any of these sections to be omitted (Cresswell, Murphey, and Kerchner, 1980).

Collective bargaining may lead to improvements in the quality of education. Proposals and counterproposals have differing characteristics; some are mutually beneficial to teachers and pupils, some are aimed at establishing administrative prerogatives, others seek to widen the scope of teachers' influence, and still others are included purely to enhance the public image of one side or the other. An example of a pupil benefit-enhancing proposal would be one that seeks to shift from standardized testing to criterion-referenced tests, which provide for participation of teachers in the design of tests to ensure a better match between curriculum and tests (Webster, 1985).

Step 3: Impasse Resolution

Impasse signifies that bargaining is no longer progressing toward agreement. Cresswell, Murphey, and Kerchner (1980) state:

> *The existence of an impasse is a threat to the bargaining relationship and the public interest since it implies that, rather than make any concession, the parties are ready to risk open hostility, long delays in reaching agreement, and perhaps a strike and its related costs. Somehow the stakes at the bargaining table have become so high that any retreat from a position is quite difficult. When the stakes are that high, the parties are more likely to engage in extreme forms of behavior that may damage the bargaining relationship and impose serious costs on the clients of the school and the public. Peaceful resolution of impasses is, therefore, usually treated as a public policy problem. (p. 176)*

The resolution of impasse may be achieved in any one or combination of ways: mediation, fact finding, arbitration, or in-

TABLE 10.1 • *Basic School System Contract Provisions*

Sections	Contents
Preamble	Identification of bargaining unit and membership therein Agreement to forgo individual negotiations
Union's rights and security	Protected organizing activity Dues deduction, agency shop, union shop Meetings, officers, general information
Employees' rights and security	Discipline Personnel file access Academic freedom Employee evaluation Seniority Employee termination Nondiscrimination
Manager's rights	
Work rules and conditions	Work load School calendar and workday Work assignment and transfers Promotion and position notification Pupil discipline School policy and operation decision procedure
Compensation and benefits	Salary schedules Supplementary wage schedules Extra-duty, overtime provisions Insurance (life, medical, income) Leave days (sick, personal, etc.) Sabbatical leaves and leaves of absence Association
Grievance procedures	Detailed description of criteria and actions
Impasse procedures	Detailed description of criteria and actions
Contract terms	Length of agreement No strike—no lockout Reopen or waiver provisions

Source: From Anthony Cresswell and Michael Murphy, *Teachers, Unions and Collective Bargaining,* ©1980 by McCutchan Publishing Corporation, Berkeley, CA 94702. Permission granted by publisher.

junctions. *Mediation* is the least formal approach to resolution. It consists of a neutral third party who meets with both parties and tries to bring them back to bargaining. However, the mediator has no power apart from persuasion to compel the parties or to impose an agreement. *Fact finding* involves the work of an individual or team to study the bargaining positions and gather information about the relative merits of each position. The fact finder prepares a report which, when made public, is intended through reason and public pressure to cause a change of positions. *Arbitration* is the process by which agreement is reached through a neutral third party, but in which the arbitrator's decision may be binding. One form of "final (or at least best) offer" arbitration found in some states requires parties in impasse to submit "their final offers to an arbitrator who is bound by law to choose, *without modification,* one or the other of the offers" (Cresswell, Murphey, and Kerchner, 1980, p. 179).

Last, an *injunction* is a court order issued to prevent serious disruption in public services. The injunction may impose fines and imprisonment against union officers and members who continue strike activity. It is a powerful tool of management but one with potentially far-reaching costs in the form of embittered labor-management relations.

Step 4: Contract Agreement and Ratification

The final stage of the contract bargaining is contract agreement. Once a contract has been negotiated, it is then sent to the union membership and the school board for ratification. If ratified, it then becomes a legally binding contract for a specified term, usually two to four years. Table 10.1 provides a summary of the types of provisions contained in a typical contract.

Step 5: Contract Communication and Education

Next, labor-management relations enter the realm of contract administration. This begins with communication of the contract to the union members and education of union and administrative representatives who will be bound by its conditions. The details of the contract need to be thoroughly reviewed and each item discussed and clarified. This is often best accomplished by those who were members of the bargaining team.

Step 6: Contract Implementation

At this point, the provisions of the contract begin to be implemented. For example, the contract may call for labor-management consultative committees on curriculum to be established in each school site. Grievance procedures may need to be developed. Directives should be issued by the school district to effect these provisions.

Step 7: Contract Dispute and Grievance Resolution

One of the main features of any contract is dispute and grievance resolution. The reason for this is that a contract can be no more effective than the means for enforcement since if either party chooses to ignore any part of it, its value is greatly diminished. The purpose of a grievance procedure is to provide a mechanism for peaceful resolution of disputes related to the provisions of the contract. The contract usually defines what constitutes a grievance, the procedural steps to be taken to resolve the grievance, and the time limitations applicable to each step. The following is a sample definition of a grievance:

> *Any claim by the Association, a teacher, or a group of teachers, that there has been an alleged violation, misinterpretation, or misapplication of the terms of the Agreement, an alleged violation of their rights, or alleged violation of any School Board policy or practice shall be a grievance, and shall be resolved through the procedure set forth herein. (Professional Negotiations Agreement between Moline (Illinois) Board of Education, District #40 and Moline Education Association, 1976–78, Article V, cited in Cresswell, Murphey, and Kerchner, 1980, p. 322)*

Once filed, the grievance may progress through several steps, however, it may be settled at any point. The initial step is the filing of a grievance by a meeting of the grievant with the union representative and informing the administration. Next, an informal meeting between the grievant and the supervisor to attempt an informal resolution usually occurs. If unsettled, the grievant may appeal to the next higher level in the process. At each step, time limits must be observed by both parties for filing and responding.

If unresolved at each step, the grievance may be referred for determination by the board of education or arbitration by an outside arbitrator.

Step 8: Contract Evaluation

The final element of contract administration is evaluation. This involves review of the contract while it is in force to determine the extent to which each party's goals and objectives are being met, what types of problems are evident, and what changes should be sought when the contract comes up for renegotiation.

Guidelines for Effective Contract Administration

A good working relationship is essential for effective contract administration. If there is a lack of trust between union and administration, the potential for a large number of costly and time-consuming grievances is large. Therefore, site administrators should endeavor to follow certain practices, such as:

1. *Become familiar with every aspect of the collective bargaining contract, and make sure that your subordinates are familiar with the contract.*
2. *Let subordinates know that you support the contract, and make a "good faith" effort to implement the contract in a fair and impartial manner.*
3. *Seek clarification when uncertain about contract provisions.*
4. *Maintain an open door and encourage administrators, teachers, and classified employees to resolve grievances informally wherever possible.*
5. *Know and respect the grievance process and procedures.*
6. *Keep the union informed of any matters that pertain to contract items.*
7. *Allow union representatives access to employee work areas and means of communication (mail boxes and bulletin boards) in accordance with the contract.*
8. *Respect the confidentiality of grievances.*
9. *Make an effort to resolve grievances in a manner consistent with the contract.*

10. *Do not threaten or impose, or convey any impression of opposition to union representative or collective bargaining. (Webster, 1985)*

The Impact of Collective Bargaining

Perhaps the issue of greatest concern for the educational policy maker is how collective bargaining has affected the quality of public education. What gains have teachers made and how have they affected the nature of teaching? How has the negotiation between school boards and teachers' unions changed the management of schools? Finally, how has collective bargaining affected the learning process and ultimately students?

Collective Bargaining Gains by Teachers

Perhaps the most comprehensive studies of how collective bargaining has affected the economic and professional status of teachers were those carried out by RAND's Center for Policy Research in Education. An initial study by RAND researchers Lorraine McDonnell and Anthony Pascal found significant gains for teachers during the 1960s and 1970s. The pattern of collective bargaining gains encompasses three stages (McDonnell and Pascal, 1979). Stage 1 involves bargaining over increases in salary and fringe benefits, stage 2 progresses to working conditions and job security, and stage 3 confronts issues of educational policy. McDonnell and Pascal's fieldwork indicated a tendency toward gradual professionalization of negotiations on both sides. Nevertheless, they state that rank-and-file teachers generally have substantial influence on bargaining agendas and settlements. In the first decade of substantial bargaining, teachers significantly improved their working conditions and enhanced their influence over the length and composition of the school day, the manner of teacher evaluation, and the use of supplementary personnel (see Table 10.2).

During the 1980s, according to a 1988 study by McDonnell and Pascal, organized teachers continued to expand the areas of influence. By 1980, a majority of bargaining units had included in their contracts provisions for regulating the length of the school day, allowing teachers to respond formally to administrators' evaluations, permitting teachers to exclude disruptive students from

TABLE 10.2 • Percentage of Districts Attaining Key Provisions, 1970, 1975, 1980, 1985

Provisions	1970[a] (N=151[b])	1975[a] (N=151)	1980 (N=151)	1985 (N=155)
1. Teacher can respond formally to administrator's evaluation	42	64[c]	77[c]	76
2. Duration of school day is specified	44	70[c]	68	73
3. Teacher can exclude disruptive student	28	50[c]	54	55
4. Teacher can refuse assignment outside of normal grade or subject	21	14	10	7
5. Maximum class size is specified	21	28	27	28
6. Involuntary transferees are selected on specific criteria	23	36[c]	40	40
7. Instructional policy committee (IPC) established in each school	16	29[c]	31	34
8. Reduction-in-force (RIF) procedures are spelled out	11	44[c]	70[c]	77

Source: L. McDonnell and A. Pascal, *Teacher Unions and Educational Reform* (Santa Monica, CA: RAND Corporation (JRE), April 1988), p. 61.

[a] These percentages differ slightly from the data in McDonnell and Pascal (1979), particularly for 1975. However, substantive interpretations of the trends in the earlier period are not different from those reported, except in the case of provision 4, which registered a decline in 1975 instead of the small rise that was reported earlier.

[b] In 1970, 18 of these districts had not yet begun collective bargaining and thus would necessarily scored 0 for attainment of the provisions.

[c] Indicates a proportion significantly different from the proportion for the immediately preceding year at a confidence level of 5 percent or better.

their classrooms, and outlining clear procedures for districts to follow if they must reduce the size of their teacher force (McDonnell and Pascal, 1988, p. v).

Changes in School Management

There was a time when the principal was unquestionably accepted as the supreme authority in the school (Johnson, 1984). Since the wide dissemination of collective bargaining, however, that is no longer the case. Collective bargaining gains of the last three decades have given teachers a level of formal authority that compels administrators to recognize that they can no longer function successfully without sensitivity to the needs and interests of the teachers. For example, Mitchell and colleagues cite a district in their sample in which 80 percent of the principals were changed in a six-year period! The reason for the personnel changes, according to the superintendent, was to bring in administrators who had the necessary skills required in a contractual environment (Mitchell, Kerchner, Erck, and Pryor, 1981).

Collective bargaining has made important changes in the way schools operate. Perhaps most significant is the effect of formal grievance procedures that allow teachers to challenge managerial demands through a judicial review process. This forces principals to formalize and regularize their relationships with teachers so as to avoid disruptive grievances. Principals must be fastidious in the application of contractual requirements. For example, one superintendent who tried to reassign several teachers because it was his managerial philosophy to introduce "change for change's sake" found himself embroiled in a prolonged grievance that he ultimately lost and that undermined his credibility with teachers and the school board.

As a result, the free-wheeling personality style of educational leadership is no longer viable. In their study, Mitchell and colleagues came to the conclusion that principals now must take pains to rationalize their decisions and offer reasons for their actions. Care must be taken to ensure that managerial directives are "consistent, logical and explicitly related to contract language, district-wide policies, and/or accepted educational goals" (Mitchell et al., 1981, p. 163). When a principal fails to be seen as rational and reasonable, the administration will tend to lose legitimacy to the union, which will be seen as the true defender and interpreter of educational policy.

It is apparent that these changes over the last two decades

have produced some movement in the direction of greater degree of collegiality and shared responsibility within the school environment. However, as bargaining moves to consider a broader range of educational policy concerns, the need for enlightened approaches to school leadership will become more acute (see Chapter Three).

Changes in the Teaching Profession

Several types of changes that pertain to the professionalization of teaching have come about as a result of the extension of collective bargaining. Each of these is related to the degree to which teachers have control over their working conditions. We have classified these as (1) changes in work rules, (2) changes in evaluation and accountability, and (3) professionalization.

Work Rules and the Use of Teacher Time
Among the more dramatic consequences of collective bargaining has been the change in the character of teachers' work responsibilities and the use of teachers' time. These changes range from contract provisions that limit the length of the work day and assignment and transfer policy to the specification of regular and extra duties. Collective bargaining has resulted in the explicit recognition of regular work duties as distinct from extra duties, which teachers may choose to perform or decline (and in some contracts earn extra pay for so doing). Prior to collective bargaining, many of these extra duties were considered by principals to be part of the job. Collective bargaining has had the effect of defining what is an appropriate work load. Limitations of the nature or extensiveness of such duties will imply that more employees will be needed or that less service may be forthcoming. One example of how collective bargaining has sharply curtailed the demands that can be placed on teachers is illustrated in the following provisions of the Philadelphia Federation of Teachers' 1972 and 1976 contracts:

1. *Teachers shall not be required to attend meetings outside of their regularly assigned hours for which there is no compensation.*
2. *Two faculty meetings per month may be extended by a maximum of 30 minutes beyond school time.*
3. *Teachers are not required to participate in more than two night activities per school year.*
4. *Teachers are not required to perform street corner*

duties unless the corner's sidewalk is immediately
adjacent to the school building; unless police crossing
guards, or NTSs are unavailable; and unless teachers
have traditionally performed these duties in that
school. (Perry, 1974, pp 59–60)

Evaluation and Accountability

Although the impetus for changes in work rules has largely occurred at the behest of teacher organizations, contract provisions that treat evaluation and accountability have come both from unions and management. On the one hand, teachers' organizations have sought evaluation procedures that would strictly define the process and make it subject to arbitration so as to limit the scope for arbitrary decisions by school administrators. On the other hand, management has sought contractually to define performance standards and evaluation procedures in order to give principals the tools they need to control teacher quality. Thus both sides have placed increased emphasis in this area. Collective bargaining has not generally changed basic evaluation policies, but it has introduced procedural requirements designed to protect teachers from arbitrary action and introduced a greater degree of due process. For example, most contracts prohibit the placement of derogatory material in a teacher's file, entitle teachers to receive copies of evaluations in a reasonable time period, provide for self-evaluations and the examination of one's own file, and stipulate conditions under which a teacher's performance may be rated unsatisfactory.

Meanwhile, the next stage of bargaining will be marked by pressures to have teachers submit their work to closer direct scrutiny (Mitchell et al., 1981; see Chapter Eight). Educational policy makers have made it clear that additional benefits should be granted only in exchange for performance-based evaluation (McDonnell and Pascal, 1988).

Professionalization

Teachers' organizations have argued for some time that the route to greater professionalization is through a strong contract. As we noted in Chapter Two, professionalization involves formalizing and broadening the base of authority to control the conditions of work. The RAND study (1988) examined the extent to which 15 professional teaching conditions had been incorporated in their sample of 151 contracts. Among the indicators of professionalism were the following items: equal or majority representation of teachers on instructional policy committees, maximum class size, controls on classroom interruptions, and the contractual protection of academic freedom (see Table 10.3). Although there was some progress between 1970 and 1980 on the indicators, little evidence occurred between 1980 and 1985. This is attributed to the fact that the drive to strengthen teacher professionalism began in earnest around 1985.

TABLE 10.3 • *Professional Teaching Conditions and Attainment of Them in 1980 and 1985 Contracts*

Professional Teaching Conditions	Percent of Districts Attaining Items	
	1980	1985
1. Assistance provided to teachers judged unsatisfactory	59	57
2. Provisional teachers to be evaluated	65	63
3. Teachers can refuse assignments outside of grade or subject area	10	7
4. Administrators cannot intervene to change teachers' grades	9	10
5. Controls on administration of standardized tests to students	2	1
6. Limits on number of subjects, grades, or ability groups teachers must teach	52	50
7. Establishes academic freedom for teachers	49	52
8. Teachers comprise half or more of instructional policy committee (IPC) membership	39	46
9. IPCs established in each school	31	33
10. IPCs empowered to review curriculum	33	38
11. Class size mandated	27	28
12. Teachers can exclude a disruptive student	54	54
13. Limits on teachers' paperwork load	16	18
14. Controls on number of classroom interruptions	31	29
15. Salary paid during sabbatical leaves	77	73

Source: L. McDonnell and A. Pascal, *Teacher Unions and Educational Reform* (Santa Monica, CA: RAND Corporation (JRE), April 1988), p. 7.

Impact on Students

Perhaps for all parties concerned with education, the question of how collective bargaining has affected students is the most crucial. This is an area in which strong views separate the opposing positions. McDonnell and Pascal (1979) noted that "how any of these consequences of collective bargaining influence the rate of learning or other student interests remains largely unknown" (p. xiii). Opponents of teacher unionism have declared that teachers, in their fight for higher wages, have abandoned their sense of duty and lost sight of the larger educational goals. One study noted the rise of teacher absenteeism as some teachers sought to view sick leave as an entitlement to be absent (Mitchell et al., 1981). Others have decried the reduction in regular teaching days. In contrast, proponents have argued that professionalizing teaching has improved the quality of teachers, and, by extension, student learning.

In 1979, the National Institute of Education began a seven-year study of the impact of collective bargaining on student performance. The study considered the effects of bargaining on teacher mobility, resource allocation, working conditions and teacher attitudes, teacher characteristics, and how these affected student achievement. The study concluded that schools in districts with collective bargaining are "more productive for the average elementary school student" (Eberts and Stone, 1986, p. 13). The schools were more productive in that students scored 5 percent higher on standardized tests. The reasons for this is that unionized districts rely to a greater degree on standard classroom instruction techniques that work best with the majority of students, and because instructional leadership by principals in these districts is marked by superior communication and coordination. Additionally, unionized school districts spend on an average about 12 percent more per pupil than nonunionized districts. However, for students who are significantly above or below the average, nonunionized schools are more productive for the reason that these students benefit from nonstandardized approaches, such as the use of teachers' aides, specialists, and independent programmed instruction. With greater instructional flexibility, nonunionized districts can better meet the needs of exceptional students (Eberts and Stone, 1986). Meanwhile, another study found evidence that unionized districts had higher class size as school boards offered higher salaries in exchange for larger classes (Hall and Carroll, 1976).

What one sees, then, is a mixed set of results from collective bargaining as it has traditionally been practiced. There have been appropriate enhancements to the economic and professional status of teachers, and there have been significant concomitant gains in working conditions and workplace guarantees. There have also been some initial steps taken toward professionalization. Meanwhile, these gains for teachers have not been without cost— inflexibility in educational programs and poorer performance by gifted as well as developmentally limited students. The following section explores some of the problems with conventional collective bargaining.

The Limits of Traditional Collective Bargaining

As education enters into the fourth decade of collective bargaining, the issue of educational reform is imminent. Does the traditional adversarial approach provide avenues for answering some of the critical areas in need of restructuring? In their 1988 study, McDonnell and Pascal conclude, "The collective bargaining process and resulting contract can either serve as one of the most effective vehicles for promoting and implementing educational reforms and change or as a major obstacle to change" (p. x). The key lies in whether unions and school managers can identity mutual interests within the context of the bargaining process.

Zero-Sum Bargaining

One of the major liabilities of the collective bargaining process is its adversarial nature. "In collective bargaining," writes Dimitri Liontos of the Oregon School Study Council, "part of the problem is that 'the players' often see themselves as members of two opposing teams engaged in a win-lose match" (1987, p. 3). In the win-lose game it is not uncommon for both sides to incur damage: Damaged self-respect, damaged collegiality, damaged public relations, or a damaged school system are not uncommon. The damage to personal relationships, which we pointed out in the preceding chapters are the quintessential components of teamwork and effective management, can take many years to repair. This is especially true when the negotiation has been prolonged or where a strike occurred.

Deception, Secrecy, and Threats

Among the common negotiating strategies are the use of deception, secrecy, and threats. Most professional negotiators receive training and learn to use this arsenal of available weapons to achieve their bargaining goals. For example, a typical text on collective bargaining for educators recommends such tactics as the following:

> *Third Party Threat . . . when one team learns that the other team has strong feelings against the use of fact-finders, mediators, and arbitrators, it is sometimes possible to use the threat of calling in such outsiders to advantage.*
> *Use of Public Sentiment . . . the strongest case that can be made to the public is one made on emotional grounds. There is only one basis for such a case: children. Put another way, the opposing side must be made to appear as though it is obstructing or opposed to what is best for children. (Webster, 1985, p. 83)*

Whatever the merits of such tactics in the context of a bargaining process, it will be clear that the ultimate impact on the level of trust between teachers and administrators is likely to be damaging.

Reduced Flexibility

A further feature of the traditional labor-management relations is the tendency toward reduced flexibility. For example, in order to protect the jobs of workers in an adversarial environment, industrial unions have resorted to featherbedding and inflexible work rules. The same process has begun, albeit on a small scale, among teachers through contracts that concentrate on limiting teachers' work obligations through rules that reduce flexibility and ultimately limit the scope of teachers to share responsibility for the full range of educational activities.

In addition, what appears to have occurred in a number of school districts is the institutionalization and elaboration of outdated and inherently inefficient systems of management. Within the confines of the traditional adversarial system of labor relations, it is unreasonable to expect that employees will act to protect management or the public where to do so would require a change in the very scope and limits of the administrative framework. The responsibility for system redesign and undoing a web of nonproductive rules and procedures must initially rest with management.

Public Pressures for Change

The traditional adversarial approach to bargaining in education seems to be approaching its limits due to several converging forces. First, the taxpayer revolt promises to limit the ability of school boards to find the tax dollars to pay for any substantial gains for teachers. This is one of the main reasons behind RAND's finding that teacher unions had made few economic gains since 1975 (McDonnell and Pascal, 1988). Meanwhile, a second current is the public's perception that education is not able to perform to its expectations. This growing frustration with public education placed added pressure on the two main teachers' organizations, the NEA and the AFT, to respond. As a result, the unions responded in the late 1980s by embracing a policy they had previously opposed—school-based decision making. In 1985, Albert Shanker, President of the AFT, made a remarkable statement: "Collective bargaining has been a good mechanism, and we should continue to use it. But we now must ask whether collective bargaining will get us where we want to go" (cited in Peck, 1988, p. 33). Theodore Sizer, Brown University Professor of Education, saw school-based decision making as a development that would eventually undermine collective bargaining as teachers take on more managerial functions.

Conventional bargaining remains a barrier in the path toward shared responsibility in educational management. The reason is that both union representatives as well as school board members operate under political and financial constraints on what they may discuss, offer, or accept. Although the adversarial method may be effective for dividing limited resources in response to political realities and relative power, the structural conditions are not favorable for devising innovative approaches to old problems.

These trends together have provoked a search for new approaches to bargaining. As teachers search for an avenue that will take them to professional status and as the public searches for schools that work better than the present generation of public schools, new models of labor-management relations are appearing. In the next section we review several of these participatory models of labor-management relations.

Why Participatory Approaches to Labor-Management Relations in Public Education Are Necessary

In the course of the 1980s, it became apparent to teachers and union leaders that collective bargaining was not working as hoped. It is true that substantial economic gains have been made, but the professional gains once hoped for were not, as the RAND study pointedly demonstrated, achieved (McDonnell and Pascal, 1988). Furthermore, administrators have found that traditional collective bargaining complicates the process of school management and may actually impede achievement of the kind of reforms that require trust and cooperation to achieve. Two influential studies of educational management, the Carnegie report entitled *A Nation Prepared: Teachers for the 21st Century,* and the California Commission on the Teaching Profession, highlighted the need to find new, less adversarial approaches to labor-management relations in the schools. Subsequently, both the AFT and the NEA have joined their voices in sponsorship and support of initiatives to find alternatives to the traditional model.

The problem with the traditional model in the eyes of Douglas Mitchell, a former director of policy support services at Far West Laboratory for Educational Research and Development, is the assumption that teaching is akin to industrial labor and does not include artistic, craft, or professional elements (Mitchell, 1986). Although traditional collective bargaining tends to protect the laboring aspects of teachers' work roles, it does so at the expense of its artistic, craft, and professional components. By adopting an effective but circumscribed approach to contract negotiation, teacher organizations have strengthened job security by establishing a system of tightly defined work rules. However, work rules, such as a limitation on the number of meetings teachers can be required to attend per month, may reduce educational flexibility while denying teachers responsibility and decision-making authority.

Mitchell views union organization in terms of a matrix that relates areas in which unions control access to those that they seek to control (see Figure 10.4).

FIGURE 10.4 • *Models of Union Organization*

| | | Control Over Access to: | |
		Workplace	Task Performance
	Job Security (Rights)	Industrial Labor	Skilled Craft
Seek to Establish Control Over:	Personal Autonomy (Value)	Artistic Performance	Professional Practice

Source: D. E. Mitchell, E. T. Kerchner, W. Erck, and G. Pryor, "The Impact of Collective Bargaining on School Management and Policy," *American Journal of Education* (February 1986):9. Reprinted with permission from The University of Chicago Press.

Industrial unions control access to the workplace and seek to establish control over job security. Organizing through the work site, they seek to control the conditions under which members work. Meanwhile, craft unions, such as plumbers and airline pilots, organize workers with similar training or skills to gain control over the right to perform these tasks. Contractual agreements forbid nonunion members from performing the craft. Artistic and professional unions, in contrast, focus on guaranteeing the independence of workers and seek to assure that all members earn a minimally acceptable wage. Members can earn a higher wage if their proficiency is superior. However, artistic organizations concern themselves more with controlling when and where they work than with the conditions of work. Artistic work is not readily supervised, hence work rules are kept to a minimum to preserve maximum flexibility over the performer's time. Turning to professional organizations, the distinguishing characteristic of professionals is that they take personal responsibility for how best to serve their clients. If they cannot exercise the right to decide when and whether certain tasks are in the best interests of their clients, they lose their claim to professional status. They seek to set the goals of their work, and their negotiations focus on the limits of professional autonomy and the relationship to the organization (Mitchell, 1986).

Teaching involves elements of all types of work. Teachers work as laborers when they perform tasks that require no special skill or ability, such as collecting lunch money or supervising the cafeteria. They use craft skills in planning lessons and grading papers. And artistic aspects are evident when teachers "perform" a lesson, dramatize important points or, like an artistic director, cast a play for an open house. And still beyond these areas there is a large professional component to teachers' work. When the classroom teacher structures learning components to meet the needs of a particular student or analyzes the merits of a particular curriculum, the teacher acts as a professional. What is apparent is that the traditional industrial approach to labor relations may fail to take into account the broad professional and artistic responsibilities that demand flexibility and recognize the role of the teacher in establishing learning goals. Tightly structured work rules may protect the teacher from administrative abuses, but will do so at the cost of achieving the broad educational goals that the public expects for each individual student. One consequence has been a substantial exodus from public education to private schools, as parents search for more individual attention.

This has led Mitchell and others, including AFT president Albert Shanker, to argue for a system that supports the joint involvement of teachers and administrators in developing educational goals. However, since traditional collective bargaining is adversarial, each side tends to be committed to defending positions rather than addressing concerns and solving problems. Fisher and Ury (1981) argue that the traditional adversarial approach creates incentives for defending positions, generates distrust, and impedes exploration of mutual interests and the development of options that can solve problems.

There is yet another aspect to consider in the next phase of labor-management relations in education. While union leaders have tended to judge effectiveness by winning concessions, teachers' perceptions of effectiveness centers on the ability of the union to develop a more credible and cooperative relationship with management (Maitland and Kerchner, 1986).

A system of labor-management relations is needed that reaches beyond the treatment of teachers as mere industrial laborers to include recognition of the professional, craft, and artistic components and allows for teachers' involvement in key areas of educational policy. There are a host of critical educational policy issues in which unions could be involved if the nature of the bargaining process were altered. For example, in the area of performance standards, what can be done about an incompetent teacher? Although professionals enforce standards of performance, in education this is a matter in which typically the school board and the teachers' union are on opposite sides, with the union occasionally defending a teacher who is commonly known to be incompetent. Could the union become involved in the process of establishing and enforcing standards of performance? Such action would involve the union explicitly in what is normally considered to be a management activity. It involves moving beyond traditional collective bargaining.

Achieving Participatory Educational Administration

Two models or alternatives to achieving participatory school-labor relations, collaborative bargaining and policy trust agreements, have emerged from negotiations in several districts. Each of these approaches makes substantive contributions to better labor relations and school management.

Collaborative or Mutual Gain Bargaining

Pueblo, Colorado, school board member, R. Michael Holmes, found much of his experience in contract negotiations and implementation to be frustrating and counterproductive. Rather than resolving conflict, he found that, in some instances, collective bargaining accentuated conflict. Some board members adopted the unhealthy attitude of "If an adversary relationship is what teachers want, that's what they'll get—and they'll be sorry for it at the bargaining table" (Holmes, 1981, p. 23). As a result of this type of thinking—that management should win every argument and seek to maintain the upper hand to punish and defeat teachers—there is now some credence to an old Persian proverb: "If you seek revenge, dig two graves." School board victories proved hollow and were followed by a climate of rancor equally unpleasant to both sides.

According to Holmes, the negotiations would occasionally follow a course of compromise, with each side listing an inordinate number of demands, many of which were unreasonable and without any merit, but included for their "trade-off" value. After a great waste of time and expenditure of energy, these frivolous items would be eliminated and serious bargaining might begin. However, it was still a process crippled by faulty communication. As in win-lose negotiation, the two sides were not listening attentively to each other, and they were misinterpreting each others' positions.

Fisher and Ury (1981) make the point that without effective communication there cannot be meaningful negotiation. They identify three stumbling blocks:

1. Negotiators are playing to the gallery. Rather than talking to each other, they are talking only to impress third parties or their own constituency.
2. Negotiators are not hearing what the other side is saying.
3. Negotiators misunderstand and misinterpret the other side's position.

The alternative suggested by Holmes and implemented in several Oregon school districts is collaborative or mutual gain bargaining. The essence of this approach involves communicating and understanding the concerns of each side at the bargaining table. Instead of taking *positions*, each side should try to explore and understand the *interests* and concerns of the other party. These concerns then become identified as problems and "the negotiating process becomes a matter of solving these problems in reasonable, acceptable ways. Both sides offer suggestions to solve the problems, and both sides commit themselves to consider seriously each question" (Holmes, 1981, p. 29).

Liontos (1987) provides a vivid illustration from Oregon's West Linn School District, which was in the midst of adversarial contract negotiations that had been going on with no end in sight. Dea Cox then took over as the new superintendent.

> *The turning point . . . occurred when he began sitting in on the negotiations as an observer. At one session . . . a board member responded tangentially to a question asked by a member of the teachers' association team. Cox quietly intervened, saying to one member: "You didn't answer Marilyn's question. If you folks are going to solve this issue, you're going to have to listen to each other. Now, Marilyn, say it again." This time the board member addressed the question and communicated a clearer understanding of the issue. The logjam had broken. "Just a little thing," admits Cox, but the most positive thing to come from a superintendent—that he'd be willing to tell a board member to pay attention. (Liontos, 1987, p. 9)*

From this first incident, Superintendent Cox established a style of cooperative bargaining. Every month a "problem identifying" group of teachers and administrators meet to discuss ways of reaching solutions in order to defuse potential conflicts before they become critical. With input from the group, issues are aired and resolved prior to formal bargaining. Teachers participate informally in setting district goals and resolving problems and determining priorities. Importantly, this ongoing discussion produces a climate of trust and amicable negotiations have been the rule.

A similar approach has been implemented by Oregon Superintendent Don Charles in several districts. Charles's approach consists of five elements (Liontos, 1987):

1. Each side would bargain without an outside negotiator.
2. Each side would have a team of no more than eight members.
3. Teachers would bargain only on issues that are locally relevant.
4. The district would sponsor monthly meetings to discuss labor-management problems and maintain open ongoing communication—a type of "continuous bargaining."
5. The parties could renegotiate whenever necessary.

Collaborative bargaining proceeds by way of discussing *interests* behind issues as opposed to taking *positions*. Techniques such as brainstorming, consensus building, and problem solving are employed in seeking to define options and option packages. The options may then be evaluated by using a mutually agreed upon standard (e.g., the least number of people are hurt). In order for a district to use collaborative or win-win bargaining, both parties must be committed to this method and be trained in its techniques. The U.S. Government's Federal Mediation and Conciliation Service and the U.S. Department of Labor Management Relations provide workshops and training to interested parties. In the state of California, the Public Employment Relations Board provides these services to school districts (see Box 10.1).

Policy Trust Agreements

A policy trust agreement is a signed agreement between a school district and a teachers' association to undertake jointly an

BOX 10.1 • Conflictual versus Cooperative Labor Relations

Elements of the Labor Relationship Which May Promote Conflict	Elements of the Labor Relationship Which May Promote Cooperation
Attitudes	**Attitudes**
1. Managing is done "around the contract".	1. Managing is done "through the contract".
2. "Distributive" bargaining of separate interests with compromise.	2. "Integrative" bargaining of mutual interests.
3. Mediation takes place only after impasse is formally declared.	3. Informal mediation processes are built in so they happen continuously.
4. The other side is viewed as a problem in an involuntary relationship.	4. The other side is accepted as a necessary part of a bilateral process.
Financial Structures	**Financial Structures**
5. Budgetary information is restricted by the district.	5. Open budget processes and/or financial formula are used.
Bargaining Processes	**Bargaining Processes**
6. Bargaining is done from positions.	6. Bargaining is done from problem statements.
7. One person talks for each side, or communication is restricted.	7. Open communications with everyone encouraged to talk.
8. Caucuses are frequent, and the purpose and outcome is kept secret.	8. Caucuses are held less frequently, with each side openly explaining the reason for the caucus and the outcome.
9. Bargaining chips are used frequently.	9. Both sides strive for consensus and the elimination of bargaining chips.

10. Bargaining consists of a "package" of small, tentative agreements into which each side is fixed.
11. Negotiations planning involves the selection of positions.
12. Each sides sits directly across the table from the other.
13. Communications to the constituencies and general public are frequently conflicting and divisive.

Working Relationships

14. The labor-management relationship evolves as a by-product of the collective bargaining process.
15. Relationship issues and substantive issues are mixed and traded off for one another.
16. Field representatives and consultants are perceived as outsiders.
17. Formal bargaining is the only problem solving mechanism.
18. The superintendent and board are insulated from the labor relations process.

10. Bargaining involves conceptualizing the "bigger picture" and withholding commitments until an appropriate and mutually agreeable time.
11. Process planning tools are utilized to analyze interests, options, and parameters.
12. Participants are arranged in a circle or around a mutual focal point such as a flipchart.
13. Communications with constituencies and the general public are developed together.

Working Relationships

14. The two sides work together to plan and develop a relationship which supports the achievement of mutual goals.
15. Relationship issues and substantive issues are addressed separately and independently.
16. Field representatives and consultants are perceived as insiders, or as bringing unique mediation and dispute resolution skills.
17. Mechanisms for solving problems are developed, including communications and issue focussed committees and brainstorming strategies.
18. The superintendent and board are involved in the labor relations processes.

Continued

BOX 10.1 *Continued*

Elements of the Labor Relationship Which May Promote Conflict

19. There is a positional approach to work-site problems.

20. There is a reliance on formal grievance procedures, un-fair hearings and concerted job actions for resolving conflict.

Shared Decision Making

21. Bargaining is narrowly confined to scope.

22. Employee groups feel excluded from decision making.

Elements of the Labor Relationship Which May Promote Cooperation

19. There is a "consensus" approach to work-site prob-lems.

20. There is a reliance on problem-solving techniques for resolving conflict.

Shared Decision Making

21. Discussions and decisions address all aspects of the mutual relationship (even beyond scope).

22. Employee groups feel included in relevant decisions.

Source: John Glaser, "Alternative Labor Relations Practices: A Second Look." From the February/March 1989 issue of *Thrust for Educational Leadership,* published by the Association of California School Administrators.

educational project. Whereas collective bargaining contracts comprise two key sections (work rules and grievance procedures), policy trust agreements focus on shared goals and implementation procedures. Traditional collective bargaining seeks to define or limit the scope of teachers' work responsibilities, whereas policy trust agreements typically expand teacher involvement and responsibilities (see Figure 10.5).

The first policy trust agreement commenced in 1987—a pilot program initiating several trust agreements in California school districts as a collaborative effort by the California Federation of Teachers and the California School Board Association under the auspices of the University of California/Stanford University Policy Analysis for California Education program. The purpose of the trust agreement project was to develop new patterns of relationships between teachers and school administrators while expanding the focus of labor-management discussions to substantive areas of educational policy. In the first year, six districts participated. Three districts designed programs to address the issue of peer assistance and peer review, two districts chose staff development, and one district focused on staff evaluation. Perhaps the best way to comprehend this new form of labor-management relations is to examine some representative agreements.

FIGURE 10.5 • *Comparing Contracts with Policy Trust Agreements*

Contracts Establish:	*Trust Agreements Establish:*
1. **Work rules** that specify: • **Required work** activities for various tasks, • **Rights** granted to individual workers.	1. **Work goals** that specify: • **Purposes** to be pursued and criteria for assessing progress, • **Resources** of time, money and authority to be held in trust.
and,	and,
2. **Grievance procedures** developed to: • **Create procedures** for hearing disputes, and • **Assign authority** for adjudicating disagreements.	2. **Execution procedures** developed to: • **Assign responsibility** for implementation of the agreement, and • **Create trustees** to resolve disagreements and insure fair and full implementation.

Source: Douglas E. Mitchell, "Policy Trust Agreements: A Better Approach to School Labor Relations," *Thrust* (September 1986):11.

The Statement of Purpose of the Trust Agreement in Shared Decision Making between the Petaluma Federation of Teachers and the Petaluma School District makes it clear that a new relationship is being created.

> *The purpose of this educational policy trust agreement is to express the District's desire to create the organizational culture and style that supports the growth of character in students and staff through the building of self-confidence, self-reliance, and mutual respect. In order to bring these abstract qualities to concrete reality, the District and the Federation agree to implement models of shared governance. To these ends, we must create a special relationship among administrators, parents, students, and teachers. (Draft Trust Agreement in Shared Decision Making, no date)*

The agreement then specifies actions that will be taken to implement it, resources that will be made available by the District, and responsibilities of the District Trust Agreement Team. An additional element of the agreement is an extraordinary mechanism for dispute resolution:

> *When it is clear that resolution cannot be reached by continuing conversations between parties, either party may request that a third party be called in for consultation. The selection of the consultant(s) will be by mutual agreement. If agreement cannot be reached with the help of the consultant(s), the agreement is null and void. (Draft Trust Agreement in Shared Decision Making, no date)*

The experience to date with these agreements is that they serve as catalysts to change. They can lead to significant role changes among teachers and school administrators. This has occurred as teachers are included as partners in decisions about the structure and method of operation of a school district. Trust agreements differ substantially from traditional contract negotiations; they move the opposing parties from defending positions to discussing mutual interests. Dale Kinsley superintendent of Santa Cruz, City Schools in California, stated it succinctly:

> *[As a result of the trust agreement process], union and management now have a sense of shared responsibility*

that didn't exist before. Moreover, preliminary evidence suggests that trust agreements are reaching out to alter the scope of all bargaining in at least one district where negotiations are far more collegial than at any time in the past. (Koppich and Kerchner, 1988)

Strong union and district leadership are nevertheless essential ingredients for success. The risks involved in following the trust agreement course requires that leaders be willing to bear the risks. Meanwhile, as pointed out in Chapter Five, those involved in collaborative decision making need to learn new skills, and the parties to a trust agreement need to master the skills of cooperative goal setting and consensual decision making.

To summarize, there are four steps in developing a policy trust agreement. First, identify the goals and purposes to be covered by the trust agreement. This should include an explicit statement of the criteria for measuring progress. Second, identify the resources to be allocated or set aside, personnel time, and money. Work units or project teams need to be identified and their responsibilities defined. Third, develop the implementation process to be used, assign responsibilities to participants (teachers, administrators, departments, parents), and establish a schedule of activities. Finally, develop the trusteeship arrangements, which include a dispute resolution procedure and an evaluation and review process.

Policy trust agreements are important complements to participative management and collective bargaining. They form a bridge between the articulation of notions of teacher professionalism and shared teacher-administrator decision making, and the implementation of such notions in the real world of collectively bargained contracts. By actually transferring money and authority to joint teacher-administrator teams, policy trust agreements facilitate improvements in the functioning of the schools.

Summary

The introduction of collective bargaining during the last three decades has restructured the role of the educational administrator, limiting the scope for unilateral decision making while providing a range of contractual protections for teachers. Collective bargaining, which affects an estimated 90 percent of all districts, has resulted in substantial improvements in salary and working conditions in schools. The union contract is a legal document that is a product of contract negotiation. Site administrators must endeavor to be fully conversant with the contract.

Despite the substantial gains that have come about as a result of collective bargaining, there is a growing concern that the adversarial nature of collective bargaining is, in some respects, counterproductive with regard to achieving broad-based educational goals, cooperation in solving problems, and achieving genuine shared decision making. This has led a growing number of school districts to explore new models and approaches that can produce improved trust and understanding between union and administrators. Such approaches can be grouped under the rubric of mutual gain bargaining.

Mutual gain bargaining and a close variant, policy trust agreements, involve negotiation that is based on principles, concepts, and procedures that permit both sides of a dispute to emerge as winners. The principles involved are:

- Focus on issues, not personalities.
- Focus on issues, not principles.
- Seek options that satisfy the expressed interests of both parties.
- Evaluate the results by using objective standards.

The assumptions that underlie this approach are distinct from traditional adversarial bargaining in several respects. Traditional bargainers accept settlements with winners and losers because they believe the fundamental nature of bargaining is competitive. They believe that whatever damage is done to interpersonal relationships can be repaired later. Since bargaining is over scarce resources, they define success as a settlement favorable to their side and see their opponent's dissatisfaction as an indication that the settlement favored their side.

In contrast, collaborative bargainers believe that a prime consideration in achieving a successful agreement is the interpersonal relationship between both sides. They believe that both parties have some area of mutual interests and that both should win, and they should help each other to do so. Because of their emphasis on a respectful and trusting relationship, mutual gain bargainers are committed to open and frank discussions of interests. This permits identification of an expanded area of mutual interests. They believe that the parties valuing things differently provides a basis for packages of options in which both sides win.

Case Study _____

Poway School District

(Authors' Note: The Poway Unified School District and the Poway Federation of Teachers developed and implemented a peer assistance and review program for first-year teachers. Why did the union, district, and school board seek a new approach in their labor relations? What common interests did the district and the union share? What did the union give up and what risks did it take? What rights did the district relinquish? What appear to be results of this process?)

Poway is a rapidly growing suburban San Diego County school district of more than 20,000 students and 850 teachers in 19 school sites. The communities that feed into Poway schools are upper-middle class; 72 percent of the families are classified as professional or semiprofessional. Only 16 percent of Poway's students are nonwhite.

As a rapidly growing school district, Poway is now beginning to hire many new teachers. In 1987–88, for example, 125 new teachers were hired at 11 schools, and similar patterns are expected in successive years as older teachers retire and housing development accelerates. Historically, labor negotiations in Poway have been protracted and tense.

The problem the district faces is that school principals cannot successfully supervise and socialize this large number of teachers. To meet this problem, the union and district entered into a trust agreement process as a possible palliative to an otherwise acrimonious relationship. The district-union trust agreement team devised a teacher-supervised assistance and evaluation program for first-year teachers. Based in part on the peer review system in place in Toledo, Ohio, the Poway trust agreement involves the transfer of both money and authority in the following respects: (1) the union has agreed to allocate $100,000 over which it had contractually negotiated authority to the new teacher project; (2) the district agreed that three senior teachers, jointly selected by the union and district, would be released from their regular teaching duties to implement the new peer assistance and review program; and (3) the union and district agreed to form a joint governing board to study the findings of teacher reviewers and make recommendations about continued employment to the superintendent and school board.

To create reasonable work loads, the trust agreement team decided to apply the new supervision system only to novice teachers in elementary and middle schools. New high school teachers and teachers entering the system with experience in other school districts were not included in the program. Each of the three supervising teachers worked with 38 novice teachers during the 1987–88 school year. In early fall, supervising teachers primarily provided logistical assistance to new teachers, helping them order books, find supplies, and meet more senior teachers. This assistance stood in vivid contrast to the "sink or swim" introduction to classroom life that has historically greeted new teachers in Poway and elsewhere.

The fall visits by the supervising teachers were informal and their observations largely unstructured. Beginning just before the Christmas break, however, supervising teachers began to conduct rigorous evaluations of novices in their charge. These evaluations centered on three aspects of teaching: (1) classroom management, or the ability to establish an orderly learning environment; (2) knowledge of subject matter; and (3) familiarity with at least the rudiments of pedagogy.

Supervising teachers demonstrated different techniques for the novices, provided informal feedback on individual lessons, offered support when beginning teachers wanted to "try something new," and even substituted in novices' classes to enable new teachers to observe more experienced teachers at work. This type of assistance and evaluation is in sharp contrast to traditional administrator evaluation, which typically lasts only a few minutes and is often quite superficial. In Poway, new teacher evaluations lasted for several hours, covered more than one subject area, and were interspersed with frequent informal visits and much assistance.

The review panel, consisting of the assistant superintendent for instruction, assistant superintendent for personnel, president of the union, a teacher appointed by the union, and the project's director (an administrative appointee who is a teacher and former union president), began in the spring to review supervising teachers' evaluations of the novices. Supervising teachers presented their "cases" to the review board in the form of written summary evaluations of each candidate. The panel discussed each case and made decisions. Of the 38 novice teachers, 3 were denied second-year contracts, 3 received marginal evaluations with specific suggestions for improvement, and 32 were "graduated" to second-year probation.

The Poway agreement is significant for several reasons. First, the new intensity of evaluation for first-year teachers signals to novices that the process of becoming a teacher is not simple or automatic; it requires work and skill. Second, Poway's program institutionalizes a support system for beginning teachers. Third, the involvement of senior teachers in assisting and evaluating novices sends a message to experienced teachers that their expertise is valued.

Certainly it is not the norm for unionized teachers to participate in dismissing one of their own. However, the three teachers whose contracts were not renewed in Poway had such obvious problems that dismissal was nearly rendered a nonissue. Of more significance, perhaps, is to focus on the 10 or so teachers whose performance was marginal before the intervention process began. These novices received substantial assistance, significantly more than that which would have been available without the program. Their school district and union made a substantial investment in these teachers' professional development and success in the classroom. As several principals noted, without this program, at least some of these novices would not have survived their first year of teaching. Now, say the principals, these new teachers can begin to contribute to the district and to their profession.

Finally, at least some circumstantial evidence exists that Poway's trust agreement process may offer the potential for improving a tense relationship between district administration and the union. Poway teachers began school in September 1988 with a negotiated contract, an event that has occurred only once in the past decade. While it may be a leap of faith to attribute conclusion of contract negotiations to participation in the Trust Agreement Project, it is the case that the essential ingredients of the new contract were developed during the March trust agreement conference. Thus, Poway offers evidence that even in districts in which labor-management relations may be characterized as less-than-cordial, trust agreements may provide a vehicle for substantial organizational change.

Source: Julia E. Koppich and Charles T. Kerchner, "The Trust Agreement Project: Broadening the Vision of School Labor-Management Relations," Policy Analysis for California Education (PACE), Berkeley, CA, September 1988.

References

Apple, M. W. *Teachers and Texts.* New York: Routledge, 1986.

Cresswell, A.; Murphey, M.; and Kerchner, C. *Teachers, Unions and Col-*

lective Bargaining in Public Education. Berkeley, CA: McCutchan, 1980.

Eberts, R., and Stone, E. *The Effect of Teacher Unions on American Education.* National Institute of Education, Washington, DC, March 1986.

Fisher, R., and Ury, W. *Getting to Yes.* Boston: Houghton Mifflin, 1981.

Glaser, J. "Alternative Labor Relations Practices: A Second Look." *Thrust* (February/March 1989):32–37.

Hall, W. C., and Carroll, N. E. "The Effect of Teachers' Organizations on Salaries and Class Size." In A. Cresswell and M. Murphey (Eds.), *Education and Collective Bargaining.* Berkeley, CA: McCutchan, 1976.

Holmes, R. M. "Reduce Hostility: Use Teacher Negotiations to Solve Mutual Problems." *American School Board Journal* (August 1981).

Johnson, S. M. *Teacher Unions in Schools.* Philadelphia: Temple University Press, 1984.

Koppich, J., and Kerchner, C. "The Trust Agreement Project: Broadening the Vision of School Labor-Management Relations." PACE Policy Paper No. PP88–9-7 (September 1988).

Liontos, D. "Collaborative Bargaining in the Schools: Case Studies and Recommendations." *Oregon School Study Council* 31 (September 1987).

Maitland, C., and Kerchner, C. "The Tone of Labor Relations in Schools: Correlates of Teacher Perception." Paper presented to AERA, San Francisco, April 1986.

McDonnell, L., and Pascal, A. *Organized Teachers in American Schools.* Santa Monica, CA: RAND, February 1979.

McDonnell, L., and Pascal, A. *Teacher Unions and Educational Reform.* Santa Monica, CA: RAND, April 1988.

Mitchell, D. "Policy Trust Agreements: A Better Approach to School Labor Relations." *Thrust* (September 1986):8–12.

Mitchell, D.; Kerchner, E. T.; Erck, W.; and Pryor, G. "The Impact of Collective Bargaining on School Management and Policy." *American Journal of Education* 89 (February 1981):147–188.

Peck, L. "Today's Teachers Unions Are Looking Well Beyond Collective Bargaining." *American School Board Journal* 175 (July 1988):32–36.

Perry, C. *Labor Relations Climate and Management Rights in Urban School School Systems.* Wharton School Industrial Research Unit, University of Pennsylvania, 1974.

Quinn, J. B. "Strategies for Change." In J. B. Quinn et al. (Eds.), *The Strategy Process.* Englewood Cliffs, NJ: Prentice-Hall, 1988.

Smith, P., and Russell. "An Alternative Form of Collective Bargaining." *Phi Delta Kappan* (April 1986).

Tyack, D. B. *The One Best System: A History of American Urban Education.* Cambridge, MA: Harvard University Press, 1974.

Tyler, G. "Why They Organize." In A. Cresswell and M. Murphey (Eds)., *Education and Collective Bargaining.* Berkeley, CA: McCutchan, 1976.

Urban, W. *Why Teachers Organized.* Detroit: Wayne State University Press, 1982.

Webster, W. G. *Effective Collective Bargaining in Public Education.* Ames: Iowa State University Press, 1985.

Zakariya, S. B. "How Carnegie and the Unions Would Transform Your Schools." *The Executive Educator* (September 1986).

CHAPTER ELEVEN

Restructuring for Participatory Management: Change and Stability

Introduction

Restructuring is a highly fashionable word in the world of education today. Consider the case of Central-Hower High School before reading this chapter. Do you think that the school's governance structure has been restructured? In what ways has decision making been significantly shifted to the faculty? Who was responsible for change in this case? Do you think Central-Hower has taken on too much or too little in the move to site-based management? What is necessary in terms of resources to sustain this change over the long run? How long might this restructuring effort need to be in place to have an impact on the school's academic program? What are some of the problems the new Faculty Senate may encounter in establishing itself as a permanent and well-functioning element of the school management process? Will the role of principal change dramatically under this type of management arrangement?

Site-Based Management at Central-Hower

In 1984, the faculty of Central-Hower High School was charged by district administrators with developing a school improvement plan that would involve teachers in decision making. One of eight high schools in the Akron, Ohio, public school system. Central-Hower is an inner-city school whose population during the past five years has declined to about 970 students: approximately 45 percent black, 45 percent white, and 8 percent Asian. About 33 percent of our students participate in the free or reduced price lunch program. Average stanines on the California Achievement Tests are 4–5, but our students' abilities range from the lowest to the highest. While the majority of our students live in our attendance district, about 36 percent have elected to attend Central-Hower in order to pursue courses in vocational and preprofessional programs.

During the past five years, we have struggled with a number of questions about how to do school-based management, three of which we will discuss here: What organizational structures will provide for the broadest participation by staff members? What procedures will ensure responsiveness, fairness, and efficiency? How is the role of the principal affected?

The Faculty Senate

Early in the project, we recognized the need for some kind of representative body to promote participation by our staff. We considered various forums, including "town meeting" sessions, which we concluded would be too time consuming. We finally agreed upon a Faculty Senate, to be composed of the principal and eight members elected from the staff. Our staff is divided into eight groups by related curricular areas, and each group elects a member of the Senate for a three-year term. Terms are staggered so that no more than three new members are elected each year.

Although the need for a representative body is readily apparent, the accountability provided by the group structure may not be so obvious. For example, if members of a group are dissatisfied with their representative, Senate procedures provide for a recall election. When members are elected at large to a governing body, however, it is difficult in practice to identify a "culprit." Also, in a traditionally structured school, teachers do not have effective ways to indicate their unhappiness over building-level decisions affecting them. Singly or in groups they can complain to the principal or to each other in the faculty lounge, but if the principal does not follow their advice, they have little recourse, aside from grievance procedures. (While it is true that major issues are subject to contractual agreements, these issues are more likely to be systemwide problems, and the process can take years).

Our school constitution spells out election procedures, officer responsibilities, and types of committees. In addition, it provides an appeal process for the principal, who has one vote on the Senate and can be outvoted by the other members. If the principal had the right to veto a Senate decision, many staff members felt, the Senate would have no real power and would become a pointless exercise. During discussions about what would actually happen if there were serious disagreement in the school, a compromise emerged when staff members recognized that someone with higher authority would intervene. So we incorporated into the appeal process the provision that the principal can appeal a Senate decision to the Director of Secondary Curriculum or the Assistant Superintendent for Curriculum and Instruction. We thereby created a natural check on the Senate and the principal. The purists were not fully satisfied, but the process has worked, in the sense that it has not been invoked during its three-year life.

The Senate's main function is to set the educational policy and agenda for the school (in accordance with school board policies). It oversees the work of departments and committees and determines the budget allocations. By working with and through small groups, as well as the faculty at large, the Senate allows a consensus to emerge. Some examples of decisions made during 1988–89 will help clarify these generalities. For example, during the summer, a committee revised the school philosophy and recommended the amended document to the Senate, who arranged for faculty discussions at a staff meeting. At this meeting, the staff voted on the revised document. Another committee, specially appointed for the task, developed a set of five-year goals for 1989/90–1994/95. After Senate deliberations, the goals were presented to and voted on by the staff. On a more practical level, the Senate approves teacher requests for texts and instructional materials, additional staff, equipment, and the like.

The Curriculum Council

At first, we thought the Senate would deal with all curricular issues as its major responsibility. However, the Senate soon discovered how time consuming the combination of curriculum matters and overall policy implementation is. As a result, we formed the *Curriculum Council* as a subcommittee of the Senate, to which it reports. (The Senate meets daily, with Senate responsibilities taking the place of supervisory duties.) The Curriculum Council is composed of elected department chairpersons. A Senate member serves as liaison between the Senate and the Council.

Because the Council is new, its functions are still evolving, but some of its activities provide insights into the shape its functions are taking. For example, this is the group that spearheaded the revision of our school philosophy in order to provide a guide for making curriculum decisions. To learn national, state, and local trends, its members heard presentations from curriculum specialists. Further, the Council examined two programs, one which teachers felt should be added and one dropped, and made recommendations to the Senate. The group is also grappling with overall issues such as what a Central-Hower graduate should know.

Yearly Plans and Five-Year Goals

In addition to these two new groups, we have instituted two
new procedures that help us to be responsive, fair, and efficient. First, in the spring, each department or committee
develops a plan for the following year. Much like a funding
proposal, each plan spells out why something should be
done; what the specific objective is; what activities, staff,
and money are involved; and what evaluation methods will
be used. This written document informs staff members
about the plans of other departments and helps all departments set realistic goals.

The second procedure involves developing five-year
goals and then tying them to the budget. (This process is
based on a plan originated by the Girl Scouts, U.S.A., and is
used by many United Way agencies across the nation.) The
five-year goals for 1989/90–1994/95 were developed by a
faculty committee during a three-day conference that examined local, state, and national trends affecting education,
current educational programs, student achievement and
needs, and probable funding.

Once the five-year goals have been adopted, we weight
them in relation to each other; that is, goal #1 is twice as
important as #2, and so on. Then the budget is divided accordingly: here, goal #1 would get twice as much money as
#2. Although we have just begun to use this model, we hope
it will help us allocate our resources wisely and in accordance with group consensus.

The Principal's Role

Early in the project, many questions arose about the role of
the principal. Faculty opinion ranged from maintaining the
traditional top-down structure to eventually eliminating the
position entirely. However, we now have a new understanding of and appreciation for the principal's role in the successful operation of the school.

At Central-Hower, the principal is responsible for all
the usual tasks; however, as a result of shared decision
making, his role vis á vis the educational program has
changed. Because our faculty has agreed that the educational agenda will be determined by consensus, the principal facilitates the building of that consensus. Thus, he
provides information or finds sources of information, serves
as a clearinghouse so committees are not working at cross

purposes to each other or systemwide goals, assists staff members in providing for accountability, and encourages staff development and experimentation. These are specific responsibilities related to developing consensus on the instructional program and methods that best serve students.

While these, too, are traditional tasks of the principal, the difference in our setting is that our principal works more indirectly. As he oversees all the work, he is helping others to accomplish it. Sharing decision making may imply that the principal loses authority. However, since the principal's sphere of communication is much greater, our principal's influence has actually increased. After all, when a principal makes a decision alone, he or she is also alone in trying to implement it. By contrast, when the group makes the decision, the group is ready to get to work on it.

From Our Experience to Yours

We do not claim to have figured out all the answers; indeed we recognize that many questions lie ahead. But our rising student achievement scores and our own sense of joy in our accomplishments have us convinced we are heading in a good direction. In a way, of course, every school is unique, but we recognize that Central-Hower is in many ways a "normal" school and has problems similar to other schools. Indeed, it is this very ordinariness that makes Central-Hower's experience with site-based management useful to others. If it works here, it will work elsewhere. And it works here.*

Throughout this text we have described, analyzed, and examined the theory and practice of a participatory approach to management within the education sector. Although individual schools, some districts, and even certain states have embarked on model programs of participatory management, this is yet to be the norm nationwide. Clearly, however, it is the wave of the future. Many superintendents and school principals are asking: How can we

---

*Sandra Strauber, Sara Stanley, and Carl Wagenknecht (1990), "Site-Based Management at Central-Hower," *Educational Leadership*, April 1990. Reprinted with permission of the Association for Supervision and Curriculum Development. Copyright © 1990 by the Association for Supervision and Curriculum Development. All rights reserved.

build a more participatory organization? Who is responsible for initiating change? What changes should come first? What do we actually need to do to get started, and how long will it take to change from our present system of management to a new one? These are the basic questions that this concluding chapter addresses. To answer them, we draw on the examples of organizations within the education sector that have embarked on a process of induced change.

Who Is Responsible for Change?

Increasing the involvement of teachers in key aspects of managing their professional activities at the school-site level has been a basic theme throughout this book. Repeatedly, teachers have indicated that they wish to have a say in evaluation procedures, new hiring decisions, staff development programs, and the allocation of professional time within the school day, as well as curriculum and instructional materials matters (Turner, 1987).

Some critics of the participatory approach to school management and shared leadership argue that by "increasing the number of decision makers in schools would create a need for additional procedures, and policies, thus increasing the bureaucratic obstacles to school improvement" (Geisert, 1988). Moreover, they suggest that the participatory approach leaves organizations leaderless, distributing responsibilities among a number of individuals, none of whom is accountable at the time of reckoning.

In fact, as we have shown, the rationale behind the participatory approach to management is the opposite. It searches for ways to delegate both responsibility and accountability to individuals within the organization. Involving staff, individually and collectively, is a strategy for increasing action that will improve the organization's overall well-being as well as the individual job performance. Participatory organizations, as we discussed in Chapters Two and Three, are not leaderless. The participatory school does not do away with the role of central functions or the principal. There are, to be sure, small schools that are without a principal (e.g., see Chapter Eight, the Orion School). Although these are effective educational organizations, they are not the only or primary model.

Creating a participatory organization is, in fact, the responsibility of all members of the school team. However, in practice, it is almost invariably the principal who takes the initiative and leads the way from the more traditional superintendency model of administration (see Chapter One) toward new ground. Without the commitment of the line manager (i.e., the principal) it is very difficult for the school to move from old practices to new ones. Although participation suggests greater decentralization and a more democratic approach to management, developing a participatory organization requires strong leadership where traditional structures and procedures run counter.

Included in the question of who is responsible for initiating changes in management style and procedures are the roles of the school district and state educational authorities. Over the past five years, we have witnessed an increase in districtwide efforts to reform both the schools and the general approach to educational management. For example, in Lake Washington (Washington), Rochester (New York), Miami-Dade (Florida), and Redwood City (California), change has been swept in via initiative or considerable support from the superintendent's office. District leadership can stimulate (or retard) change at the school-site level, but it must be matched with leadership and commitment at the site level.

By contrast, there is yet relatively little indication that state educational authorities can do much to bring about changes in the routine management practices of schools. This is the conclusion of a comparison of state-led attempts to introduce major educational reforms, including managerial changes, in Texas, California, and South Carolina (Timar and Kirp, 1989). Each state took a different approach to try and induce change at the school-site level. Texas used a rational-planning, top-down model whereby the state formulated policies that were drawn up as regulations and mandates with which schools had to comply. California used a market-incentive model, creating artificial markets in which implementation of specific policy provisions can be bargained between state and local officials. However, adherence to state policies is a matter of local choice. South Carolina chose a midcourse between California and Texas, sometimes referred to as a *political interaction model.* Policy formulation occurs at the state level, but compliance is at the discretion of local districts. Careful examination of these efforts shows that on its own, none is sufficient to engender change. Organizationally competent schools may take advantage of the reforms, but the organizationally incoherent schools are unable to integrate them into their own programs. Far-reaching change or reform will necessitate an integration of the state, local, and school-site effort.

What Changes Must Take Place?

The entire education community is rapidly converging on the view that schools, as organizations, are in need of fundamental changes—both structural and managerial (Timar and Kirp, 1989; McNeil, 1988; Shanker, 1988). These are the types of fundamental changes that do not come about quickly or easily. A careful evaluation of the Ford Foundation's $30 million effort to support first-order reforms in a wide range of schools—urban, rural, and suburban, as well as large and small—found the following:

- *Innovations took root in schools where the objectives and techniques used were limited in number and very clearly defined.*
- *More substantive changes took place when the school staff agreed from the outset on the nature, extent of limitations, and specific purposes of the project.*
- *Success was related to the presence of a project leader involved throughout the project cycle: from planning to implementation to final evaluation.*
- *Innovation and change required both intellectual and financial resources from the district as well as the funding agency.*
- *The less complex a school system's structure, the more easily and rapidly changes were introduced and accepted. Small schools changed more quickly than larger schools, but were less likely to sustain their innovations. (Orlich, 1989)*

Managing Change

These findings strongly suggest that managing the change process is the key to successful change. Introducing changes in management approach require the same planning, consensus building, specificity of objectives, and careful monitoring of implementation than any other innovation, for example, the introduction of a new curriculum, or the creation of a new department within the school. Schools will do best to choose a specific area of the management process, such as staff development, problem solving, planning, resource planning and allocation, or evaluation, and focus on introducing a more participatory approach rather than tackling the entire system at once.

Where to Begin: Creating Action Space

Many employees implicitly or explicitly regard change as equivalent to a change of manager. However, if one views management as embedded in an organization's structure, then one can begin to understand that a change of face may not necessarily bring about a change in management approach.

An action space, either within the existing organizational framework or parallel to it, is needed. This action space is the launching pad for a new idea or way of doing things. It can be generated by the principal, a teacher, a group of teachers, or perhaps someone outside the organization altogether. Action space is necessary for experimenting with new ways of doing things. It must be relatively free from the "rules of the game" that apply to the organization in general in the initial phases.

Action space becomes available in two ways: intentionally and unintentionally. It can be created by setting up an ad hoc task force, such as a special implementation team, or establishing a parallel structure such as a school-within-a-school. It may also be created inadvertently through crisis, a vacuum, or a rebellion within the organization. A *crisis,* such as a threat of school closure, may bring a staff together in an ad hoc fashion outside the normal ways in which they interact within the school to fight for a common objective—the preservation of their school. The loss of a staff development officer at the district level due to budgetary constraints may create a *vacuum* for a group of teachers to initiate their own staff development committee at the site level. A *rebellion* from the ranks of employees can also be the impetus for change. A group of teachers, highly dissatisfied with an alcoholic principal, may band together informally at first to complain to each other. The group may eventually emerge as a force of rebellion and pressure the central administration until the principal is removed. The group may find, however, that that is only the beginning of the change process. Their revolution merely creates the space needed for transformation to occur. If the group obtains a new, dynamic principal at the helm, it will have to work hard to remold an organization that had deteriorated badly.

Managers are also capable of initiating a change process by creating the conditions in which change can occur. They must be careful to remember that they are not likely to encounter success if they expect to be able to *mandate* change. Some principals who have been successful change agents in their school have done so by seeking outside funding to support an innovative idea. Others have just acted or supported the actions of their staff. Judy Kell of Hawthorne Elementary (see Chapter Three) says, "It is easier to ask forgiveness than permission." Trust agreements (described in Chapter Ten) are examples of an "experimental" space created between school-site personnel and district-level management.

In addition to a space for experimentation, efforts for changing a management style should be linked to a real problem, one that most members of the staff want to solve. For example, if a school chooses a peer coaching program simply because it sounds interesting, rather than out of specific need to provide support for a young, relatively inexperienced teaching staff (see the Orion School, Chapter Eight), then the initiative is likely to fizzle early in the process.

Choosing the vehicle for a change in management practices is the first real step forward. The process of choosing is, itself, critical. It can be the school's first experience in exploring the complexities of participatory management. It is likely to be studded with some false starts and promises, but is important in terms of building organizationwide commitment to a departure from the status quo. In this regard, it is a political process as much as it is a managerial process. It also gives the proponents of a more participatory approach the opportunity to launch a trial balloon that is likely to indicate the source as well as magnitude of some of the obstacles that are likely to arise once a choice has been made and an implementation strategy devised.

Barriers to Change

We have already examined and discussed some barriers to introducing participatory approaches in Chapter Two. Some of these barriers are within the organization itself. In the case of schools, barriers may come from among teaching staff; for example, some teachers may be highly risk adverse. Risk aversion is usually closely connected with a fear of failure or other negative consequences that could possibly result. The importance of a safe space to experiment with new processes can help to alleviate some of these anxieties. Another point of resistance among the teaching staff may emanate from lack of time. In a recent survey of teachers regarding the critical problems in teaching, finding the time to accomplish all one's professional objectives was rated as the number one major problem by 59 percent of the 1,000 respondents (Turner, 1987).

Another barrier is the actual availability of resources. Involving teachers more actively in the professional aspects of school-site management will take time. Teacher time is the education sector's most costly resource. Nearly one-fifth of teachers surveyed by *Learning* in 1987 indicated that they are already concerned about having too many nonprofessional duties (Turner, 1987). One of the most pressing problems will be for educational managers to help find ways of reallocating teachers' time to enhance their involvement in the school on an organizationwide basis as well as to improve the quality of classroom performance. Reallocation of time may cost some money. However, the potential benefits in terms of teacher morale and student learning may well offset the costs associated with reorganization efforts that depart from the traditional organization of school rather radically (for example see Box 11.1).

Barriers are also embedded in the districtwide organizational practices. For example, a school that wants to have more control over the hiring, retention, and promotion of staff may find itself in conflict with districtwide procedures. Equally adverse to change may be the basic policy mandates of state educational authorities. McNeil (1988) argues forcefully that minimum bureaucratic standards set for teachers and schools by outside authorities—usually at the state level—make it organizationally impossible for teachers to fulfill the requirements and, at the same time, meet the educational needs of the students. Along with the pressure toward standardization of teaching practices is the pressure toward uniform management practices in schools on a district and statewide basis. The push to standardization has some advantages, but in an organizational system where bureaucracy is already well established, it does little to further the possibility of innovation or reform (see Chapter One).

How Long Will It Take?

Contemplating changes is always easier than making changes. Unfortunately, most efforts to change schools have been ephemeral and have left little lasting impact. In this respect, Katz's thesis (1971) that schools, as organizations, have changed precious little since the late 1800s when bureaucracy gained hegemony may be fundamentally correct. Fortunately, there is no indication that educators—or even the general public—have tired of trying to improve the schools. Since the 1950s, at least three revolutions have

---

BOX 11.1 • *Holweide Comprehensive School,*
Cologne, West Germany

Not long ago, I visited a public school, the Holweide Comprehensive School in Cologne, West Germany. In addition to German children, the school has many children of Turkish, Portuguese, Greek and Moroccan "guest workers." Most students are not considered university or even technical school material, based on the nationwide exam given in fourth grade. But, despite this and the students' language problems, the school has an excellent record of successfully preparing students for university entrance exams. There are waiting lists for student admissions and for faculty positions.

The secret is that the school has tried something different. First, instead of the traditional programming, teachers work in teams that are responsible for the entire education of the same group of students (seven teachers for 100 students, for example), from grade 5 until they graduate at age 19. The teachers decide what time should be given to each subject and are free to change schedules as they see fit.

Stimulating Thinking

In the classrooms, there is almost no lecturing. Students are arranged in small groups with projects to do or problems to solve. The idea is to promote team effort and peer teaching. Problems are designed to stimulate thinking and creativity. For example: "Develop a theory on when and why time zones were established. Would they have existed during the Roman Empire? What opposition would there be to abandon or reduce the number of zones we now have?"

In this particular school there are only three supervisors—a principal and two assistants—all of whom, under German law, must teach at least six hours a week. Each teaching team elects one of its members to the faculty senate, and no decision of the principal is effective without ratification by majority of the senate. In addition, each team has a member on the school curriculum committee, which makes it possible for each group to exchange ideas and experiences.

Source: Reprinted with permission from "Restructuring Leadership" by Albert Shanker, President, American Federation of Teachers, in *The College Board Review* No. 149, Fall 1988. Copyright © 1988 by College Entrance Examination Board, New York.

---

swept the nation's schools. Sputnik, in the late 1950s and early 1960s, which led to the movement to upgrade science and mathematics education, was followed by the Equal Educational Opportunity movement of the mid-1960s and early 1970s and the alternative school movement of the same era. Now, the school improvement and quest for educational excellence movement of the early 1980s is giving way to a push for reform and restructuring schools in the 1990s. Through each of these, educators have learned more about what needs to be done to truly transform schools into workable organizations for students as well as teachers.

Basic Conditions for Change

There are a number of basic conditions that must be obtained in order for real change in the way we manage our schools to take place. Oddly enough, they are founded on the premise of stability—stability in leadership, stability of the exchange agents, stability of resources, and stability of policy.

- *Leadership.* A change from the superintendency to a more participatory approach to school management will require a cadre of site- and district-level administrators dedicated to initiating and implementing new practices. If change is to take hold at the site level, there must be continuity for an extended time period (four to six years). Districtwide change is far more complex. It requires not only stability in terms of the top-level district management but also a critical mass of supporters at the central and site levels.
- *Change Agents.* Change agents are the nuclei of teachers at the site level who are willing and enthusiastic enough about a new approach to management to carry it to their colleagues with or without support from the site manager. That these change agents must be fixed in their organizations and their stability is as critical to success as that of the leadership.
- *Resources.* Without resources, change is very difficult. At first glance, change in management appears to be an easy target. Unlike an educational program, it does not appear to have large-scale direct costs. As we have repeatedly stressed throughout the text, a participatory approach to management that can work has cost implications. Mentor teaching, school-based planning, site-level evaluation, and peer coach-

ing all take teacher time and cost money. A stable resource base needs to be planned for, acquired, and maintained to underpin a participatory organization.

Policy. Policy is nothing more or less than a framework or set of guidelines for action. The translation of educational policy into action depends ultimately on school-site managers and classroom teachers. Their actions are the litmus test of effectiveness of any given educational policy. We have already pointed out that policy alone is an insufficient condition for a change in actual management practice. Nevertheless, continuity in educational policy at the state and district levels can make important contributions to management change efforts. Rapid or continual shifts in policy confuse and frustrate those required to implement them, particularly when they have not been involved or consulted at the formative stage. Moreover, these shifts often produce a lack of confidence and even cynicism among teachers. District or statewide policy to support participative management are perhaps best formulated after the fact—that is, after several schools have had sufficient time to experiment with their own unique solutions to their own unique problems. A number of unique cases over time will produce enough districtwide experience to begin to generate into a policy. Meanwhile, individual managers and teachers will need to collaborate to determine where to begin. In some schools, the site planning process may be the springboard. In others, problem solving and decision making will open many avenues. In still others, an organizational evaluation may launch the school on the path of greater participation in management, whereas greater client involvement or a redesign of teacher-administrative relations may be the motor in other instances. The point of departure is nothing more than a beginning. The manager and staff together must chart the course of the journey.

Case Study

San Diego City School District

(Authors' Note: It may be instructive for readers to compare and contrast this concluding case, which focuses on San Diego City School District, with the Lake Washington case at the end of

Chapter Two. Who are the key players in each case with respect to initiating a plan for change? Who are the important figures when a district actually moves to implement change? Given the 12-year experience in Lake Washington, and nearly 15 years' experience in Vallejo Unified School District, how long might it take for San Diego to see some results from the restructuring effort it has undertaken? What stability factors will play a role in making possible the kinds of changes sought in this district? As an exercise, you might want to draw up a change strategy for your own district, identifying the major steps in the process, the key players at each stage, and a realistic time table for each stage.)

When Tom Payzant took on San Diego's beleaguered school district in 1982, he faced a difficult situation. The district, with 153 schools and 117,000 students, had just ended a period of intense labor strife that culminated in a teacher's strike. The demographics of the district had changed dramatically from a predominantly white population to one in which the combined Hispanic, Black, and Asian minorities comprised nearly 60 percent of the student population. Added to this was Payzant's perceptive recognition that students were emerging from the school system with a "I-can't-do" attitude. With the changing nature of work that requires higher levels of literacy and numeracy for entry-level jobs today than in the past, the outlook for San Diego's students was not auspicious.

During an initial period, Payzant cut $1 million from the district's rapidly growing budget. Adversarial relations with the teachers continued and was the subject of teacher protest and pickets. Payzant gradually shifted his focus toward a school-based, teacher-centered approach. In part, this was a result of his realization that the old approach would not work. His new focus was also prodded by external events such as California's Proposition 98 ballot initiative campaign, which was designed to protect education's share of the state's budget. Both teachers and the district shared an interest in seeing the proposition pass and they realized that open hostility between teachers and the district would have been inimical to the success of the initiative. The election of a new president of the teacher's union provided a further opportunity to begin to establish a new relationship of trust between teachers and the district's administration.

The opportunity for restructuring was ripe and Payzant recognized the need to alter the fundamental "assembly-line" structure. In an article he wrote,

> *Most schools in America are structured today much as*
> *they were at the turn of the century. They function like*
> *factories. They select, sort, grade and process*
> *students. . . . There is an assembly line process that pro-*
> *pels students through a maze that, if successfully negoti-*
> *ated, leads to annual promotion and ultimately a high*
> *school diploma. Too many fall off the assembly line. We*
> *call them dropouts. And in the name of quality control, we*
> *test to emphasize failure rather than success.*

Payzant seized the moment to call for restructuring that places "much more of the decision making authority, responsibility, and accountability for student achievement, with teachers at each school. The idea is that teachers, working with the advice and involvement of parents and other staff members know best how to meet the particular needs of the school's students."

He initiated the process of change in May 1986 by appointing a group of 17 community leaders to study the impact of changing demographic and economic conditions and to recommend appropriate changes. Following the group's report, the Board of Education committed itself to the development of model programs in school-centered management. In order to implement this decision, in October 1987 the superintendent appointed the Innovation and Change Leadership Group (ICLG). The ICLG was comprised of 11 teachers, 11 administrators, 3 classified employees, the president of the Board of Education, and 7 knowledgeable community representatives including PTA leaders and dean of the University of San Diego's School of Education.

The ICLG spawned a series of school restructuring seminars that culminated in "Super Saturday." On April 18, 1988, teams of five representatives (one administrator, two teachers, one classified staff representative, and one parent) from each of 38 self-selected schools attended an all-day school restructuring program. Of these, 25 school teams chose to participate in "Super Planning Week."

Among the actions that emerged was a waiver process whereby the ICLG would assist schools with requests to waive local, state, and federal policy, laws, and regulations, and waive collective bargaining agreements to facilitate school restructuring efforts by recommending approval to the board of education of the employee organization. Proposals have been developed for financial support from educational foundations, such as the Stuart

Foundation, to plan and develop specific participatory projects at various school sites.

Although it is too early to report on the success of the restructuring process, there are several favorable signs. First, as a result of the superintendent's efforts, the term *restructuring* (meaning the schools have license to develop school-based management) is now in every employee's vocabulary. Teachers are thinking about how they might restructure their schools, and they have permission and encouragement to do so. Second, the district's bureaucracy is beginning to shift its perception of its role. As an example, for the first time in recent memory, the district's purchasing department sent its buyers out to the schools to view their service from the field, as a first step in viewing the schools as their customers, marking a very significant change.

However, resistance of the central office has been one of the major problems standing in the path of restructuring. Assistant superintendent for personnel services, George Russell, told *Education Week*, "There was a lot of alarm. If you tell a central office manager that he can't say 'no' to a school—well there were a lot of questions. 'What are we going to be doing if we can't say no'?" Director of second-language education, Timothy Allen, added that in a school-focused initiative "there really was not, as I saw it, a clear role for the Central Office" (Olson, 1988, pp. 1, 8–11). Middle managers expressed the concern that teachers lack the knowledge and information needed to make the best decisions on the children's behalf.

With the shift in emphasis, central administrators had to change their style and content. Timothy Allen observed, "Previously, I could get up in front of a group of principals and say, 'This is what is required, and this is the way you're required to implement it.' Now you think twice before you tell people what to do at a school because there is a certain amount of power at the school" (Olson, p. 9).

The move in the direction of school-based management is not smooth sailing for other reasons. For one, notes superintendent Payzant, restructuring requires additional resources. For example, one school came up with an innovation that would have required students to arrive at the same time, instead of at staggered times. This would have entailed additional transportation costs, but the money was not available. Second, there are still substantial pressures for top-down action and accountability. Representatives of minority students expressed a concern that decentralizing decisions to the schools would make it difficult for them to tell whether their objectives were being met. They would need to contact each of the district's 153 schools instead of just the central administration. Finally, the reward and motivation system will need adjustment to respond to the anticipated changes.

In the final analysis, restructuring is building trust. It is not something that happens easily or overnight. It is a process that calls for careful leadership at all levels of the district, from the superintendent to the district's middle managers to the principals.

References

Caldwell, S. D., and Wood, F. H. "School-Backed Improvement—Are We Ready? *Educational Leadership* (October 1988):50–53.

Geisert, G. "Participatory Management: Panacea or Hoax?" *Educational Leadership* (November 1988):56–59.

Katz, M. *Class, Bureaucracy and Schools: The Illusion of Educational Change in America.* New York: Praeger, 1971.

McNeil, L. "Contradictions of Reform," *Phi Delta Kappan* (March 1988):478–485.

Olson, L. *Education Week* (March 1988):1, 8–11.

Orlich, D. C. "Educational Reforms: Mistakes, Misconceptions, Miscues." *Phi Delta Kappan* (March 1989):512–517.

Scarr, L. E. "Lake Washington's Master Plan—A System for Growth." *Educational Leadership* (October 1988):13–16.

Shanker, A. "Restructuring Leadership." *The College Board Review* 149 (Fall 1988):14–17.

Timar, T. B., and Kirp, D. L. "Educational Reform in the 1980s: Lessons from the States." *Phi Delta Kappan* (March 1989):504–511.

Turner, R. R. "What Are the Critical Problems in Teaching?" *Learning* (March 1987):58–63.

Appendix:
A Guide to Using
the Case Method

What Is a Case?

A case study is a model of the real world. Included in this book are situational cases that describe events relative to a school or district that can be seen as contributing to a positive or problematic situation. Exercise and decision cases require the reader to utilize and/or apply techniques and procedures presented in the case, whereas background cases are intended to convey information and familiarize the reader with real-life illustrations of concepts and theories in action. All are written descriptions of actual situations that educators have experienced or are based on real-life situations. In most instances the real names of the schools, districts, and individuals are used. In others they have been disguised; this does not, however, change the value of the case. Each case study illustrates one or more definable issues. Some cases provide models that illustrate the application of theory in concrete situations. Others call for decisions and critical thinking. All provide an opportunity to talk about an interesting situation.

Educational Functions of the Case Method

Through its realism, the case method allows the reader to participate actively in analyzing problems and assessing solutions. The method illustrates theory, imparts information in an interesting way, and provides opportunities to exercise analytical thinking and judgment. The experience gained by using cases can increase an individual's capacity to work effectively. Some cases build one's awareness that the axioms of management cannot be mechanically applied. The case method enables an individual to become a keen observer, one who can analyze and determine the potential consequences of various courses of action.

Using the Case Method

In using the case method, the student should be instructed first to read the case carefully and master the facts, identifying all crucial information. Second, the reader should identify the key issues or actions, evaluate each, and consider their relative importance. Where a case asks one to suggest a course of action, the student should list as many alternatives as possible and evaluate their consequences. Students should come to class fully prepared and ready to discuss the issues. The instructor may ask students to respond individually to the case or choose to discuss the case with either the whole class or in small groups. Participants in group discussion should be encouraged to speak freely and openly. When discussing the case study with the entire class, the instructor may begin by asking one student to summarize the case. The questions that precede each case are designed to focus the discussion on key points. If small groups are used, they should be instructed to prepare a summary of their discussion to report back to the entire group. Students may be asked to write a one-page executive summary, to prepare a detailed discussion of the issues, or to answer the questions at the beginning of the case.

The case method is best used in group discussion. Groups should be encouraged to contrast the case with their own experiences. The instructor may have several objectives in utilizing the case and should clarify which objectives are dominant. The aim may be to illustrate theory, to present an opportunity to apply a technique, to provide a decision-making experience, to improve inquiry skills, or to cause the student to reevaluate his or her own attitudes. The use of cases in classroom settings provides an opportunity for the practice of interpersonal and communication skills.

Index